HOW TO BUILD KILLER CHEVY

SMALL-BLOCK ENGINES

Mike Mavrigian

CarTech®

CarTech®

CarTech®, Inc.
6118 Main Street
North Branch, MN 55056
Phone: 651-277-1200 or 800-551-4754
Fax: 651-277-1203
www.cartechbooks.com

Edit by Bob Wilson
Layout by Hailey Samples

ISBN 978-1-61325-489-9
Item No. SA456

Library of Congress Cataloging-in-Publication Data

Names: Mavrigian, Mike, author.
Title: How to build killer Chevy small-block engines / Mike Mavrigian.
Description: Forest Lake, MN : CarTech, 2019.
Identifiers: LCCN 2019025209 | ISBN 9781613254899 (paperback)
Subjects: LCSH: Chevrolet automobile–Motors–Design and construction.
Classification: LCC TL215.C5 M383 2019 | DDC 629.25/04–dc23
LC record available at https://lccn.loc.gov/2019025209

Written, edited, and designed in the U.S.A.
Printed in China

10 9 8 7 6 5 4 3

DISTRIBUTION BY:

Europe
PGUK
63 Hatton Garden
London EC1N 8LE, England
Phone: 020 7061 1980 • Fax: 020 7242 3725
www.pguk.co.uk

Australia
Renniks Publications Ltd.
3/37-39 Green Street
Banksmeadow, NSW 2109, Australia
Phone: 2 9695 7055 • Fax: 2 9695 7355
www.renniks.com

Canada
Login Canada
300 Saulteaux Crescent
Winnipeg, MB, R3J 3T2 Canada
Phone: 800 665 1148 • Fax: 800 665 0103
www.lb.ca

CONTENTS

Acknowledgments 5

Chapter 1: The Small-Block Chevy 6
  OEM Crankshaft Journal Size 8
  Today's Options 10

Chapter 2: The Block: Where It All Begins 11
  Cast Iron Versus Aluminum 11
  OEM Blocks 12
  Advantages of an Aftermarket Block 15
  Dart 15
  Brodix 17
  Donovan 18
  Chevy Performance Blocks 21
  World Products 21

Chapter 3: Crankshafts 23
  Crankshaft Stroke 23
  Factory Stock Crankshaft Stroke 23
  Popular Aftermarket Bore/Stroke
    Combinations 24
  Bore and Stroke Combinations 27
  Selecting Crankshaft Stroke 27
  Forgings and Billet 28
  Crankshaft Durability Treatments 29
  REM Finishing 29

Chapter 4: Connecting Rods 30
  Rod Ratio 30
  Types of Rods 31
  Connecting Rod Length 34
  Rod to Block Clearance 35
  Rod Side Clearance 35
  Beam Design 36
  Rod and Cap Numbering 37
  Rod Bolt Tips 37
  Tightening Rod Bolts by Monitoring Stretch 38
  REM Finishing 39

**Chapter 5: Today's Performance
  Cylinder Heads** 40
  Edelbrock 43
  Trick Flow Specialties (TFS) 44
  Dart 45
  Brodix 51

Air Flow Research 52
World Products 52
Racing Head Service 53

**Chapter 6: Advancements in Camshaft Design and
  Technology** 54
  Roller Cam Advantages 54
  Camshaft Patterns to Compensate for Intake
    Manifold Runners 55
  Symmetrical Versus Asymmetrical Camshafts 56
  Surface Finishing Technology 56
  Lobe Separation Angles 57
  Base Circle Diameter 58
  Special Firing-Order Camshafts 58
  Camshaft Needle Bearings 58
  Choosing the Correct Distributor Gear 59
  Check for Runout 60

Chapter 7: Induction 61
  Manifolds 61
  Selecting Carburetor Size 63
  E85 Fuel 64
  EFI 65
  Fuel Pressure 67
  Fuel Injectors: Low Impedance
    Versus High Impedance 67
  Choosing Injector Size 68
  Forced Induction 69
  Supercharger Basics 70
  Fuel System 71
  Compression Ratio 71
  Upgrading the Engine to Accommodate the New-
    Found Power 72
  Fuel Injection Tech 72
  Injector Impedance 74
  Injector Harness Adapters 75
  Injector Physical Dimensions 75

Chapter 8: Rockers and Lifters 76
  Roller Rockers 76
  Shaft-Mounted Rockers 77
  Rocker Arm Materials 77
  Rocker Arm Ratio 79
  Lifters 80

CONTENTS

Chapter 9: Pistons 86
  Piston Skirts and Major/Minor Thrust...............86
  Offset Pin 88
  Match the Valve Angle 88
  Examples of Piston Choices 89
  Piston Dome Shape..90
  Coatings...91
  Piston Features and Options 92
  Piston CD and the Oil Ring 95
  Piston Dome Volume 96
  Combustion Chamber Volume 96

Chapter 10: Sample Engine Build: 422 CI 97
  Block Prep and Modifications 98
  Crankshaft Balancing 103
  Block Plugs..105
  Cam and Bearings 105
  Crankshaft Installation...............................107
  Dry Belt Care 113
  Crank Balancer Installation 114
  Piston and Rod Installation 115

Oil Filter Adapter 119
Wet Sump Oil Pumps 119
Cam Timing...121
Roller Lifters 122
Timing Pointer 124
Crank Trigger 124
Cylinder Heads 125
Rockers 130
Pushrods 132
Intake Manifold 134
Carburetor...135
Distributor...136
Valve Covers..137
Oil Pan 138
Vacuum Pump 138
Racing Alternator 139
Water Pump 140
Dyno Run..140
Parts Used in This Build 141

Source Guide 143

ACKNOWLEDGMENTS

Thanks to the following for their participation and input: Zac Kimball and Chris Raschke, ARP; Bill McKnight, Mahle; Ron Rotunno, Fel-Pro; Sean Crawford, JE Pistons; Tom Lieb, Scat Enterprises; Don Meziere, Meziere Enterprises; Mike Osterhaus, Melling Select; Cody Smith, Cloyes; Jodi Holtrey, Medina Mountain Motors; Scott Gressman, Gressman Powersports; Tony Lombardi, Ross Racing Engines; Bill Tichenor and Jeff Teel, Holley and MSD Performance; Silver Gomez, MSD Performance; John Callies, John Callies Inc./Morel Lifters; Richard Maskin, Dart; Jack McKinnis, World Products; Dick Boyer, World Products/Erson-PBM; Trent Goodwin, Comp Cams and RHS; Duane Boes, Callies Crankshafts; Air Flow Research; Al Rebescher, Trick Flow Specialties; Bob Fall, Fall Automotive Machine; Glen Schierholt, UEM/Icon Pistons; Swain Tech Coatings; Thor Schroeder, Moroso Performance; Lynn Livermore, Fluidampr; Bullet Cams; Permatex; Dave Monyhan, Goodson Shop Supplies; Ryan Kilpatrick, Oliver Rods; Tom Lieb and Alex Gonzalez, Scat Crankshafts; Jennifer Woods, Brodix; Randy Becker, Harland Sharp, CJ Jones, Jones Racing; Rob Remesi and Mike Mullen, Jesel; Robin Manton, Manton Pushrods; Wilson Intake Manifolds; Jim Smaaladen, Bryant Crankshafts; Kathy Donovan, Donovan.

HOW TO BUILD KILLER CHEVY SMALL-BLOCK ENGINES

THE SMALL-BLOCK CHEVY

Hot dogs, baseball, apple pie, the flag, Mom, and the small-block Chevy engine. Collectively, we're talking about all things America. Shortly after the birth of the performance industry to the present day, the beloved SBC (small-block Chevy) continues to be one of the most, if not *the* most, prolific and intensely-developed, go-to engine platform in the performance and racing communities.

The first small-block Chevy engine was introduced in 1955 and was available in the Bel Air and Corvette in 265 cubic inches of displacement. Small-block engines, featuring a cylinder bore spacing of 4.40 inches, produced from 1955 to 1974 were referred to as Turbo-Fire or High Torque engines. The 350-ci engine, one of many iterations of the platform, was introduced in 1967 and helped the small-block Chevy become one of the most popular platforms for performance use. The 350 is widely considered as the standard platform for the small-block family.

The 265-ci engine debuted in 1955 and was the foundation for decades of performance that followed. (Photo Courtesy GM Media Archives)

The 1965 327-ci engine with fuel injection is shown. The Rochester Ramjet fuel injection system was first offered as a high-performance option on the Corvette and GM passenger cars in 1957. It was discontinued partway through 1965 in favor of the Chevrolet big-block as a performance option. This is a purely mechanical system, unlike modern electric systems today. (Photo Courtesy GM Media Archives)

Shortly after the debut of the small-block engine, the aftermarket began introducing components that were primarily designed to work with the OEM factory blocks to improve performance. Beginning with upgrades to camshafts, intake manifolds, carburetors, and tubular exhaust headers, hot rodders and racers began to experience and enjoy substantial performance improvements. This continued with upgraded cylinder heads in both cast iron and aluminum, forged pistons of various dome configurations, superior ignition components, stronger valvetrain components, stronger connecting rods, stronger crankshafts, stronger main caps, different crank strokes and connecting rod lengths, etc.

As racers continued to stretch the engine speed and load parameters, weak links that became apparent were quickly addressed, resulting in increasingly stronger parts in addition to components and systems that offered power enhancements. Since those early days, the small-block Chevy engine became firmly established as the standard of performance engines for street rodders, drag racers, oval track racers, and road racing competition. Aftermarket manufacturers also began producing stronger engine blocks that offered superior strength, rigidity, and cooling, in addition to providing the ability to increase cylinder bore diameters and to accept longer crankshaft strokes. In the effort to reduce weight and to improve cooling, aluminum blocks became available for specific racing applications.

General Motors continued to evolve engine platforms from the early 1970s' LT1 and later LS-series designs to the current LT platforms, but despite this ever-evolving development of newer and more sophisticated platforms, the performance industry never abandoned the venerable Generation I small-block. It was just the opposite: development continues to this day to address the needs of enthusiasts and racers who steadfastly continue to take advantage of this engine platform.

The SBC has long been considered an iconic symbol of American performance, representing a standard to which all other V-8 engines are compared. In other words, the small-block (Gen I) Chevy engine was, and continues to be, an established workhorse and is unlikely to ever fall by the wayside. Taking advantage of all that the performance aftermarket industry has to offer, today's builders are able to create 1,000-plus-hp beasts. One of the greatest benefits to consider is that everything you need or want is readily available. It all boils down to how much you want to spend.

The early small-block 265 engines featured a 3.00-inch stroke and 3.750-inch bore that produced around 162 hp and about 257 ft-lbs of torque when equipped with a 2-barrel carburetor. The 283 engine moved up to a 3.875-inch bore and increased power to 185 hp. When fitted with dual 4-barrel carbs, a higher compression ratio of 9.5:1, and dual exhaust, the power level rose to around 270 hp. In 1962, the 327-ci design debuted, featuring a 4.00-inch bore and 3.250-inch stroke with OEM power levels that reached the 340-hp level (360 hp at 11.25:1 compression in the injected Vette version). Along came the 302 engine, famous for its application in the 1969 Camaro Z28 that offered around 370 to 465 hp, depending on the intake and fuel setup.

While the basic design platform for the small-block Chevy engine hasn't changed significantly, the performance aftermarket continues

Displayed is the infamous 302-ci high-winding engine that powered the iconic 1969 Camaro Z28. This engine was created in 1967 specifically to meet SCCA rules for Trans Am racing. The 302 is the byproduct of dropping a 283 crank into a 327 block. (Photo Courtesy GM Media Archives)

Thanks to ongoing aftermarket development, today you can configure a small-block Chevy for just about any application and degree of power. This example is a 422-ci build, featuring 100-percent performance aftermarket components that easily spit out over 700 hp.

Stronger and more efficient blocks, cranks, rods, threaded fasteners, and main caps have been developed to withstand today's demands for extreme power and torque. Assembly methods have changed as well with builders paying closer attention to real-world connecting rod bolt stretch as opposed to following torque specs.

Weight-reduced aluminum blocks are readily available for the SBC for replacement of the OEM design as well as specialty applications and for weight savings and superior cooling.

One of the most popular engine platforms for professional Sprint car racing continues to be the SBC designed for running alcohol fuel.

to develop components and procedures for boosting power and torque.

Along came the 350 small-block in 1967, and the die was cast. The 350 became the go-to standard platform for performance applications. The original crank stroke was 3.480 inches and was coupled with 4.00-inch bores. With a variety of bore and stroke combinations, cubic inch displacement choices grew. Yes, you can alter bore and stroke on any engine, but the 350 became extraordinarily popular as a basis of performance mods. The following chart provides examples of combinations.

OEM Crankshaft Journal Size

Be aware that Chevy small-block versions were initially available with different crankshaft rod and main journal sizes. Early 265 through 327 engines featured small journal cranks, while later versions featured medium journals, and the 400 version featured what is referred to as a large journal.

To provide a boost in cubic inches, and in an effort to make more torque, General Motors debuted

CI	Bore	Stroke
355	4.030	3.480
364	4.000	3.622
383	4.030	3.750
402	4.125	3.760
408	4.030	4.000
410	4.135	3.820 (one example)
422	4.165	3.875

Note: 410 Sprint Car rules allow 410 ci with a max bore of 4.165. Various combinations of bore and stroke are used to achieve 410 ci. The above list provides mere examples of displacement combinations. Some may require the use of aftermarket blocks to achieve bore sizes not supported on factory blocks.

Also note: If you plan to increase stroke, you're moving the big ends of the connecting rods closer to the camshaft. During test fitting, if you have a clearance concern, you'll need connecting rods that are designed for strokers, featuring relieved shoulders above the rod cap parting line area and/or a camshaft with a smaller base circle. This is why aftermarket block–makers offer raised-cam blocks that place the cam bore higher, typically available at cam bore centerline rises of +0.125, +0.134, +0.391, and +0.434-inch.

Small Journal Cranks		
CI	Mains	Rods
265	2.300	2.000
283	2.300	2.000
302	2.300	2.000
327	2.300	2.000
Medium Journal Cranks		
CI	Mains	Rods
262	2.450	2.100
267	2.450	2.100
302	2.450	2.100
305	2.450	2.100
307	2.450	2.100
327	2.450	2.100
350	2.450	2.100
Large Journal Cranks		
CI	Mains	Rods
400	2.650	2.100

Thanks to the research and development of aftermarket block man-ufacturers, we no longer need to rely on aged OEM blocks. Quality blocks, such as the Dart iron block shown here, offer superior met-allurgy, improved priority main oiling, and precision casting.

Forced induc-tion along with stronger bottom-end components raise the bar in terms of potential power. This twin-turbo SBC is a prime example.

In addition to the incredible array of components designed to enhance performance, the SBC is one of the most versatile platforms for visual customization.

the 400-ci version of the small-block in 1970. This block featured siamesed bores that provided more strength but reduced cooling efficiency. The bore was 4.125 inches and the stroke was 3.750 inches. The 400 crank also featured a larger 2.650-inch main journal as opposed to the 350's 2.450-inch mains.

In the early days, performance builders began using the 400 engine's 3.750-inch stroke crank in 350 blocks to increase displacement of the 350, along with enlarging cylinder bores to 4.030 inches (383 ci), which required align honing the main bores to accommodate the larger 400 cranks. Also, while the 350 platform required internal crank balancing, the 400 crank required an external balance with a balance-weighted damper and flywheel.

Starting in 1998, NASCAR applications began using the SB2, which is essentially the second generation of the original SBC. The basic difference lies in the cylinder heads, which feature an altered valve layout, 11-degree valves, and an 8-bolt valve cover instead of the traditional 4-bolt pattern. A popular build involves 440 ci with a 4.000-inch stroke, 4.185-inch bores, and 15:1 compression.

NASCAR's SB2 is essentially a small-block Chevy with different cylinder heads that feature 11-degree valves, an altered valve layout, and 15:1 compression. (Photo Courtesy GM Media Archives)

Today's Options

Today, aftermarket cranks with a variety of stroke dimensions and choices of rod and main journal diameters are readily available for the 350 platform. This allows builders to achieve just about any displacement desired with the added advantage of superior-strength forged crankshafts. With the advent and continuing development of superior aftermarket blocks, cranks, bearings, rods, pistons, heads, cams, rockers, stronger high-grade main caps, rod and head fasteners, pushrods, intake manifolds, carbureted and injected fuel systems, and advanced ignition systems and oil delivery, the need to make do with OEM components has been eliminated.

For applications that plan to use a crank-driven supercharger, small-block aftermarket cranks are available with longer, larger-diameter big-block snouts to accommodate the added stress. Many choices are available in terms of component design depending on the final goal, such as shorter-angle cylinder heads, larger valves, rocker arms of various ratios, valve springs of various metallurgy, design and rates, lightweight titanium retainers and valves,

Superior ignition timing is available by referencing directly from the crank via flying magnet crank trigger systems.

connecting rods in steel or aluminum, lightweight crankshafts with profiled counterweights, both wet and dry sump oiling systems, superior wet sump oil pumps, stronger and more precise timing systems, etc. The list goes on. There may be no other engine platform that has benefited from persistent, ongoing, and never-ending development than the stalwart small-block Chevy, and there appears to be no end in sight.

The small-block, especially the 350 platform, has become, in essence, the performance industry version of a Lego set. If you can imagine it, you can build it, all thanks to the efforts of early to present-day racing engine builders and the spectacular support of the entire automotive performance parts aftermarket.

The increasingly common use of CNC machining allows block blueprinting on a single machine, something unheard of in days past. Rather than consuming many hours and multiple machining operations, CNC block machining can be accomplished in a matter of minutes, with an incredible level of precision.

Despite the OEM development of current-day sophisticated engine platforms, such as the LS and LT series, the Gen I small-block Chevy engine continues to enjoy widespread acclaim and popularity for both street performance and racing applications. You simply can't go wrong with the beloved small-block platform. It's a true American icon.

The array of superior engine components available for the SBC is truly mind-boggling. All of today's high-level aftermarket components evolved from the initial OEM designs to offer incredible advancements in performance and durability.

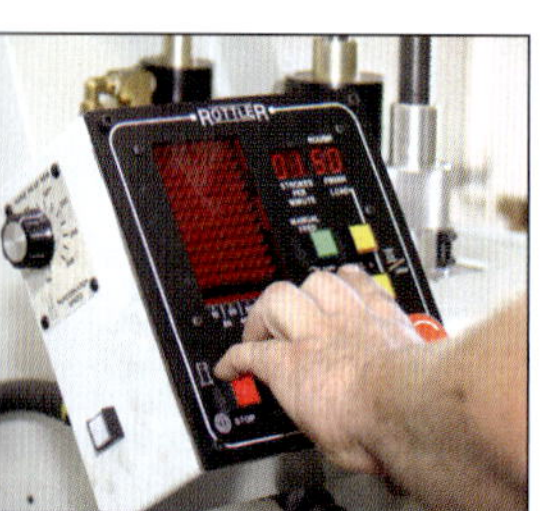

Engine building machinery has evolved by leaps and bounds over the years in the pursuit of not only efficiency but also high-precision results from cylinder bore and lifter bore corrections to main bore sizing and alignment, bore honing, crank balancing, cylinder head seat and guide work, head porting, and beyond.

Whether for a racing application or for powering a custom street rod, the small-block Chevy remains one of the most popular choices.

THE BLOCK: WHERE IT ALL BEGINS

From the inception of the Gen I small-block Chevy engine to the current LS and Gen V LT variants, they all share a few common basic traits: a 90-degree V-8 platform, 4.4-inch cylinder bore spacing, a single overhead valve camshaft, and a pushrod connection between the lifters and rocker arms.

As most enthusiasts already know, the small-block Chevy engine has been around since 1955. Over the years, displacement, strength, durability, and machinability (in terms of allowing modifications) variations have proliferated. Modern aftermarket blocks are available to accommodate much larger displacements and design variations than in days past in terms of both bore diameter and stroke increase increments as well as the ability to withstand higher cylinder pressures and operating speeds.

The Generation I small-block Chevy engine just keeps getting better with age. By age, I refer to non-stop development to enhance its capabilities. Refinements over the years have resulted in today's extraordinarily robust and versatile performance platform. Perhaps no other engine platform in the history of the internal combustion engine

has experienced more evolutionary enhancement changes than the venerable small-block Chevy engine. A prime example of those improvements to foundation componentry is the engine block. Currently available blocks specifically suitable for high performance include cast iron (of varying nickel content), cast aluminum, and billet aluminum.

Cast Iron Versus Aluminum

For both street and many racing applications, cast-iron blocks are perfectly acceptable. The inherent advantage of alloy blocks is obvious in terms of weight reduction: cast-iron blocks typically weigh in the area of 170 to 240 pounds, while aluminum blocks can weigh as little as 80 pounds, depending on various lightening options offered by some makers. Weight reduction is also necessary for certain forms of racing (sprint car racing, for example). Another advantage of aluminum is the relative ease/ability to be welded to repair certain failures, such as cracks, broken mounting tabs, etc.

Cast-iron blocks can be overbored within the limits of specific designs, while aluminum blocks feature iron

cylinder liners that limit bore oversizing. Today's aftermarket iron blocks typically feature thicker decks for increased rigidity, thicker cylinder walls that permit more overboring than OEM blocks, and improved cooling and oiling passages. Aluminum aftermarket blocks are available for designated bore sizes to suit just about any desired application. One major difference, aside from

While today's cast-iron aftermarket performance blocks are superior in strength and rigidity, some companies also offer compacted graphite iron (CGI) blocks, which offer increased material density and strength. (Photo Courtesy Dart)

the weight difference, is cost. Aluminum blocks are more expensive than cast iron. New cast-iron aftermarket blocks generally run in the $2,000 to $3,000 range, while new aluminum racing bare blocks can cost as much as $5,000 to $6,000.

Unless your racing application demands the use of an aluminum block, stick with cast iron. We won't waste time by delving into vintage OEM mass production cast-iron blocks. For purposes of this book, we'll only discuss currently available blocks offered by qualified aftermarket manufacturers.

A cast-iron block's material makeup can differ depending on the iron mix from gray iron or nodular iron to iron mixed with a level of nickel for increased hardness to CGI (compacted graphite iron). CGI features a molecular makeup that creates tightly interconnected graphite during the casting process that offers increased hardness, increased fatigue strength, superior ductility, and greater tensile strength. CGI is less brittle and more stable than gray iron. Several aftermarket block makers now offer CGI blocks. Due to the increased strength, a block can be machined for further weight reduction without sacrificing strength compared to a gray iron casting.

For instance, cylinder bore walls can be machined thinner without sacrificing wall integrity and strength. CGI is 75 percent stronger than gray iron and approximately 200 percent more resistant to fatigue. This makes CGI a good choice for racing blocks that need to withstand extreme pressures and temperatures. Also, due to the increased strength level, a CGI block can be machined to reduce weight by as much as 22 percent compared to gray iron.

Main Caps

For any high-performance application, a block should feature four-bolt main caps, which offer much greater rigidity to cope with the pressures of high-revving crankshafts. This reduces crank deflection and harmonics and offers superior clamping force for the main caps compared to early non-performance two-bolt main cap designs. All aftermarket performance blocks feature four-bolt main caps, many featuring splayed outer bolts at the number 2, 3, and 4 cap locations. The splayed outer bolts (usually at about a 10-degree angle) enter toward the side of the block where there's more material thickness as opposed to the bottom of the main web, which increases cap rigidity.

OEM Blocks

The use of OEM or stock blocks has served well as the foundation for street performance and racing applications. That was then, and this is now. Today's performance aftermarket now offers a dizzying array of block upgrade designs.

Aftermarket engine blocks feature superior casting materials and techniques. They are cast and raw machined to much tighter tolerances than vintage mass-produced Chevy OEM blocks. A Dart cast iron Little M block is shown here.

All performance aftermarket blocks feature four-bolt main caps. Depending on the specific block, the outer bolts may be straight on all caps, or caps number 2, 3, and 4 will be splayed at an angle.

Aftermarket performance blocks feature four-bolt main caps with the outer bolts or studs on caps number 2, 3, and 4 splayed at an angle, providing stronger fastener clamping force at a thicker area of the outer block instead of the bolts engaging into the bottom of the main webs. The example seen here is a Dart Little M block.

Aftermarket blocks (such as the Dart Little M shown here) typically feature relief cutouts at the pan rail sides to accommodate increased stroke. The block maker anticipates that the builder plans to use a longer crankshaft stroke. The block is pre-notched to provide added clearance between the connecting rod's big end and the cylinder bottom and pan rail. The block maker will specify that the block is planned for a certain stroke, for example 4.000 inches, and that additional clearance may be needed if a longer stroke or thicker aluminum rods are used. If additional clearance is required, the factory relief notch provides a starting point.

OEM iron castings were production based, which means that they're made in production batches. Because of mass-production techniques, inconsistencies and variations of design tolerances were common, such as core shifts that may have resulted in variances of cylinder wall thickness, cylinder bore on-centers, lifter bore on-centers, and machining tolerances that may have resulted in uneven deck heights and block deck squareness. By and large, these inconsistent mass-production tolerance issues were nothing that prevented the engine from running, or even running extremely well, but the path

Many aftermarket blocks feature splayed outer main cap bolts at the number 2, 3, and 4 cap locations, taking advantage of the increased mass toward the side of the block as opposed to entering the main web area.

of mass production didn't always optimize the power (and durability) potential of the wonderful design.

The mass-production tolerance issues aside, the majority were built using cast-iron main caps; some had a two-bolt design and higher-performance models featured a more robust four-bolt main cap clamping.

I am by no means trying to disparage the use of factory blocks. They served many generations of performance enthusiasts well both on the street and track. However, in an effort to make engines more durable in the process of attaining more power, performance and racing engine builders continually strove to improve and enhance the blocks by adding steel billet main caps accompanied with stronger, higher tensile strength main cap bolts or studs. Remachining factory blocks to improve the geometry involved careful align honing of the main bearing bore, oversizing cylinder bores to increase displacement, accurizing lifter bore centerlines by overboring, correcting casting-shift flaws, and installing bronze bushings back to required lifter bore diameter, etc.

In the quest for added displacement, large-stroke crankshafts were fitted and required relieving the cylinder bore edges and pan rails for clearance while being limited to stroke by potential clearance issues between camshafts and connecting rods. When chasing the demons of power, factory blocks posed other limitations in terms of block deck thickness, main web strength, cylinder wall thickness, and moderately efficient oiling circuits.

In addition to the evolutionary improvements on the original design, aftermarket blocks provide the option of starting the build with a brand-spanking new block as opposed to dealing with an aged, worn, and pitted original GM mass-produced block. Keep in mind, however, that Chevy Performance offers high-quality cast-iron racing blocks that are a cut above blocks that are produced for mass vehicle builds.

Enter the world of aftermarket performance engine blocks. Manufacturers, such as Dart, Brodix, Donovan, World Products, and Chevrolet Performance, offer small-block Chevy platform blocks in versions that range from stock-spec to racing-application-specific. These accommodate extremes of bore diameter and stroke to lightweight alloy construction and more, all featuring a vastly superior level of precision and strength compared to OEM mass-production blocks.

Today's aftermarket block makers offer variations that suit any application. No longer are you stuck with OEM designs that limit build potential. For example, today you can obtain blocks that feature tall-deck designs and raised-cam versions, both allowing the use of an increased crankshaft stroke. Raised-cam blocks, depending on the specific block, can feature the cam bore raised by about 0.391 inch beyond the OEM crank-to-cam centerline, resulting in a crank-to-cam centerline distance of 4.912 inches.

Moving the camshaft higher relative to the crank provides additional rod big-end to cam lobe clearance, which is especially critical when running fatter aluminum rods. Performance aftermarket blocks also typically feature longer cylinder walls that extend farther toward the crankcase, providing superior piston skirt support during bottom-dead-center transition. Typically, aftermarket blocks also feature enlarged lifter bosses, which allow the builder to machine the lifter bores to accommodate the lifter diameter of choice.

These are features that builders back in the day wish they had access to. Currently available aftermarket blocks are designed with all of the features and potential tweaks that allow builders to achieve the performance parameters that they want instead of being limited to what's feasible with an aged production block. Today's blocks unleash the builder's creativity to levels unheard of even a decade ago.

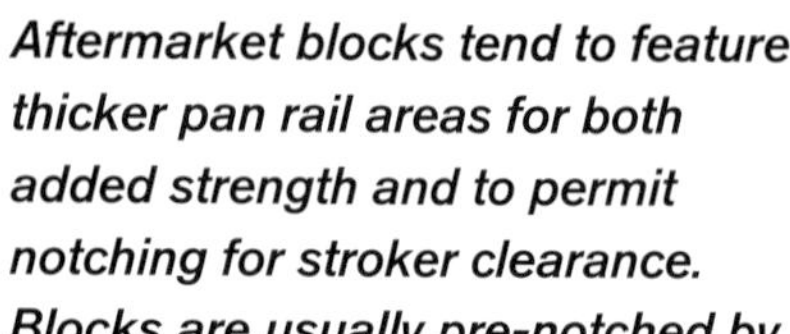

This aftermarket small-block features a 0.134-inch raised cam tunnel, providing extra clearance between a healthy larger-diameter cam core and the rod's big ends when an increased crank stroke is planned.

In essence, the Generation I small-block Chevy platform has been around for so many years and has been the basis for countless race-build variations that aftermarket block designs have evolved to reach an unprecedented level of strength and durability with superior casting processes and CNC machining. In short, today's blocks far surpass the capabilities and virtues of the original production blocks.

When it comes to small-block Chevy builds with aftermarket blocks, a common choice is between 350 or 400 main sizes. The 350 mains (2.45 inches) are fine for the street and high-performance builds, while the 400 mains (2.650 inches) are generally a better choice for extreme-duty builds because there's more cross-sectional mass

Aftermarket blocks tend to feature thicker pan rail areas for both added strength and to permit notching for stroker clearance. Blocks are usually pre-notched by the block maker in anticipation of the stroke that the builder has in mind. For instance, if the block was ordered for a 4.000-inch stroke, the factory clearance notches are usually sufficient. If additional clearancing is needed, it involves minor material removal.

In addition to thicker cylinder walls, beefy pan rail and main web areas, aftermarket blocks usually feature cylinders that extend toward the crankcase to offer additional stability for the pistons, reducing piston rock during the transition from bottom dead center.

between main and rod pin areas. The 400 main size provides a bit of added insurance against crank breakage.

When ordering most aftermarket blocks, lifter bores are usually slightly undersized, allowing you to bore to accommodate the desired lifter diameter. While 0.842-inch lifters are considered stock size, high-performance and race-engine builders tend to go larger; for example, 0.905-, or even 0.937-inch-diameter, lifters could be used to obtain a larger roller wheel diameter. While many iron-block builders use bronze lifter bushings (requiring overboring beyond the lifter diameter, installing the bushings, and sizing the bushings to provide the desired lifter oil clearance) when dealing with an aluminum block, bronze bushings really aren't needed since many builders prefer the lifters to ride against the parent aluminum. It should also be noted that many aftermarket blocks are available to accommodate either one-piece or two-piece rear main seals, which depends on the crankshaft selection.

Advantages of an Aftermarket Block

Today's aftermarket blocks offer many distinct advantages compared to mass-produced factory-original blocks. The most notable differences are as follows.

OEM blocks were designed with an oiling circuit that delivered oil from the pump to the filter, then to the cam bearings, to the lifters and rockers, and finally to the main and rod bearings. For high-stress and high engine speeds, this is simply not an efficient system. New aftermarket blocks as well as Chevy's line of performance Bowtie blocks reverse this with the main bearings receiving oil delivery first. This is referred to as priority main oiling, which has become the standard in performance blocks.

Block deck thickness on OEM blocks can vary greatly, sometimes to the point of not providing the rigidity required for high compression and negatively affecting cylinder bore roundness (cylinder bore distortion). Aftermarket blocks tend to feature much thicker decks, as thick as 0.675-inches, that provide superior strength, reduced cylinder bore distortion, and superior head gasket sealing when the cylinder heads are clamped in place. Cylinder wall thickness is also improved in aftermarket blocks in terms of both minimum thickness and improved consistency of wall thickness around the entire perimeter of the cylinder wall. This increased thickness further limits cylinder bore distortion and allows the builder to increase bore diameter further without weakening the cylinder walls.

OEM blocks may feature wall thicknesses as thin as 0.194 inch in the thinnest spots, while aftermarket blocks may provide minimum thickness in the 0.220- to 0.308-inch range even when cylinders are finished to a 4.125-inch diameter. Many aftermarket blocks feature siamesed bores with no water jackets between cylinders. This provides superior rigidity to the cylinder walls with less dynamic deflection, which also helps to minimize cylinder bore distortion. Controlling cylinder wall geometry (in an effort to maintain as much uniform roundness as possible during engine operation) reduces frictional drag and improves piston ring sealing.

While the standard small-block cam bearing bores are 2.000 inches, aftermarket blocks are available in a variety of bore sizes depending on the cam journal and/or the type and size of the cam bearings. A popular move is to use a small-block cam that features big-block cam journals of 1.949 inches in diameter, requiring cam bearing bores of 2.120 inches. This allows the use of an increased-mass cam core for added cam rigidity for less deflection when using with high-pressure springs. Even larger cam bore sizes of 2.250 inches are available for the use of needle roller cam bearings. Choices of cam bearing bores include 50, 55, and 60 mm. The cam bearing bore size can be specified when ordering the block. The aftermarket offers a high level of versatility compared to working within the constraints of an aged factory production block.

Today's quality aftermarket blocks offer vastly superior strength and rigidity with less metallurgical movement under thermal and dynamic stress. With these superior blocks, coupled with the ability of today's engine builder to accurize critical dimensions with either specialty blueprinting machining fixtures or multi-capability CNC machining, we have the best that today's technology offers to produce blocks capable of running and sustaining extremely high engine speeds. They can withstand the extreme cylinder pressures obtained through the use of high compression and/or high-boost forced induction. Unless you're planning a true historic restoration where you feel compelled to salvage a vintage block, today's aftermarket blocks are the better choice performance-wise, especially considering the quality offerings from such manufacturers as Dart, Chevy Performance, Brodix, and Donovan.

Dart

Dart provides the following offerings.

SHP Pro Iron

This is an excellent upgrade or stock replacement. Designed for street high-performance or sportsman racing and special high performance (SHP), this block is ideal for hot rodders, drag/circle track, off-road, or high-performance marine applications. For a few dollars more than you'd spend on a 40-year-old core that needs cleaning, machining repairs, and upgrades, this provides a new foundation for your build.

Many features provide superior performance and durability, including a priority main oiling system, Siamese cylinder bores with extra-thick walls, thicker decks for superior head clamping and gasket sealing, blind head bolt holes that don't enter water jackets, scalloped water jacket walls that improve flow around cylinders, and pre-clearance for a 3.75-inch stroke. Other features include splayed outer bolts on the middle main bearing caps, provisions for OEM stock roller lifters and cam, the use of 0.300-inch-tall stock 1987–1995 roller lifters, acceptance of the 1981–1985 stock-style oil pan and dipstick, and all OEM-location bolt holes for the starter, clutch ball, etc.

Race Series Aluminum

This weight-saving cast-aluminum racing block is offered in deck heights from 8.850 to 9.500 inches. The casting features a premium and proprietary high-strength RMR aluminum alloy. Cylinders are extended at the bottom for better piston support when used with long-stroke cranks. A raised cam tunnel provides added clearance for strokers. The cam tunnel is raised by 0.391 inch with an option for a 0.434-inch raise. Siamesed bores are offered in 4.000 inches or 4.125 inches and can be safely bored to as much as 4.165 inches. Ductile-iron cylinder sleeves and extra-thick walls provide an excellent ring seal.

The oil pan rails have been spread out by 0.400 inch at each side for more stroker clearance. This small-block platform features big-block cam bearings, allowing the use of larger base circle cams to reduce twisting with cam-driven pumps. Rear external oil inlets with crossovers and restrictor provisions located in the center of the lifter valley simplify external oil pump plumbing. This block has no provision for a block-mounted oil filter, so a remote filter is required.

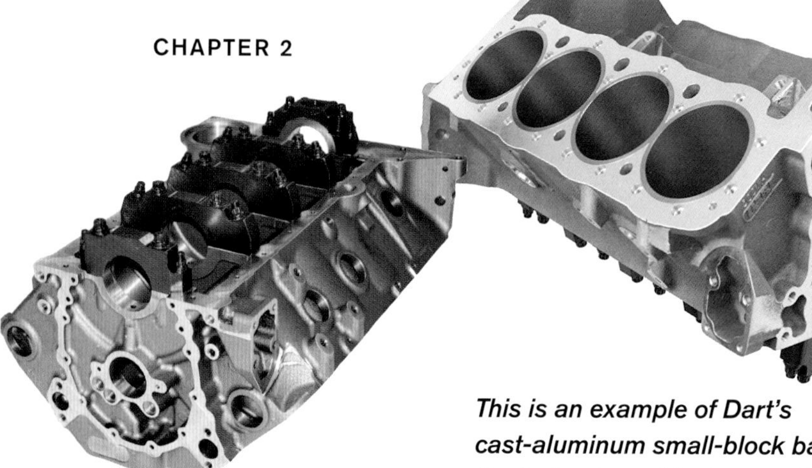

Dart's SHP Pro Iron block is pictured. (Photo Courtesy Dart Machinery)

Race Series 4.500 BS Aluminum

This enhanced version of Dart's cast-aluminum racing block is similar to the aforementioned race series aluminum block but features a 4.500-inch bore spacing and permits bore diameters up to a whopping 4.250 inches. Head bolt patterns are offered in either a standard 17-bolt or optional 19-bolt version. Deck height choices include 8.850, 9.025, or 9.075 inches. Tall-deck versions are also available at heights of 9.325 inches or 9.500 inches. The range of deck heights allows greater versatility for the preferred rod angle and ratio. Standard is a 0.391-inch raised cam tunnel, which provides a camshaft-to-crankshaft centerline of 4.912 inches. An optional 0.434-inch raised cam is also available.

Little M Sportsman Iron Block

This block is another offering from Dart that is ideal for a serious street performance build, sportsman racing, or a marine application when the builder wishes to use standard-type Chevy small-block parts, such as the cam, timing chain, oil pump, oil pan, oil filter, motor mounts, mechanical fuel pump, clutch linkage, etc. Improvements over a factory block, in addition to Dart's stronger casting and higher

This is an example of Dart's cast-aluminum small-block bare block. Cast-aluminum blocks are slightly more expensive than cast iron but cost substantially less than billet blocks. If weight savings is important and you can't afford billet, this is a great choice. (Photo Courtesv Dart Machinerv)

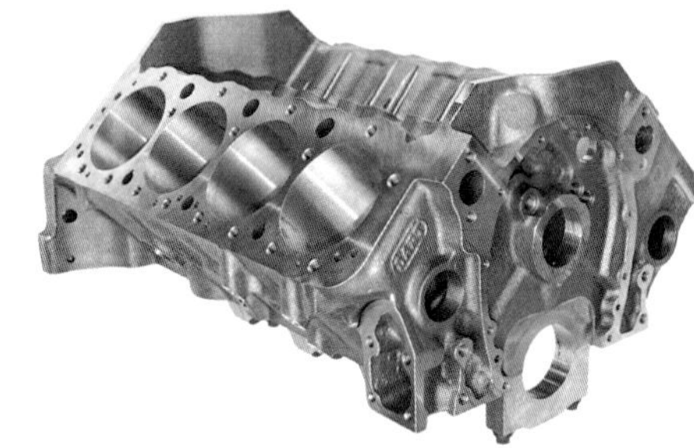

Dart's Little M Sportsman iron block is shown. Like all Dart blocks, options include the desired bore size, deck height, and standard or raised-cam versions. (Photo Courtesy Dart Machinery)

precision machining, include priority main oiling, where the main bearings are fed first, Siamese cylinder bores with extra-thick walls (a minimum of 0.275-inch thick even with a 4.185-inch bore), scalloped water jackets, an open lifter valley for improved oil return, enlarged lifter bosses that accommodate offset and oversize lifters, blind head bolt holes that don't enter water, splayed outer main cap bolts on middle caps, a rear external oil feed, and crossover and restrictor provisions.

Little M Iron Block

The Little M is a true cast-iron racing block suitable for street or track.

Like the Little M Sportsman block, it accepts standard SBC parts with all of the features of the Sportsman version. The Little M is fitted with billet steel four-bolt main bearing caps and is available in a CGI (compacted graphite iron) version that doubles strength without adding weight, making it a good choice for boost applications (turbo, supercharger, or nitrous). The Little M is beefed up in critical areas and designed from the ground up as a true racing block that can be used with off-the-shelf SBC components.

Little M 305 Water Iron

This block is legal for 305 Race-saver Sprint Series racing and is suitable as a stock replacement or performance upgrade block. To accommodate race classes that require stock displacements, this block features non-siamesed 3.750-inch cylinder bores and also has priority main oiling, thicker decks, blind head bolt holes, and splayed four-bolt main caps. It accepts standard SBC parts and has a rear external oil feed, crossover and restrictor provisions, an open lifter valley, and enlarged lifter bosses.

Iron Eagle 4.500 BS

The Iron Eagle is targeted at advanced engine builders for unlimited late-model or off-road truck maximum competition. The spread-bore spacing of 4.500 inches requires special 4.500-inch cylinder heads and components. The 4.500-inch bore spacing (as opposed to the standard 4.400-inch spacing) allows larger bore diameters and gasket sealing surface between bores. The maximum recommended bore size is 4.250 inches.

This block features a 0.391-inch raised cam tunnel, but an optional 0.434-inch raise is also available.

Oil pan rails are spread out 0.400 inch at each side for reduced windage and added stroker clearance. Oil pan bolt holes are in line with the main caps to eliminate interference with stroker setups. Other features include big-block cam bearings, dual starter mounts to provide a choice of left or right location, front and rear external oil inlets, and crossover and restrictor provisions.

Aluminum Billet Block

In addition to the wide variety of iron and aluminum cast blocks offered by Dart, the firm also offers an aluminum billet block that is machined from one huge chunk of dense forged 6061 aerospace aluminum alloy. These full-water-jacket blocks are custom ordered to your specs in terms of bore diameter, bore centerline, standard or 4.500-inch bore spacing, the deck height of your choice, the standard or raised cam bore location, cam tunnel options up to 60 mm, and custom lifter bore diameter and location. They are equipped with either steel or optional aluminum main caps. For a block that can be custom engineered to a builder's custom specifications, this is the trick pony.

Dart's Iron Eagle small-block iron block is shown here. (Photo Courtesy Dart Machinery)

This is an example of a Dart billet block that is ready to ship. The builder then final-hone-sizes the cylinder bores, cuts decks to desired height, and sizes lifter bores to accommodate the lifters of choice. (Photo courtesy Dart Machinery)

Brodix

All Brodix blocks are CNC machined from A-356 high-strength virgin aluminum castings and are popular choices for drag, late-model, and sprint car racing applications. A wide variety of deck heights, bore sizes, and main cap materials is available in addition to CNC-lightening options that carve unneeded material

Some block manufacturers, such as Dart, offer the option of billet aluminum blocks that are CNC machined starting with raw dense aluminum forged billets. Shown here are raw billets and semi-finished CNC machined blocks. (Photo Courtesy Dart Machinery)

from the blocks, effectively skeletonizing to reduce weight where possible.

Main bore and cylinder bore options include a 400 main/4.125-inch bore, 350 main/4.125-inch bore, 400 main/4.000-inch bore, and 350 main/4.000-inch bore.

Cam bearing choices include a small-block babbit, a big-block babbit, a standard 2.250-inch OD roller bearing or 50-mm roller bearing, and standard or +0.391-inch raised cam bearing locations. Note that the use of babbit-style cam bearings requires the use of wide cam bearings with 1/4-inch locks in the center bearing locations and spiral locks on the two end bearings. Roller cam bearings require spiral locks on all five bearings.

A host of custom-order versions of blocks are offered, including those with either wet or dry sump applications, with or without the fuel pump boss, standard or wide-pan rails, side water reverse cooling, front oil scavenging, lifter bore locations, spark plug holes, 350 or 400 mains, standard light steel or titanium main caps, deck heights of 9.000 to 9.300 inches, 9.000 to 9.500 inches, and 9.020 inches.

Stroker clearance is provided for 4.125-inch crank strokes if the block has a standard cam location. For raised-cam blocks, clearance is already set for a 4.250-inch stroke. The 410 sprint car blocks are clearanced for a 3.800-inch stroke.

Note: As shipped, cylinder sleeves are left slightly above the deck intentionally, allowing the builder the choice of surfacing the sleeves flat with the deck or not. As you can see, Brodix blocks are intended for serious pro-level racing applications with a multitude of options available to suit specific build requirements.

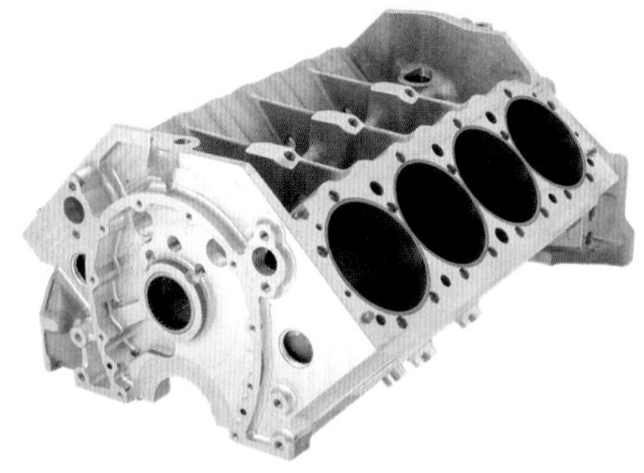

Brodix blocks are cast aluminum and intended for racing applications. Standard platforms are weight relieved via CNC cutouts, but additional weight relief is available as an option. (Photo Courtesy Brodix)

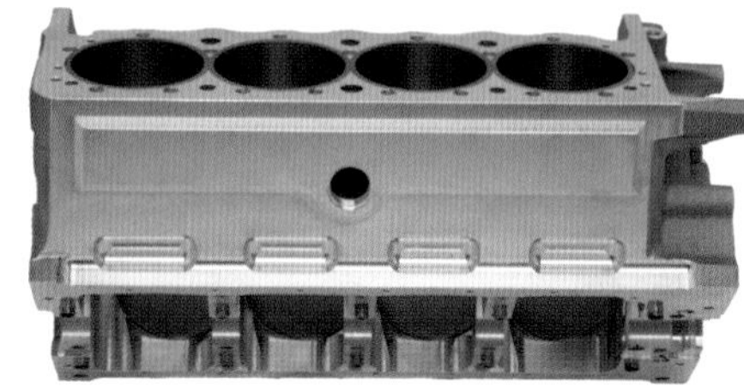

An example of optional block side lightening is shown where material has been removed without compromising block strength. (Photo Courtesy Brodix)

Brodix offers specific head stud kits for their blocks based on the builder's choice of specific Brodix cylinder heads.

Note that block versions are also available in solid form with no water jackets for extreme drag applications.

Basic order part numbers for blocks, not including the many options mentioned earlier, are as follows:

400 main/400 bore...............8011000
350 main/350 bore................8011001

Donovan

All Donovan blocks are made from high-strength aluminum castings with incredibly intensive and intricate CNC milling and feature priority-main oiling. Each block is custom made to suit the engine

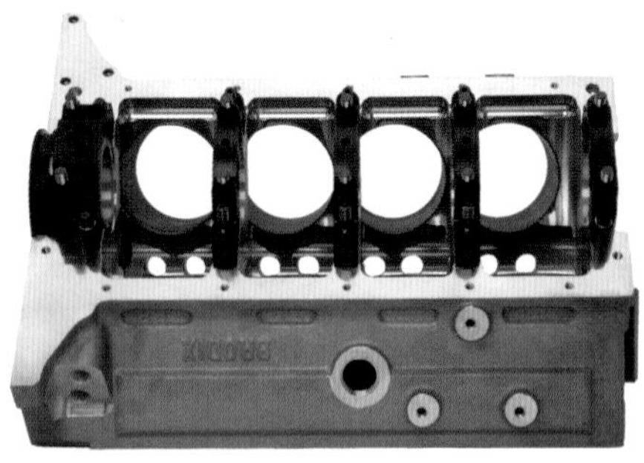

Note the as-cast block side. Although weight is reduced, blocks can be ordered with additional material removal for further lightening. (Photo Courtesy Brodix)

Aftermarket racing blocks typically feature added material at the lifter bore bosses to allow the builder to enlarge the bores to accommodate the lifter diameter of choice. When using roller lifters, lifters must stay in plane with the cam lobes and cannot be allowed to rotate, requiring either individual lifters guided in plane with dog bone guides or lifters that are paired together with a link bar. Note that this block features tapped holes between lifter bores, allowing the option of using individual or link-bar roller lifters. (Photo Courtesy Brodix)

builder's requirements. All blocks include a head stud kit, core plugs and dowels, ductile iron sleeves, main caps, and main cap studs, washers, and nuts. When first examining a Donovan block, it seems as if it was milled from a chunk of billet aluminum. The entire block (decks, lifter valleys, sides, front, main webs, etc.) is precision milled on CNC stations with the exception of the rear face, which is the only area that gives a hint that the block began as a casting. These are serious blocks intended for racing only (sans fuel pump and filter bosses, lightened exterior sides, etc.). All holes are threaded to accept –AN straight thread O-ring fittings.

Three basic configurations are available, including the HC400, 410, and 350/400.

HC400 Block

The basic features of the HC400 block include a weight of 105 pounds, the cam tunnel raised 0.390 inch, the deck height available to 9.500 inches, the pan rail 1/2-inch wider than stock, a fuel pump boss, an oil filter boss, and standard Chevy-type motor mounts. Custom pan rail patterns are available.

HC410 and 410 Block

Popular for sprint car builds, the HC410 block weighs in at a mere 83 to 88 pounds and is designed for dry sump oiling only. The blocks feature a 0.390-inch raised cam location and a fully machined exterior with a standard pan rail width. The 410 version weighs a paltry 80 pounds and features the standard cam location and removal of the fuel pump and motor mount bosses.

350/400 Blocks

This block is available to accommodate either a 350 or 400 main bore and features a 9.025-inch deck height, a fuel pump boss, standard motor mount bosses, and an oil filter boss. It is offered for either a 4.000 or 4.125-inch cylinder bore size. Weight is 100 pounds. Custom options include gear drive accommodation; full, half, or solid castings; and a special cam bore size on request.

Lightweight options are available for all Donovan blocks, such as removal of engine mount bosses and oil filter and/or fuel pump bosses, lifter valley and exterior shaving/profiling, etc., where weight savings is a priority.

Note that the HC designation indicates a raised cam configuration, which raises the cam 0.390 inch to

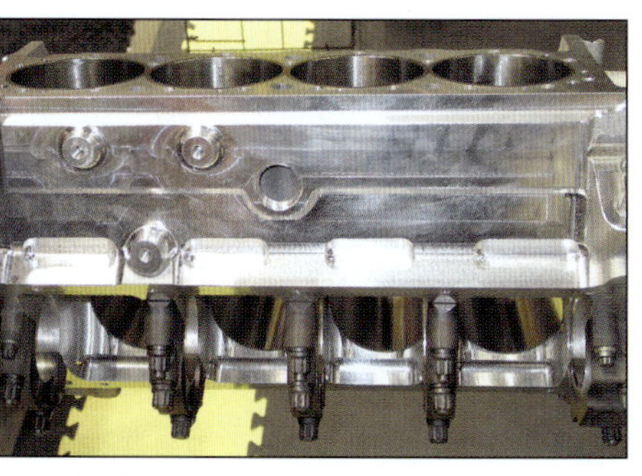

Aluminum engine blocks provide obvious advantages in terms of weight and are mandatory for some racing classes. The Sprint car series, for example, requires a cast block that is finished to a 410-ci displacement. Shown here is a popular Donovan aluminum block.

The Donovan aluminum 410 block is fully CNC machined except for the rear face, which is the only indication that it's a cast piece.

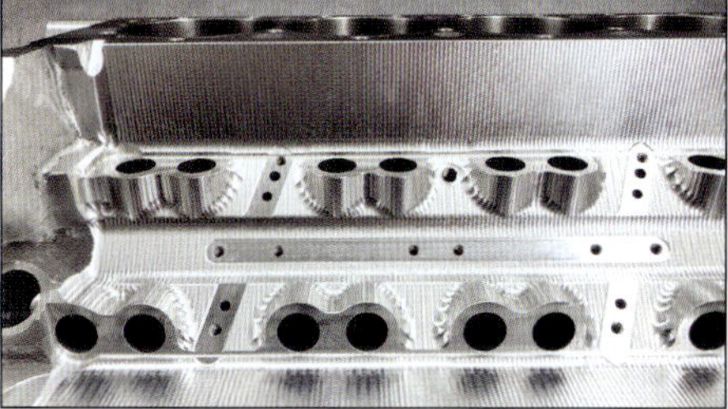

This Donovan racing block has been CNC machined even in the lifter valley, removing all material that is unnecessary while leaving enough material at the lifter bosses for the builder's plan to use the lifter diameter of choice.

The Donovan 410 block is fully machined on a CNC machining center, including the exterior sides, which are shaved down to reduce weight. Because of the dedicated racing application, there is no need for side motor mount bosses, fuel pump bosses, a starter boss, filter boss, etc. This is a good example of a racing-only block that is purpose-designed for racing function only, eliminating as much weight as is practical in the process.

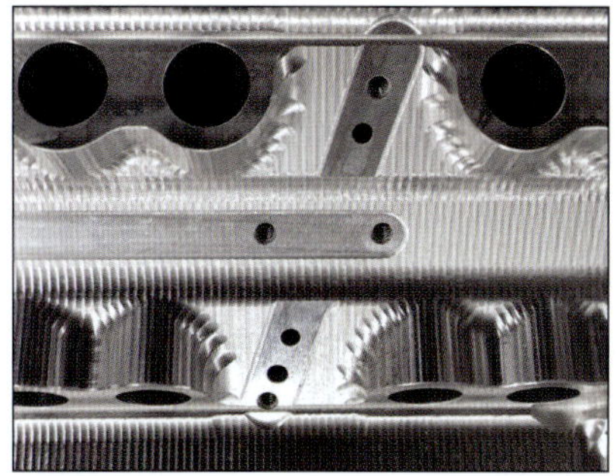

A close view of the lifter valley in this Donovan aluminum block reveals a series of tapped holes in the center. Since builders of these blocks tend to use needle roller cam bearings, these holes allow the insertion of stopper bolts that prevent the roller cam bearings from walking out of their bores during operation, which is possible due to the thermal expansion rate differences between the aluminum block and the baring cages.

While traditional small-block Chevy main caps provide a mount for a wet sump oil pump, when the builder elects to use a dry sump system, the pump holes in the rear main cap must be plugged. For blocks that are intended for dry sump applications from the very start, block makers provide rear main caps that have no such wet sump oil pump provision.

Makers of racing blocks often offer weight reduction options that include the removal of unnecessary material. This Donovan aluminum block is a good example. The block is so extensively CNC machined that it initially appears to have been machined from a solid billet of aluminum.

Main caps for high-performance or racing blocks will feature either nodular iron or billet steel main caps. Some builders prefer steel for its strength, while others prefer nodular iron for its combined strength and ductility, or resistance to breaking. One builder I spoke with, for example, prefers nodular iron because, "They tend to bend instead of break," he said, citing his experience with regard to extreme-duty engine failures.

Aftermarket block makers tend to design their blocks with added mass at the pan rail areas to allow for increased crankshaft stroke. Notice the healthy relief notch on this aluminum block for the big end of the rod's clearance.

When ordering an aftermarket block, in many cases you can specify an option regarding camshaft bore diameter, depending on your planned cam bearing application: standard (2.000 inches), big-block journal (2.120 inches), or roller bearing (50, 55, or 60 mm). In some cases, the block maker will produce the cam bore in a standard size, noting that the bores may be enlarged to accommodate the desired bearings. This example shows a block fitted with roller bearings.

Dedicated racing blocks, such as the Donovan aluminum 410, feature external coolant transfer plumbing due to material removal for weight reduction. The fitting in the center allows the racer to inject hot water into the block before firing the engine.

allow for increased stroker crank and rod to cam clearance, which can be sized for either 350 or 400 cranks. Special cam bore sizes are also available. The Donovan blocks are truly custom-order race blocks to accommodate the builder's preferences.

Chevy Performance Blocks

Chevrolet Performance offers a wide range of blocks specifically intended for racing use that receive more detailed prep compared to the regular street blocks.

Cast-Iron Bowtie Race Block

Features include the use of "premium" castings with thicker deck surfaces, priority main oiling, improved coolant flow, splayed four-bolt steel main caps secured with "premium" fasteners, and precision CNC machining to within 0.005 inch.

Chevy Performance Race Blocks

Racing blocks with applications for NASCAR and NHRA are reportedly CNC machined with closer tolerances than their Bowtie blocks (within 0.001 inch) and are reportedly capable of handling up to around 1,200 hp. Features include priority main oiling, four-bolt splayed steel main caps secured with premium studs, and a minimum cylinder wall thickness of 0.225 inch (at 4.155-inch bore). A sonic bore check data sheet is provided with each block. Nominal wall thickness is 0.340 inch. Extra-thick deck surfaces have blind holes that are not open to water.

Enlarged cam bosses allow custom machining for larger bearings, and extra-thick main bearing bulkheads provide greater strength. Main bearing cap inner bolts are spread 0.210 inch to allow machining

for the use of 400 journal cranks. The billet steel rear main cap is designed for wet sump use but can be plugged for dry sump applications. The rear main seals are the two-piece style, requiring pre-1986 style oil pans. Lifter bores are tall, requiring clearancing for some aftermarket solid roller lifters. The oil dipstick boss is not drilled, giving you the option of running a dipstick.

Chevy Performance Iron Bowtie Race Block

The Bowtie blocks, rated at handling 700-plus-hp, are CNC machined to within 0.005-inch tolerance. Designed to accommodate 350-size crankshafts, features include four-bolt splayed steel main caps, a deck height of 9.025-inch, two-piece rear main seals, 2.000-inch OD cam bearings, and 3.980-inch finished bores. Maximum overbore is 4.155 inches; maximum stroke is 3.750 inches.

Race blocks and Bowtie race blocks are available for use with one-piece or two-piece rear main seals and a wide variety of bore sizes and stroke accommodation. All feature four-bolt main caps. Examples include part numbers:

10066034	Two-piece rear seal, 4.000-inch bore
10105123	One-piece rear seal, 4.000-inch bore
88962516	One-piece rear seal, 4.000-inch bore, for 383 stroker
24502503	Bowtie, two-piece rear seal, 3.98-inch unfinished bore
12480175	Bowtie, one-piece rear seal, 4.117–4.155-inch bore
24502572	Two-piece rear seal, 4.500-inch bore
12480157	Bowtie Sportsman, two-piece rear seal, 4.117-inch bore
366300	Bowtie, aluminum, 4.000-inch bore, splayed nodular caps, for 2.45-inch journal cranks
366287	Bowtie, iron, 3.980-inch bores for 4.125 bore max, four-bolt nodular caps

World Products

World Products offers a variety of performance small-block Chevy blocks under the Motown II label. All blocks are a high-density cast-iron alloy and feature a deck height of 9.025 inches. Available bore sizes range from 3.995 to 4.120 inches, and some enable as much as a 4.200-inch overbore. Most blocks are pre-clearanced to accept a 4.000-inch stroke. Selections among the 18 variants offered include choices of cam journal sizes of 2.000 inches, big-block Chevy, and 50 mm. The available cam tunnel location is standard SBC or plus 0.134-inch raised. Bronze-bushed lifter bores are offered in either standard or 0.904 inch. Main bore size options include 350 or 400.

Depending on the specific block part number, main caps are ductile iron, nodular, or billet steel. In addition, a series of Motown Pro Lightweight iron blocks are offered with a bare weight of 178 pounds. With 18 different block part numbers from which to choose, the selection offers applications from street to full race.

Iron aftermarket blocks are often supplied with bronze lifter bore bushings already installed, requiring finish machining to the necessary diameter size and top trimming. (Photo Courtesy World Products)

Aftermarket block makers often use varying oil delivery designs specific to their blocks. This World Products Motown II block features oil crossovers for the lifter oil feed and is tapped for NPT plugs. If solid lifters are planned, deeper-located threads in the holes allow the use of plugs that are drilled to restrict oil delivery. (Photo Courtesy World Products)

Depending on the manufacturer, blocks may be ordered with either nodular iron or steel billet main caps, depending on builder's preference. Shown here is a World Products Motown II block fitted with nodular iron caps. (Photo Courtesy World Products)

This is an example of a World Products Motown II cast-iron block. As with other makers, these blocks are available with standard height or raised cam bores, standard or tall decks, and a variety of raw bore sizes. (Photo Courtesy World Products)

Iron blocks are often fitted with bronze lifter bore bushings, which are raw finished on the tight side, allowing the builder to machine the desired lifter clearance based on the diameter and type of lifters being used. Depending on the link-bar lifters, the top exposed bushing material may need to be trimmed to provide link bar clearance.

This is an example of a Motown II block with steel billet main caps. (Photo Courtesy World Products)

CRANKSHAFTS

Over the years, the evolution of performance crankshafts has experienced a high level of development in terms of materials, manufacturing processes, dimensions, weight reduction, windage concerns, oil delivery, surface finishes, counterweight aerodynamics, and quality control. Gone are the days when a racer is forced to make do by modifying a factory OEM crankshaft.

This is an example of a Scat lightweight forged crank with a scalloped flywheel flange, fully gun drilled, and with bullnosed and knife-edged counterweights.

Crankshaft Stroke

Crankshaft stroke refers to the distance from the crankshaft main centerline to the centerline of the rod journal. Published crankshaft stroke refers to the total sweep of the rod journal from top dead center (TDC) to bottom dead center (BDC). For example, a crankshaft that features a 4.000-inch stroke indicates that the rod journals will move 4.000 inches from TDC to BDC.

However, when we are planning a stroke, rod, and piston combination to determine the crank stroke, rod length, and piston compression distance (CD) relative to the block deck height, we consider only half of the total stroke of the crank. With the rod journal at TDC, the half-stroke distance plus the rod length plus the piston CD will dictate where the piston dome is located relative to the deck at TDC. If our goal is to achieve a zero deck, we refer to the deck height as our target.

Deck height is the distance from the main bore centerline to the block's head deck surface. If our deck height is 9.000 inches, the combination of half-stroke plus the connecting rod length plus the piston CD must equal the target 9.000-inch deck height. Connecting rod length refers to the distance from the centerline of the rod's big end to the centerline of the rod's wrist pin bore. Piston CD refers to the distance between the centerline of the wrist pin bore of the piston to the piston's top dome edge.

As an example, again referring to a deck height of 9.000 inches, if our crank features a crank stroke of 4.000 inches, we use half of the total stroke, which in this case is 2.000 inches. If our connecting rods feature a center-to-center length of 6.000 inches, our piston CD needs to be 1.000 inch. If our deck height is 9.025 inches, along with a 2.000-inch half stroke and 6.000-inch rod, piston CD would be 1.025.

Factory Stock Crankshaft Stroke

When building a high-performance small-block engine, we typically take advantage of changes to the stroke to obtain increased performance. Simply as a reference, the following tables show the factory-original stroke, rod length, and piston CD found in original Chevy small-block engines.

Factory Stock Crankshaft Stroke					
Engine (CI)	Year	Bore	Stroke	Rod Length	Piston CD
262	1975–1976	3.671	3.000	5.703	1.750
265	1955–1956	3.750	3.000	5.703	1.800
267	1979–1981	3.500	3.484	5.703	1.560
283	1957–1967	3.875	3.000	5.703	1.800
302	1967–1969	4.000	3.000	5.703	1.800
305	1976–1994	3.735	3.484	5.703	1.560
307	1968–1973	3.875	3.250	5.703	1.675
327	1962–1967	4.000	3.250	5.703	1.675
327	1968–1969	4.000	3.250	5.703	1.675
350	1967–1994	4.000	3.484	5.703	1.560
400	1970–1980	4.125	3.750	5.565	1.560

Popular Aftermarket Bore/ Stroke Combinations

When planning a build to deliver increased horsepower and torque, we're certainly not going to adhere to factory specs. Depending on the limitations of the block at hand, a wide range of cubic inch displacements is possible. Listed on this page are a few examples. Other limiting factors involve the crankshaft strokes available from specific manufacturers.

Aftermarket performance crankshafts for the SBC are available in a dizzying array of strokes, including 3.000, 3.250, 3.335, 3.480, 3.500, 3.562, 3.625, 3.750. 3.800, 3.875, 4.000, 4.125, and 4.250 inches.

Standard deck height for a small-block Chevy block is 9.025 inches. If a specific stroke, rod length, and piston CD combination exceeds stock deck height, a tall-deck aftermarket block is required to accommodate the extended distance from the main bore centerline to the piston dome. While stock deck height is 9.025 inches, aftermarket tall-deck blocks are available, usually with a deck height of 9.325 inches, permitting a longer stroke and longer rods.

Deciding crankshaft stroke involves several factors, including

Aftermarket Bore/Stroke Combinations		
Engine CI	Bore	Stroke
302	4.000	3.000
327	4.000	3.250
346	3.900	3.620
350	4.000	3.480
355	4.030	3.480
364	4.000	3.620
377	4.155	3.480
383	4.030	3.750
406	4.155	3.750
410	4.130	3.800
414	4.125	3.875
427	4.125	4.000
434	4.155	4.000
441	4.125	4.125
447	4.155	4.125
454	4.125	4.250

the physical dimensional variables of rod length, piston compression distance, block deck height, and the desired operating characteristics. Speaking in general terms, a longer crankshaft stroke provides increased torque, while a shorter stroke provides the ability for the engine to generate higher engine speed (RPM). For example, a drag racing application may call for a longer stroke, while a road race application may call for a shorter stroke.

We also need to consider crankshaft weight. A lightweight crank, due to a decrease in mass, allows the engine to rev quicker, which is an advantage in drag or sprint car applications. However, in racing where endurance plays a major role, a heavier crank that is not highly modified for weight reduction can provide increased stability with less harmonics, providing increased durability for long runs at high engine speeds, especially where engine RPM doesn't vary a great deal as the engine tends to run at a fairly consistent RPM. As you can see, choosing the crank stroke and weight involves a variety of factors.

In a small-block Chevy build, you have the option of running 350 main journals or the larger 400 main journals. Today's aftermarket blocks are available with either main bore size.

A crankshaft with 350 mains will feature a main journal diameter of 2.450 inches, while a crank with 400 mains will have a main journal diameter of 2.650 inches. Builder preferences differ depending on their experience and opinions. The small 350 main results in a lower bearing speed, which is preferred for better oil delivery to the bearings. The larger 400 main crank, while slightly beefier, results in additional loss of block material to accommodate the larger journals. My preference is the 350 main.

Always keep in mind that increases in the crankshaft stroke decrease the clearances between the connecting rod's big end and the block and between the rod's big end and the camshaft. In terms of cam clearance, rod big ends designed for stroker clearance are vital. They often require rods that feature shorter rod cap bolts, which lowers the profile of the big end's shoulder. This is the reason that aftermarket block makers offer raised cam blocks that position the cam tunnel about 0.300 inch or more, providing additional cam to the rod's big end clearance.

Just as the dynamic effect of aerodynamics plays a role in how the vehicle cuts through the air at speed, the profile shape of crankshaft counterweights can affect windage drag inside the crankcase. Although the crankshaft counterweights don't rotate through the sump's oil bath, oil that drains down from the top back to the oil pan wet sump or even a dry sump's pan can drain onto or across the counterweights. The counterweights don't need oil and should be kept as dry as possible to avoid unwanted parasitic oil drag.

Many builders prefer to knife edge the counterweights, which typically involves creating a rounded/radiused nose on the counterweights' leading edge, tapering down at the trailing edge, very much like the cross section of an airplane wing. This allows parasitic oil that tends to cling to the counterweights to skim over the counterweight and evacuate quicker, theoretically reducing oil cling and drag, providing what you might call a slipstream effect. While not necessary for a street-driven performance engine, profiling the counterweights can often provide an advantage in a high-revving racing crankshaft.

Another method of reducing drag caused by parasitic oil cling is to have the counterweights treated with a slippery specialty coating that prevents oil from sticking to the counterweights. Specialty coating firms, such as Swain Tech Coatings, PolyDyn Performance Coatings, and others, offer these services for racers who are looking for every possible advantage.

Many aftermarket performance crankshaft makers gun drill a hole through the center of the mains to reduce weight. This photo was taken during the manufacturing process at the Callies Performance Products factory.

OEM factory crankshafts were notorious for journal oil holes that featured no chamfering and had sharp edges. Performance builders commonly addressed these ports by softening the hole edges and grinding a chamfer to promote better oil flow. Today's aftermarket cranks are already prepped and generally have no need for further modification as seen in this main journal example.

While older OEM factory cranks featured a square-cut fillet at the journal-to-counterweight intersection, aftermarket performance cranks feature a radius transition. This provides superior strength, vastly reducing or eliminating the potential for a stress fatigue.

Rod journal oil holes are also lightly chamfered for better oil delivery to the bearings. Addressing and improving oil flow is just one of the features that aftermarket crank makers provide, eliminating modifications normally needed when dealing with yesterday's factory cranks.

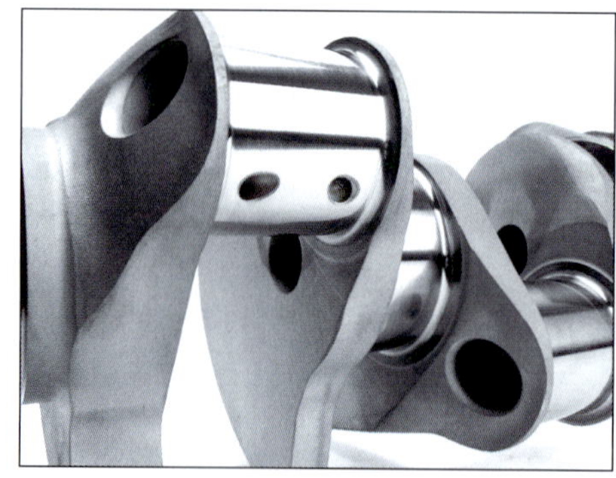

Aftermarket cranks commonly feature generous fillet radii that eliminate potential stress risers. (Photo Courtesy Lunati)

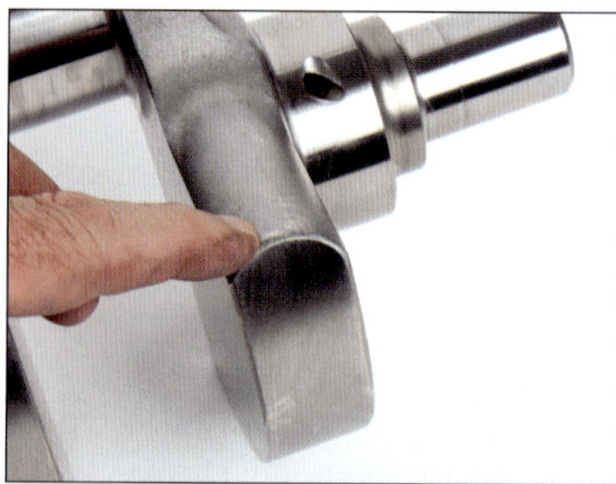

The leading edge of this counterweight is bullnosed to reduce drag, providing less resistance than a square-cut edge.

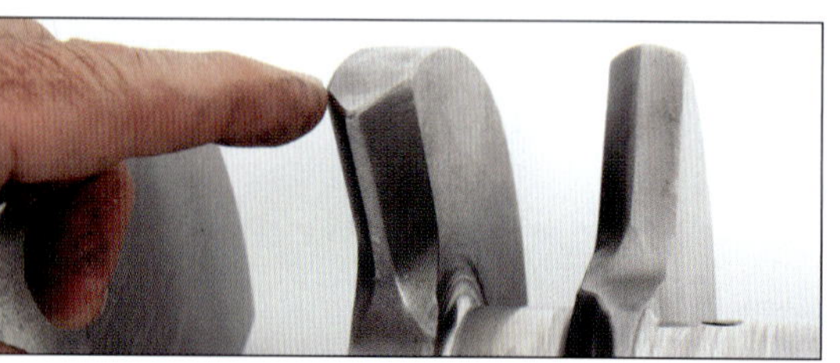

The trailing edge of this counterweight features a knife edge cut. This slows an increased slipstream effect. Coupled with a bullnosed leading edge, this approaches the aerodynamic effect similar to that of an airplane wing and provides less windage drag during revolution and faster evacuation of parasitic oil.

Finish-grinding journals is performed with a high degree of precision on state-of-the-art grinders that are constantly checked for calibration.

Unlike mass-production factory cranks of years gone by, today's aftermarket crank journals commonly feature very precise and consistently machined journal dimensions. It's rare to find a crank made by a reputable manufacturer that features out-of-tolerance diameters and taper. While measuring journals and installed bearing dimensions for fit and oil clearance is always necessary to verify, it's rare that corrections will be needed.

This closeup shows the extreme scalloped profile of the Callies Performance Products Magnum XL. Unneeded counterweight material is removed, providing a drastic weight reduction while maintaining a high strength-to-weight ratio. It is designed for lighter-weight rods and pistons, in terms of balancing accommodation. (Photo Courtesy Callies Performance Products)

Note the star-cut flange for reduced weight. This is a feature offered by several crank makers. (Photo Courtesy Lunati)

This is an example of a forged steel crankshaft from Scat. Standard-weight cranks feature full-size counterweights, while gun drilling provides a level of weight reduction. Unless extreme lightening is required for certain racing applications, a standard-weight crank is an excellent choice for all high-performance street and a wide range of racing applications as well. The critical elements include precision machining and journal hardness that are offered by leading crank makers.

An example of extreme lightening of a racing crankshaft is shown. The Magnum XL series features lightening profiles where counterweight material has been machined from non-stress areas, greatly reducing parasitic material and weight. This minimizes windage within the crankcase. Oil control is improved through the elimination of disruptive undercuts, resulting in smooth-sided, free-flowing counterweights. Each main and rod journal is gun drilled for additional weight reduction and improved throttle response. Magnum XL cranks are shipped fully balanced to the builder's exact assembly weight, requiring the builder to supply bobweight information. (Photo Courtesy Callies Performance Products)

Examples of the Lunati Signature Series are shown. They are made from a non-twist 4340 forging and are rated at handling over 1,500 hp. Features include gun-drilled mains, lightened rod journals, micropolished journals, and windage-reducing, contoured-wing counterweights. Signature Series blower applications are also available and are designed for use with Roots-type superchargers. Features include 0.125-inch fillet radii on rods and mains, duel keyways, larger nose bolt threads, and enlarged flexplate flange threads. (Photo Courtesy Lunati)

Bore and Stroke Combinations

Determining a bore and stroke combination for cubic-inch displacement involves a very simple formula:

Bore x Bore x Stroke x 0.7854 x number of cylinders.

Example: Let's say that the planned cylinder bore size for an 8-cylinder engine is 4.125 inches and your planned crankshaft stroke is 4.000 inches.

4.125 x 4.125 x 4.000 x 0.7854 x 8 = 427.6503

Selecting Crankshaft Stroke

Too many enthusiasts tend to choose the bigger option as the best choice for just about everything—a bigger cam, bigger heads, a bigger carb, etc. Increasing crankshaft stroke provides greater torque down low. Shorter strokes allow the engine to rev higher. It all depends on where you want the peak power and torque. Especially for forced induction engines that utilize supercharging or turbocharging, a longer stroke simply isn't needed because the increased dynamic compression under boost is making the power.

Consider the relationship of cylinder bore diameter and crankshaft stroke, wherein we refer to the "square" of the engine. If the bore diameter and stroke are equal, for example if bore size is 4.000 inches and stroke is 4.000 inches, the engine is square. If the bore diameter is greater than crank stroke, the engine is referred to as over-square. If the bore size is less than stroke, it's under-square.

With the bore size as a constant, increasing the crankshaft stroke tends to produce greater torque and low-RPM power but is more limited in engine RPM. Going to a shorter stroke allows increased engine speed and moves power higher in the RPM band. If your goal is to obtain more torque for street driving, building the engine square or under-square is preferable. If you're planning a road racing or oval track build, moving to an over-square platform is likely the better choice.

There's no magic formula to determine which stroke and/or bore size is ideal because other factors, such as cylinder head flow, valve size, valve angle, camshaft profile, etc., influence the final outcome. However, speaking in very basic terms, when selecting the crankshaft stroke, longer strokes suit higher-torque requirements, while shorter strokes are better suited for higher engine RPM. Many street builds call for maximum displacement and maximum torque, which is why many opt for the biggest bores and longest strokes that will fit into the confines of a specific block package.

A very generic view of stroke selection is that a longer stroke provides increased torque with the powerband moved toward the lower RPM range, while a shorter stroke provides the capability of higher revs with the powerband moved into the higher RPM range.

Forgings and Billet

Steel forged crankshafts can be made using either a twist or non-twist method. A twist forging takes a raw forged crankshaft and, while heated and malleable, twists the forging to orient the rod throws in the proper clock position. A non-twist forging forges the crank with rod throws already in the proper clock positions. The difference is that a non-twist forging has a more uniform grain structure and is therefore stronger.

High-performance forged cranks intended for extreme applications are made using the non-twist method. This is followed by finish-machining, heat treating for strength and stability, and nitriding for increased surface hardness. Examples of makers include Callies Performance Products, Crower, Scat, Winberg, Eagle, and Lunati.

Billet crankshafts are, as the term implies, CNC machined from a solid blank of high-quality dense steel. Billet crankshafts are, not surprisingly, more expensive due to the material waste and the increased CNC machining time. Billet cranks are available from several manufacturers, including Scat, Callies Performance Products, Winberg, and Bryant Racing, to name a few.

The advantage of choosing a billet crankshaft is twofold: strength and custom application. The molecular structure is consistent because the process begins with a dense forged billet. Depending on the specific application, a crank machined from billet stock may be as strong or stronger than a crank that is forged and finish machined.

One of the real benefits of a billet crank is the ability to create exactly the crank you want. Since it's being machined from a blank at the outset, all dimensions can be achieved to suit your specific needs. That includes main and rod journal diameter and width, stroke, counterweight shape, snout diameter and length, etc. For a street application or a weekend warrior build, the cost versus function makes a billet crank a bit of overkill. However, for the pro racer who requires maximum durability and custom dimensions, the higher cost is justifiable.

Forged crankshafts are produced with a steel/alloy mix, slug heated to formability, compacted to rough shape in a hydraulic press, machined, and heat treated.

Aftermarket forged cranks are a better choice compared to OEM forged cranks. The reason: OEM forged cranks tend to have a high carbon content, but aftermarket forged cranks tend to have a higher content of chrome and nickel in the formulation, and the higher alloy content provides much superior strength.

Common debates exist in regard to strength. Some note that a forged crank offers superior strength because the grain structure has been moved and compacted, resulting in a more uniform grain structure during manufacturing. Billet cranks begin life as an already-forged chunk of billet steel, which is then machined to shape. However, the grain structure tends to run more parallel to the length of the crank. Depending on who you talk to, you'll hear that billet is stronger than a forging or that a forging is stronger than billet. We won't get into the debate here. As far as I'm concerned, a forged or billet crankshaft made by a reputable performance aftermarket manufacturer is suitable. The major difference, in my opinion, is that choosing a billet crankshaft provides increased latitude in terms of creating a custom-dimension crank in those instances where a builder's request simply can't be fulfilled by an off-the-shelf forged crank.

Today's performance aftermarket offers crankshaft features that were unheard of only a few decades ago. Thanks to ongoing development within the aftermarket, we

Shown here is Lunati's Voodoo lightweight crank with a substantial amount of material removed to reduce rotating weight while maintaining rigidity. The 430 is a non-twist forging and is nitride heat treated with lightening holes in the rod journals. Note the undercut counterweights for further weight reduction. (Photo Courtesy Lunati)

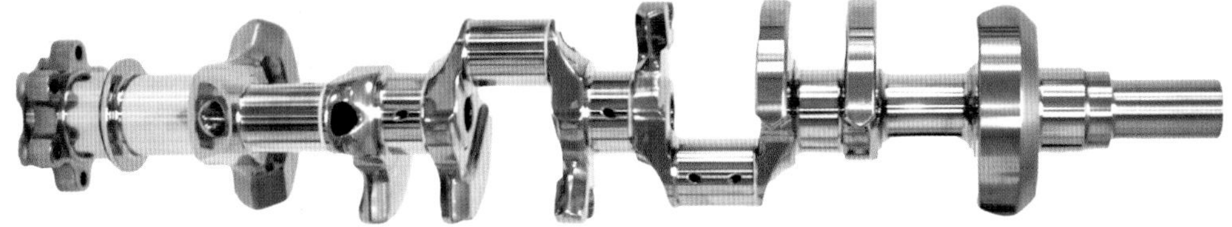

An example of a billet crankshaft by Bryant Racing is shown. Starting with a several-hundred-pound dense steel billet, the entire crankshaft is CNC machined to finished state, followed by REM isotropic finishing. (Photo Courtesy Bryant Crankshaft)

now have a greater selection of stroke dimensions, counterweight shaping, weight reduction, journal diameter choices beyond stock sizes, vastly superior metallurgy, high-precision CNC machining, surface finishes, and more, which translate into availability of performance cranks that contribute to obtaining increased power and torque along with substantially improved durability.

Crankshaft Durability Treatments

In an effort to make a crankshaft more durable, more resistant to fatigue, and to provide a hard bearing surface, a process of nitriding is commonly employed. This creates a nitrogen-infused surface treatment that creates a several thousandths of an inch thick hardness increase that allows the crank to better withstand high bearing loads. An ion plasma nitriding process produces a deep case that enhances strength while creating an extremely hard bearing wear surface.

This is not to be confused with cryogenics, which offers its own benefits. Cryogenics involves subjecting the crankshaft to sub-zero temperatures as low as -400°F and warming it back up to ambient temperature in a controlled time process. This compacts the steel/alloy steel material into a tighter, more uniform molecular "grain" to offer higher resistance to fatigue.

Another process that provides a more uniform molecular structure is vibratory stress relief, which is a non-destructive method of subjecting the part to computer-controlled harmonic frequencies that vibrate the molecules, producing a more uniform structure. Vibratory stress relief is referred to as non-destructive because the part cannot be damaged during the process, unlike cryogenics, where strict protocols must be followed to avoid making the part too brittle. Improving the grain structure and/or surface hardening a crankshaft won't produce additional horsepower, but these processes contribute to improving the durability of the crankshaft during extreme loads and speeds.

REM Finishing

REM's Isotropic Finishing process (ISF) has been in use in various industries for decades but has been more commonly used in performance and racing applications in recent years. In combination with a proprietary chemical treatment and a vibratory polishing process, an REM-finished crankshaft's appearance is extremely polished and smooth. Basically, it looks as though it's been highly polished and chrome plated. With the appearance set aside, the performance benefits are what count.

Benefits include friction reduction, increased efficiency, a horsepower increase due to reduction of parasitic friction and oil cling, lower operating temperatures, reduced lubrication requirements, and increased component durability as sharp potential stress risers are reduced. Applications for REM finishing include not only crankshafts but also connecting rods, camshafts, lifters, valve springs, rocker arms, ring and pinion assemblies, mechanical oil pumps, rack and pinion steering components, transmission gears, universal joints, etc.

The REM ISF process results in a non-directional, low-Ra surface finish, which means that the surface is extremely smooth with reduced microscopic peaks. *Ra* stands for roughness average. The lower the Ra number, the smoother the finish. Think of it this way: consider the difference between sanding a metal surface with 80-grit sandpaper compared to using 2000-grit paper.

As an example (and a good one at that), an accomplished engine builder and close friend recounted a tale of a customer's race engine. The engine was built using an REM ISF treated crankshaft. My friend's shop performed all of the machine work, and the customer assembled the engine. He installed an adjustable-height distributor that featured a slip collar. The owner of the engine forgot to tighten the slip collar. As a result, during a race, the distributor began to climb out of its location to the point where it lost contact with the oil pump drive shaft, quickly resulting in zero oil pressure. He ran the engine for another lap before returning to the pits.

After the race, he brought the engine to my friend's shop for a teardown and inspection. Incredibly, while the crank showed signs of extreme overheating and the bearings were toast, the crank's rod and main journals were scratch-free, looking like the day the crank was finished.

The typical cost for REM ISF processing is about $600 for a crank and a set of eight rods. When you consider what's at stake, that's not a bad price to pay for added peace of mind.

CONNECTING RODS

Connecting rods are one of the most critical components for any performance build. They provide the connection between the crank and the pistons and must withstand compression force and the dynamics incurred during the transition between approaching TDC and leaving TDC. Tensile strength, rigidity, and weight considerations are key factors. For engines designed to produce high levels of both horsepower and torque, only high-quality aftermarket forged steel, aluminum, or titanium rods should be considered. Cast rods should be completely ignored.

Today's aftermarket offers a mind-boggling selection of rods in terms of superior materials, design innovations, lengths, and bearing bore diameter sizes to accommodate any build that you desire.

Rod Ratio

Rod ratio is the combination of crankshaft stroke and connecting rod length. The ratio created by this combination affects both performance and durability. Rod ratio needs to be considered. Rod ratio is calculated by dividing the rod length by the crank stroke. For example, if the crankshaft features a stroke of 4.000 inches and the rod length is 6.000 inches, 6.000 divided by 4.000 equals a 1.5:1 rod ratio.

By increasing the stroke or by using a shorter rod, the rod ratio decreases. If the stroke is reduced or a longer rod is used, the rod ratio increases. Changes in the rod ratio affect the operating angle of the rods, which in turn affect piston thrust load and friction between piston skirts and the cylinder walls.

Generally speaking, for street and high-performance use, rod ratios in the 1.5 to 1.8:1 range are acceptable, and about 1.75:1 is considered by some as ideal. However, extreme performance applications sometimes use ratios as high as 1.9 to 2:1.

When generically discussing rod length, let's compare 5.700-inch rods to 6.000-inch rods while keeping the crank stroke unchanged. A shorter rod causes the piston to spend a bit less time dwelling at top dead center (TDC). A longer rod causes the piston to dwell longer at TDC, resulting in greater combustion pressure. A 5.700-inch rod allows the piston to dwell for about 2 to 3 degrees at TDC, while a 6.000-inch rod allows the piston to dwell at TDC about 9 to 10 degrees. The longer dwell time with a longer rod helps to flatten out the torque curve an allows the use of

Factory OEM rods in the past typically required machining or grinding to create a weight-matched set. Current aftermarket performance rods commonly require little, if any, weight corrections.

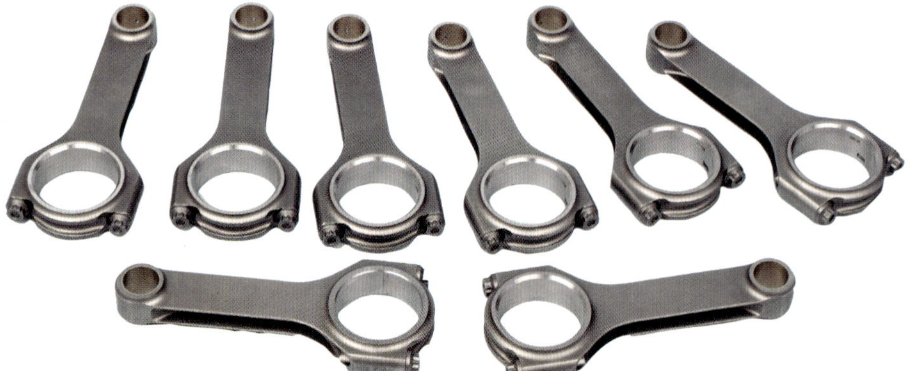

HOW TO BUILD KILLER CHEVY SMALL-BLOCK ENGINES

a higher compression ratio on pump gas. A longer rod aids the engine to pull better in a high RPM range.

The use of a longer rod also allows the use of pistons with a shorter compression distance (distance from the wrist pin centerline to the dome), which allows for a shorter skirt length, reducing weight mass. In basic terms, a longer rod provides more torque at high RPMs and reduces friction due to the reduced operational angle compared to a shorter rod.

All things considered, what is the best stroke and rod length combination? It all depends on your objectives.

Both OEM and aftermarket blocks are available in standard 9.025-inch deck heights, in addition to a variety of tall-deck configurations. Using Dart as one example, deck heights of 8.850, 9.025, 9.325, and 9.500 inches are available.

When determining the rod length that fits your build, you must consider these factors:

- Block deck height
- Half of the crank stroke
- Piston compression height

The reason we are only concerned with half of the crankshaft stroke when determining rod length is because only the TDC location of the crank rod journal influences the placement of the piston dome relative to the block deck. So, if the crank features a 4.000-inch stroke, we only factor in one half of the total stroke, which in this case is 2.000 inches. The half-stroke dimension, coupled with rod length and piston compression height, combines to place the piston dome at the block deck, whether this is desired at zero or slightly below deck according to the builder's plan.

While rod ratio is certainly a factor to consider, other factors, such as displacement, compression ratio, cylinder head flow, cam timing, and exhaust scavenging, play a bigger role.

Types of Rods

If you're planning to build a killer small-block Chevy, or any serious-performance engine for that matter, forget factory rods. Spend the dough on a set of high-quality aftermarket rods. Today's rod makers use superior materials for strength and durability with higher-precision machining and typically offer rods that are spot-on in terms of dimensions and weight-match.

Since stroke increases are so popular, leading rod makers have addressed this by featuring lower profiles at the top shoulders of the rod for clearance. This eliminates the need to modify the rods to gain needed clearance at the pan rails and cylinder bottoms.

Forged Steel Rods

Today's forged steel rods are made by heating a dense ingot of alloy steel (commonly using 4340 steel) to a malleable state at about 2,200°F, then forming the raw part under as much as 240,000 pounds of pressure in a forging die. The forging process results in an extremely strong unit

Examples of Commonly Available SBC Rod Ratios		
The examples used had a 9.025-inch deck block. Rod length is divided by crank stroke.		
Crank Stroke	**Rod Length**	**Ratio**
3.000	5.700	1.9:1
3.250	5.700	1.75:1
3.335	5.700	1.709:1
3.350	5.700	1.701:1
3.480	5.700	1.637:1
3.500	5.700	1.628:1
3.562	5.700	1.600:1
3.562	5.850	1.642:1
3.625	5.700	1.572:1
3.625	5.850	1.613:1
3.750	5.700	1.52:1
3.750	6.000	1.6:1
3.800	5.700	1.5:1
3.800	6.000	1.578:1
3.875	6.000	1.548:1
4.000	6.000	1.5:1

Examples of Commonly Available SBC Rod Ratios		
The following miscellaneous examples had a 9.500-inch-tall deck block.		
Crank Stroke	**Rod Length**	**Ratio**
4.000	6.125	1.53:1
4.125	6.200	1.5:1
4.125	6.250	1.51:1
4.000	6.250	1.56:1
3.800	6.250	1.64:1
3.562	6.250	1.75:1
3.250	6.200	1.90:1

with a tight molecular grain, which is followed by heat treating and stress relieving. This makes the metal stronger with a tighter, more-compacted grain structure. Depending on the rod maker, the rods may then be induction hardened, shot-peened, and/or cryogenically stress-relieved and heat treated.

The trimmed, rough-shape forging is then quenched and tempered. Heat treating should be done before machining because the heat treating/tempering process can deform the part's shape by as much as 0.060 inch. Manufacturer methods may vary but might involve quenching the part in a glycol solution. The raw rod is then CNC machined, the raw cap is cut away, both mating surfaces are machined to create a light undersize, the cap is installed, and the big end is machined to create a perfectly round hole at a precise diameter. Once machining is complete, the rod is stress relieved and surface hardened.

Note the contoured/low profile of the upper rod bolt shoulders. Aftermarket rod makers are aware of the need to accommodate increased stroke, offering this design to provide additional clearance. This is an example of a Scat stroker rod.

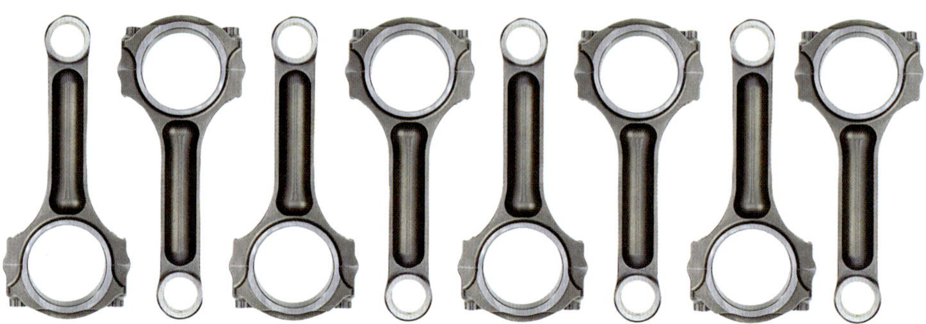

A set of Oliver Racing Parts I-beam steel rods is shown here. High-quality aftermarket rod makers offer tightly weight-matched sets. I-beam steel rods generally offer lighter weight and are more suited for high engine speeds. With that said, excellent results can be had with either beam design in terms of both high revs and torque handling capability. In many cases, the choice of beam design is dictated by a builder's personal preference. (Photo Courtesy Oliver Racing Parts)

Commonly available beam designs include H-beam and I-beam. Examples of I-beam rods are seen here. Beam design preference is often the result of the opinion and/or experience of the individual builder. Rods of both designs made by reputable manufacturers offer high tensile strength.

While most OEM rods feature press-fit wrist pins where the pins float but are press-fit to the piston pin bosses, aftermarket piston makers and rod makers offer full-floating pin designs where the pins freely rotate in both the rod's small end and piston. Some rod makers offer a choice of press or float applications. An oil-fed bronze bushing is featured in the rod small-end bore for enhanced lubricity.

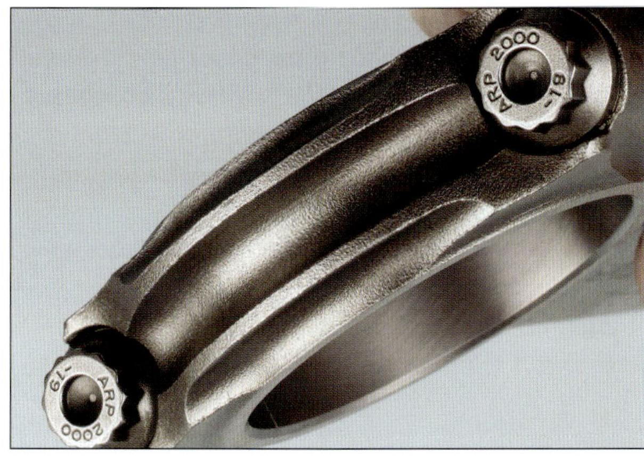

In a further effort to both reduce weight and increase strength, aftermarket rod caps often feature a ribbed design.

Aftermarket performance rods are chamfered at the side of the rod that faces the crankshaft's rod journal radiused fillet. Because performance cranks feature a generous radius fillet at each end of the journal, this chamfer accommodates the needed clearance to prevent an otherwise square-cut big-end bore from interfering with the radiused fillet.

Aluminum Rods

Aluminum rods have their advantages, but they're not for everyone. Yes, they may be lighter compared to forged steel, but they're more expensive, and they're fatter, so clearance concerns become more of an issue.

Aluminum rods start as dense forgings or dense-forged billet stock that are CNC machined to the final shape. Materials are commonly a 7075 or 7075-T6 aluminum alloy. Die-forging provides a more highly dense grain structure for added strength. During the forging process, the material is exposed to about 700°F and impacted with as much as 2,200 tons of pressure, resulting in enhanced grain flow and material density.

While weight reduction is a plus, due to the increased thickness, more attention is required in terms of clearance checking. If aluminum rods are used, just as hard washers are needed for aluminum cylinder head bolt locations, hardened washers must be installed under the rod bolt heads to prevent the bolt heads from digging into the parent aluminum. Aluminum rods are ideal for extremely high RPM and are suited for drag racing because the aluminum flexes and serves to absorb compressive and transitional energy to/from TDC.

Drag engines are run hard and then shut off at the end of the run. However, that characteristic makes them unsuitable for road racing applications where the flexing under loads is continuous. A myth is that aluminum rods stretch too much. They actually don't stretch. The material expands more compared to steel. In terms of length growth, the rod may only grow under operating temperature by only a few thousandths of an inch. Obviously, piston-to-valve clearance must be more tightly adhered to.

Aluminum rods typically feature an I-beam design for clearance reasons. Since an aluminum rod beam must be wider to begin with, an H-beam design would make the beams even wider. One downside of aluminum rods, aside from the higher price, is cycle life. Because the material grows and flexes, the fatigue life is shorter compared to steel, so the frequency needed to replace them in terms of the number of races/runs is greater.

Billet Rods

Billet rods begin life as dense-grain forged plate stock that is then CNC machined to shape. Billet rods are available in both alloy

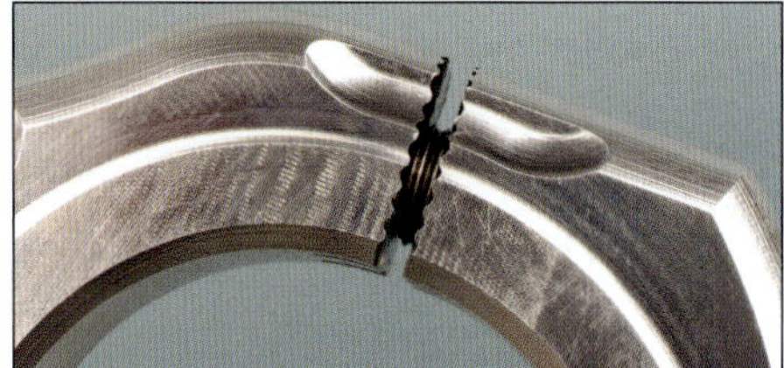

Aluminum is obviously lighter than steel, but aluminum rods need to feature a larger cross section to provide enough beefiness/strength. Aluminum rods are CNC machined from dense billet forgings and offer a very tight grain pattern. The example seen here is from GRP.

Rather than relying on the dowel sleeve and/or rod bolts to register the cap to the rod saddle on this GRP aluminum rod, radius-pattern tooth grooves have been machined into both mating surfaces for an extremely precise cap register.

Because aluminum rod material expands more than steel, the rod's big end diameter tends to slightly grow under temperature, reducing rod bearing crush. To stabilize the lower rod bearing, an aluminum rod cap will feature a small locating dowel that engages a hole in the lower rod bearing. This prevents the rod bearings from potentially rotating in the big-end bore. It is not recommended to run tighter rod bearing oil clearance in an attempt to compensate, which can be detrimental to cold engine conditions. If the builder notes a slight drop in oil pressure, the preferred choice is to run a higher viscosity oil.

steel and aluminum materials. The cost of billet rods is higher in comparison, simply due to the material wasted during machining from a blank and the increased labor/machine time involved. Billet rods also offer another advantage: since the rod is machined from a blank, custom rod dimensions are possible for those who are developing their own platforms and feel the need to experiment with specific length, width and beam shapes for those rare instances where available in-stock rods don't meet custom requirements. However, you're going to pay for that privilege in terms of CNC programming and machining time.

Titanium Rods

As with most choices of materials and design, there are advantages and disadvantages. The highlight of titanium involves its lighter weight compared to a steel or aluminum rod of the same size and its strength-to-weight ratio. Typically, a titanium rod is machined from Ti6AL4V stock, which is approximately 33 percent lighter than a comparable-sized forged steel rod. This reduces the reciprocating weight, an obvious advantage in terms of accommodating high engine speeds and in attaining quicker RPMs.

The disadvantages involve higher cost and the need for increased care and attention in terms of nicks or scratches because the material, while offering high tensile strength, is very susceptible to failure from stress risers. Titanium is also rather gummy when exposed to contact friction and can easily gall. The potential concern is at the sides of the big ends if/when they contact each other. To address this, the titanium rod's big-end sides may be either highly polished or treated to a hard-surface coating.

Connecting Rod Length

Published rod length refers to the distance from the center of the small-end bore to the center of the big-end bore, referred to as center-to-center length. Performance rods for small-block Chevy applications are commonly available in inch lengths of 5.700, 5.850, 6.000, 6.125, 6.200, and 6.250 to suit various combinations of the crank stroke, piston compression height, and block deck height.

As mentioned earlier, the combination of half of the crank stroke, rod length, and piston compression distance (CD) must add up to meet the desired piston dome location relative to the block deck surface.

For example, if your block deck height is 9.025 inches, and you want to achieve a zero-deck (where the piston dome is flush with the block deck), the combination of half crank stroke, rod length, and piston CD must stack up to meet that 9.025-inch dimension.

Titanium rods are available and popular due to their light weight. However, they are substantially more expensive and are much more sensitive to scratches or dings that can result in stress risers, so great care is required when handling. Shown here is an H-beam titanium rod by GRP.

Dimension Explanation

The following definitions explain dimension.

Block deck height: The distance from the centerline of the main bore to the deck surface.

Crank stroke factor: We consider only half of the total crank stroke, measuring from the crank main centerline to the rod journal centerline when the rod journal is at TDC.

Rod length: The distance from the centerline of the big-end bore to the centerline of the small-end/wrist pin bore.

Piston CD: The compression distance from the centerline of the wrist pin bore to the piston dome at the dome's flat area that meets the block deck.

Example: Using a block that we surfaced to a deck height of 9.000 inches and a crankshaft that features a 4.125-inch total stroke, we can easily determine required rod length and piston CD.

Since our goal in this example is to achieve a zero-deck piston to deck clearance, we know that our total crank/rod/piston combo needs to be 9.000 inches.

Since we're using a 4.000-inch stroke crank, and we're only going to factor half of the total stroke, we can immediately subtract 2.000 inches from our 9.000-inch goal, leaving 7.000 inches to be made up with our rod and piston.

Now, say that we wish to use a 6.000-inch rod. Subtracting that from our previous 7.000-inch subtotal means that we need a piston that has a 1.000-inch CD.

If we opted to use a stroke of 3.875-inch coupled with a 6.000-inch rod, using the same formula, our piston would require a CD of 1.062-inch. ■

Rod to Block Clearance

Regardless of your setup, clearance of the rod's big end to the block pan rail and cylinder bottom should always be checked during engine mockup, regardless of the stroke being used. Obviously, as you increase the stroke (or when using fat aluminum rods), the rod's big ends, usually at the rod bolt locations, are going to get closer to these block areas, so it's critical to verify clearances to determine if clearance reliefs are needed at the block.

With the crank installed on its bearings, mock install the piston/rod with the rod bearings in place. There's no need to fully torque the rod bolts at this point. Just snug them to make the cap flush to the rod saddle and slowly rotate the crank, observing the clearances. If the clearance is too tight, mark the block interference locations with a marker. Do this with each rod location. With all the components removed back to a bare block, carefully grind material to obtain clearance. Clean the block and repeat the test assembly, again verifying clearances. As a general rule, at least a 0.080-inch clearance should be at all rod-to-block locations.

Potential rod big end to camshaft clearance concerns arise when the stroke is increased, when large aluminum rods are used, and/or when a camshaft features a larger base circle. This is why aftermarket blocks are available with raised cam tunnels to move the cam away from possible rod strikes.

A rod's big end and the camshaft tunnel are visible. When the crankshaft stroke is increased and cam lobe lift is increased, closer attention to the clearance of the rod's big end to the camshaft is needed. This is why aftermarket block makers offer raised-cam blocks to move the cam farther away from the rods.

Rod Side Clearance

Rod side clearance is important. If it's too tight, the pair of rods on a common journal will rub against each other, creating friction, potential galling, and excess heat. If it's too loose, the rods can slide excessively fore/aft, which can place undue loads on the rod bearings and at the piston pin area, which can adversely affect piston skirt side loading at the cylinder walls.

During test fitting, use your fingers to spread the two rod big ends on a common journal apart against the journal fillets. Insert a clean feeler gauge between the rod sides. A generally recommended clearance is in the range of 0.014 inch. I would say 0.012 inch is the minimum, and 0.019 to 0.020 inch is the maximum.

Due to a higher degree of precision machining, high-quality aftermarket rod big end widths tend to provide proper and more consistent side play clearance. When coupled to a high-quality aftermarket crank where journal width is held to close and consistent tolerance, it's rare for the rod's big end width to require correction. Today's quality aftermarket cranks and rods simply provide better finished machining.

Beam Design

The rod beam (the area of the rod that connects the piston wrist pin bore to the big-end bore) must provide the strength, in terms of compressive and tensile forces, to withstand the forces induced during high-RPM and high-torque abuse. Common beam designs include the I-beam and H-beam.

The I-beam features a slimmer face width compared to an H-beam and has a groove relief running along the face of each side of the beam. Face refers to the sides of the beam that align with the flat side of the big end. If you cut an I-beam rod at the midpoint of the beam, the cut surface would mimic an upper-case letter *I*. An H-beam rod features the relief groove on each side of the beam in line with the rod bolt sides of the big end. If you cut the beam, the cross-sectional view would look like the uppercase letter *H*.

What's the difference? Assuming the rod was made by an established quality-minded aftermarket manufacturer, either design will provide the desired performance and durability. However, when choosing between the two designs, an I-beam style rod is theoretically better suited for high-RPM use due to its generally lighter weight compared to an H-beam rod, assuming both are made of the same steel alloy material. An H-beam rod is theoretically better suited to handle high-torque engines.

In theory, H-beam rods are stronger, but in reality, an H-beam rod *can* be lighter while being as strong as an I-beam rod. In many cases, choosing between I-beam and H-beam boils down to either manufacturer availability and/or the engine builder's preference.

A beam style developed more recently is the X-beam. The X-beam design represents a hybrid approach using a combination of I-beam and H-beam with weight-saving grooves on both the beam faces and sides. This is often available on bulkier aluminum rods to provide both a level of weight reduction and an increase of surface area for enhanced strength.

I-beam rods tend to be a bit lighter than H-beam rods and are good choices where high engine RPM is a concern as opposed to high torque. H-beam rods may offer a bit more strength and rigidity and may be better at handling higher compressive forces where the engine produces lots of torque. (Photo Courtesy Oliver Racing Parts)

The aftermarket connecting rods available today far surpass OEM rods in terms of materials, designs, construction, precision machining, closely held tolerances, accommodation of increased strokes, weight-matching sets, strength, and a broad range of lengths and big-end diameters. An example of a Scat forged steel H-beam rod is shown here.

Rod and Cap Numbering

It should be obvious that rods and their caps must always remain as a matched pair. When the rod is initially assembled to the cap, the big-end bore is final machined. If the cap was installed to a different rod, it would not register accurately, resulting in and out of round bore, unless the assembly was resized and honed. Never mix rods and caps. Again, the need to keep respective rods and caps together is critical.

In the old days when dealing with OEM rods, it may have been necessary to stamp a number, or a series of dots, into the side of the big end's saddle and cap to provide a reference. Today's aftermarket performance rods are typically laser-etched with an identical multi-numeral/letter code, at each side of the rod saddle and cap mating line, eliminating the need to perform this on your own. Also, laser etching is non-destructive, applying no pressure to the metal. Using a stamp and a hammer in unskilled hands can potentially distort the big end.

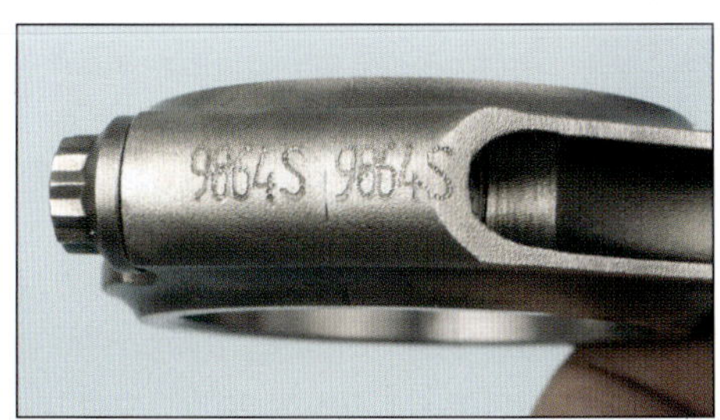

In the old days, engine builders needed to mark the rod and cap with an identifying mark or number to avoid accidentally mixing caps and rods. Today's aftermarket rods arrive pre-marked with laser-etched numbers. Since no pressure is used, laser etching avoids potential distortion as opposed to using a number or letter stamp hammered into the surface.

Rod Bolt Tips

The fit and tensile strength of the rod bolts is absolutely critical, especially for high-performance applications. While it was standard practice to upgrade OEM rods with high-quality rod bolts, such as those offered by ARP as an example, aftermarket performance rods are always assembled and shipped with high-quality/high-strength rod bolts from the get-go. These high-performance rod bolts typically feature a 12-point head design. The 12-point design provides a more secure engagement and is naturally driven by a 12-point wrench. This design also allows the use of a smaller-diameter head, which provides easier access due to the smaller outer diameter of the appropriate-sized socket wrench.

High-performance rod bolts designed for racing applications are also available in a variety of thread diameters. Shank lengths and material formulation affect the recommended installation torque and maximum allowable bolt stretch.

Thread diameter and length are specific to the design requirements of the rod itself. A numeric code is commonly featured on the bolt head that indicates the type of material. Typical materials are 8740 or 2000. The 8740 rod bolts are chrome-moly, offering a tensile strength of 180,000 to 210,000 psi that is adequate for most racing applications; 2000 rod bolts differ in alloy formulation and can provide higher clamping loads of as much as 220,000 psi.

A set of aftermarket rods includes a spec sheet that provides the recommended torque value and the "do not to exceed" amount of bolt stretch based on thread diameter, shank length, and the type of material. For example, a set of Scat connecting rods equipped with ARP rod bolts includes a spec sheet that lists the torque and max stretch for 5/16 x 1.500-inch ARP 2000, 3/8 x 1.600-inch ARP 8740, 3/8 x 1.600-inch ARP 2000, 7/16 x 1.400-inch ARP 8740, 7/16 x 1.500-inch SCAT 2001, 7/16 x 1.600-inch ARP 8740, 7/16 x 1.600-inch ARP 2000, 7/16 x 1.800-inch ARP 8740, and 7/16 x 1.800-inch SCAT 2001 cap screws. Each one is listed with its own recommended torque value and the amount of bolt stretch that is not to be exceeded. Simply measure and identify your rod bolt thread diameter, bolt length, and type of material to determine the proper tightening value.

Because the popular method of rod bolt installation involves monitoring the installed bolt stretch/degree of elasticity, performance rod bolts typically feature a dimple at each end to provide engagement points for the use of a rod bolt stretch gauge.

When installing rod bolts, pay attention to the bolt diameter, length, and material series because the torque value and/or maximum allowable bolt stretch will differ. For example, a 7/16 x 1.6-inch 8740 rod bolt may be specified for 63 ft-lbs with ARP lube and max stretch of 0.0050 inch, while a 7/16 x 1.4-inch 8740 bolt may call for 64 ft-lbs and a max stretch of 0.0046 inch.

Tightening Rod Bolts by Monitoring Stretch

While I dislike referring to the *old* days when it comes to addressing the topic of tightening connecting rod bolts, rather than applying a specified torque value alone, monitoring the amount of bolt stretch provides distinct advantages of not only achieving a more accurate degree of clamping force but also is a way to monitor and maintain records of each bolt's condition. A bolt, such as one used in a high-tensile application of connecting rod applications, can be viewed as an elastic component. When exposed to a specific amount of clamping force, the bolt slightly stretches, or elongates, displaying a degree of rubber band elasticity. If under-tightened, insufficient clamping force between the rod saddle and cap won't be achieved, potentially allowing the cap to slightly pull away from the saddle, reducing rod bearing crush. If over-tightened, the bolt may be pulled beyond the elastic state where the rubber band effect is lost, in which case the bolt becomes weakened with resulting bearing looseness and potential rod bolt failure.

As noted, checking and monitoring rod bolt stretch provides a more accurate achievement of clamping force because this eliminates the potential frictional factor that is experienced when relying on the applied torque value alone. By staying within the specified stretch, we are measuring and recording the actual elastic range of the bolt. This is extremely useful when engines are repeatedly rebuilt and/or inspected between races. By recording each individual rod bolt's location in terms of initially installed stretch, we can recheck to see how far the bolt stretches under a given torque value. For example, if a bolt initially stretched by 0.0045 inch when torqued to 70 ft-lbs, but now that same bolt stretches 0.006 inch at the same torque value, we can determine that the bolt is no longer within spec and must be replaced.

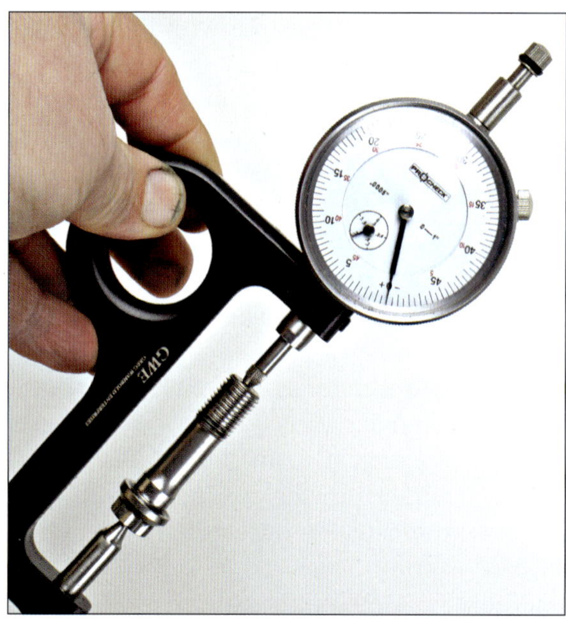

While only a torque specification was followed in years past, as part of the effort to enhance and evolve, the most precise method of securing rod bolts is to monitor rod bolt stretch. The suggested torque value can be used as a baseline, but measuring bolt stretch provides a much more accurate method of achieving and determining bolt clamping load. Each bolt is first indexed on a stretch gauge in its relaxed state with the gauge set at zero.

While it's always been common practice to lubricate rod bolts, today's high-tensile-strength rod bolts offered by firms, such as ARP, are to be coated with a high-pressure and friction-reducing lube, such as ARP Ultra-Torque lube or CMD. Lube must be applied both to the threads and the underside of the bolt head. The use of specific lubricants, as opposed to engine oil, can significantly affect the frictional level during tightening. Pay close attention to the rod maker's and/or rod bolt maker's torque values with regard to the type of lube being used. If you follow the torque value specified for 30W oil but have applied a reduced-friction lube, you can overstress the bolt by overtightening. As an arbitrary example, if the spec for a given rod bolt is 65 ft-lbs for ARP lube and 75 ft-lbs for oil, if you tighten to the higher oil spec when using ARP lube or CMD, you risk tightening the bolt beyond its max stretch spec. The specialty lubes provide reduced friction, requiring less applied torque compared to the use of engine oil.

Rod bolt stretch gauges are offered by several sources, such as ARP, Goodson Tools & Supplies, Moroso Performance Products, and others. The gauge features a dial indicator, a fixed pointed anvil, and an opposing spring-loaded adjustable centering probe. The pointed ends engage to the rod bolt at the bolt's head and shank tip dimples. Before installing the rod bolt, place it in the gauge, applying a small preload. Adjust the gauge to read zero. This provides a *static* free-length of the bolt.

Remove the bolt from the gauge, lube it, and install it to the rod. Do not change the current needle setting on the dial indicator. If the specified torque value for that application calls for 70 ft-lbs, using a torque wrench, tighten the bolt to 70 ft-lbs. Then, install the stretch gauge. Since you zeroed the gauge at the bolt's free length, the gauge will now show how far the bolt has stretched at your torque value. For example, if the rod maker's spec sheet lists a stretch not to exceed 0.0062 inch, and your stretch reading shows 0.006 inch, you know that you are within the allowable range. The engine builder may prefer to begin by torquing the bolt to 50 ft-lbs, then 60 ft-lbs, etc., checking stretch after each torque application to provide a picture of how much stretch is occurring as increased torque is applied.

Note that the stretch gauge must be individually zeroed for each bolt because individual bolt lengths and dimple depths can vary. In other words, do not assume that by zeroing the gauge for one bolt, that the remaining bolts will zero at the same point on the gauge. Treat each bolt as a unique part.

REM Finishing

REM finishing has become increasingly popular for applications, including crankshafts, connecting rods, camshafts, and more. This is essentially a chemical and tumble-polishing process that smooths out the surface finish to an almost chrome-plated appearance. The advantages include micropolishing to reduce or eliminate microscopic machining peaks and valleys. This results in a more uniform and uninterrupted surface and softens any sharp edges, which eliminates potential stress risers.

The ultra-slick finish also helps to shed parasitic oil cling, potentially freeing up power due to reduced drag. REM finishing services are available from some rod makers as an option, as well as independent metal finishing services across the country. Costs vary, but typically this process for a crank and a full set of rods may run in the range of $500 to $600.

This closeup of the REM finished rod cap gives you a better view regarding the surface finish, taking on the appearance of a highly polished or chrome-plated finish.

This is an example of a rod that has been treated to an REM finish process. This chemical and tumble-polished process results in an extremely smooth surface, eliminating microscopic peaks and valleys in the surface finish. This makes the rod stronger and less susceptible to fatigue, and it provides a slick surface to reduce parasitic oil cling, reducing windage drag.

TODAY'S PERFORMANCE CYLINDER HEADS

Given the lengthy development time frame of the small-block Chevy engine, cylinder head design represents an area that has undergone extensive research, resulting in airflow and performance gains that were unheard of in the early days. Traditionally, the Chevy small-block cylinder head employs a 23-degree valve layout. The valve angle refers to the relationship of the valve angle relative to the head deck surface.

Valve layout designs include 23, 18, 15, 12, and even 10 and 9 degree with the shallowest angles involving applications for extreme racing (Pro Stock, etc.) use. Aside from the traditional 23-degree head design, the 18-degree versions are the most popular for street and racing applications.

Moving away from the traditional 23-degree valve angle to a decreased angle moves the intake valve farther away from the cylinder bore wall, effectively unshrouding the valve, which benefits high-RPM power but may decrease low-end power. The shallower valve angle allows the builder to use smaller combustion chambers to increase compression without the need to use domed pistons. The 23-degree valve heads locate the valves 0.275 inch from the cylinder bore centerline. At maximum valve lift, the valves are shrouded by the cylinder bore and combustion chamber while 18-degree heads place the intake valves at the bore centerline and move the exhaust valves a bit closer to the cylinder wall. This layout removes the shrouding effect of the intake valve at maximum lift

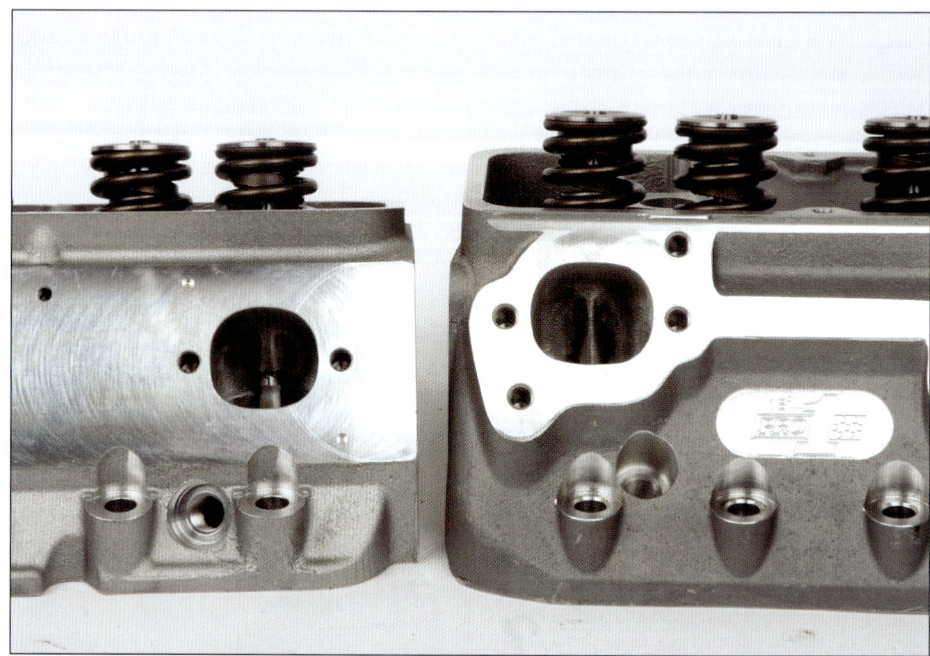

Notice that the 18-degree head on the right is taller than the 23-degree head. The exhaust ports on the 18-degree head are raised compared to the stock-height location of the ports on the 23-degree head. The 18-degree head also features longer valves.

and also allows the use of a larger intake valve.

The stock valve angle of 23 degrees places the valves away from the bore centerline by about 0.275 inch, contributing to valve shrouding in the combustion chamber at max lift. Reducing the valve angle places the valves closer to or at the bore centerline and reduces the height of the chamber wall to reduce shrouding and gain a more efficient airflow.

Further taking advantage of the 18-degree valve layout, the intake runners are raised, typically about 1.150 inch from the head deck, increasing airflow at higher engine speeds. The uniqueness of 18-degree heads includes the need for longer valves and longer head studs compared to the traditional 23-degree heads. Piston valve reliefs also must be cut to match the 18-degree valve angle, requiring the purchase of pistons that are designed for 18-degree heads. The use of 18-degree cylinder heads also requires purchasing higher-cost components, such as a solid roller cam, solid roller lifters that feature offset pushrod cups, shaft-mounted rockers with intake and exhaust offsets, and an intake manifold that features a 5-degree manifold deck compared to the 10-degree manifold deck used with 23-degree heads. If you wish to take advantage of 18-degree cylinder heads, be prepared to include these required components in your build budget.

Lower valve angles (in this case, lower than 23 degrees) that allow an increase in valve size are an advantage as long as the ports are raised to benefit high flow. Shallower valve angles can also reduce the chance for detonation. Taking it to the extreme, Pro Stock drag racing heads commonly feature 9- or 10-degree valves. Shallower angles tend to provide greater mid-valve-lift airflow, but when they are used with a cam and rocker setup that produces more than, say, 0.600-inch lift, airflow can be unstable when used for a street application.

This is a very simplistic way to look at the valve angle: the flatter the angle, the more the engine is intended for higher engine speed. When the floor of the ports is raised and a reduced angle is used, flow improves and the valves allow better breathing because the valves are less shrouded at the bores. As already mentioned, as the valve angle decreases, this allows you to run small combustion chambers for improved flame travel. The valve angle by itself is not the primary factor; it is just one of the variables with regard to cylinder head design. These shallow valve angles, which are commonly available today, were developed during the years since the inception of the small-block Chevy as race engine builders continually researched and experimented with cylinder head design.

Why are there so many choices in terms of the valve angle? As head designers moved away from the original GM 23-degree layout, the shallower angles produce superior flow as long as the ports are raised to coordinate with the angle. With experimentation and development, cylinder head manufacturers continually strive to make a better mousetrap in terms of obtaining maximum horsepower at given RPM ranges. The shallower the valve angle, the more the powerband moves up with higher engine speed. Some valve angles are mandated by certain sanctioning bodies, while variations of valve angles are selected to work with the specific application in terms of where the builder wants the power at a given engine speed. For example, 13-degree valve angles seem to be the most popular currently for sprint car applications.

Aftermarket race heads are also available with a symmetrical port layout. Instead of the center exhaust ports placed close together as is normally found on small-block heads, which concentrates heat unevenly port-to-port, some heads are now offered with evenly spaced exhaust ports, which is one of the lessons derived from GM's LS engine development. This not only eliminates heat concentration between the two center ports but also allows superior exhaust flow. Having symmetrically located exhaust ports is beneficial to endurance engines in long-distance oval track and road course environments.

To improve flow, race heads commonly feature raised intake and exhaust ports. Raising the location of the ports also allows more material deck thickness for improved rigidity.

In addition to the use of superior aluminum alloy materials, design changes that surpass the original GM designs and the incredible array of options in terms of chamber volumes, port volumes, port shapes, and valve locations, angles, and sizes all contribute to the availability of cylinder head performance that was never available in previous decades.

Note: CarTech offers a cylinder head book, *High-Performance Small-Block Chevy Cylinder Heads*, that delves into greater detail concerning cylinder head design and selection tips.

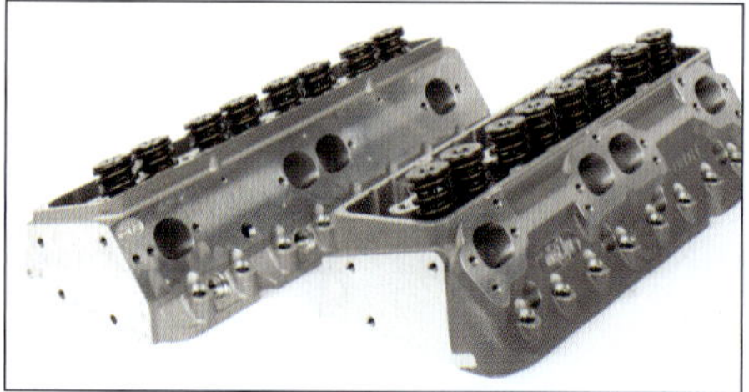

While 23-degree cylinder heads have been the norm for small-block Chevy applications, today we have access to a range of various, shallower valve angles for higher flow and improved throttle response. Shown here is a Dart 23-degree head on the left and a Dart 18-degree head. Racing heads today are offered with larger valves and valve angles of 23, 18, 16, 15, 13, 12.5, 11, and 9 degrees, as examples.

This visual comparison of a Dart 23-degree head (left) and 18-degree head (right) makes the slight valve angle difference noticeable. Even to the naked eye, you can see how the valves on the 18-degree head feature a shallower angle compared to the stock 23-degree angle.

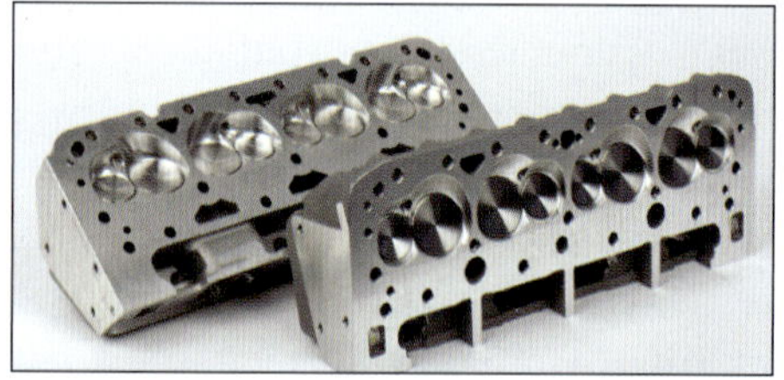

Thanks to the widespread use of precision CNC machining centers in use by today's aftermarket cylinder head manufacturers, heads are commonly available in fully-CNC-machined versions in terms of both creating specific port and combustion chamber shapes and volumes and total consistency port to port and chamber to chamber.

This is an example of a 23-degree head. Notice how the intake valve is shrouded by the combustion chamber as the valve is open.

Pictured is a 13-degree head. Notice how the intake valve is unshrouded when it is open. This allows for superior flow, aiding in horsepower gains at higher engine speed.

Shown here is a comparison between a conventional GM 23-degree head intake port location on the left and a 13-degree intake port location on the right. As the valve angle is reduced, essentially straightening the valve in relation to the deck, it's necessary to raise the location of the intake ports to achieve smooth and uninterrupted airflow.

Edelbrock

Edelbrock offers a dizzying array of small-block heads, about 30-plus in all, ranging from mild to wild. This includes its E-Series, Performer RPM, E-CNC series, in addition to select heads that are legal for specific NHRA drag racing applications and an SCCA-approved head for the American Series of road racing. Listed here are merely five examples.

PN 5089 E-Street

These cylinder heads feature as-cast ports and 64-cc combustion chambers with 2.020-inch intake valves and 1.6-inch exhaust valves. They are 23-degree heads, designed for budget-minded street performance, rated at 5,500 rpm and maximum lift of 0.550 inch.

PN 60715 RPM

As-cast ports are featured, and these heads are intended for hydraulic roller cams. They feature 23-degree valves and angled spark plugs. The effective RPM range is 1,500 to 6,500. They require a minimum 4.000-inch bore. The maximum allowable valve lift is 0.575 inch.

PN 60975 E-Tec

E-Tec-170 23-degree aluminum heads are intended as direct replacements for 302-, 327-, 350-, and 400-ci applications with Vortec-style intake manifolds and are designed for hydraulic roller cams. The LT1-style intake ports are raised and the spark plugs are placed closer to the center of the cylinder.

PN 61209 E-CNC

E-CNC 225 heads are intended for serious street and racing applications. The 23-degree heads are fully CNC ported, intended for solid roller cam applications with a maximum valve lift of 0.700 inch. Intake port volume is 225 cc with 2.100-inch intake valves and 1.6-inch exhaust valves. According to Edelbrock, these heads offer 30 to 60 hp more than Performer RPM heads.

PN 60637 RPM NHRA

The 60637 RPM NHRA heads are offered in bare form and designed for use in NHRA Stock and Super Stock drag racing applications. Features include 23-degree valve angles, 70-cc combustion chambers, 185-cc intake runners, straight spark plugs, threaded inserts for rocker studs and exhaust bolts, and they are rated for 1,500 to 6,500 rpm.

Edelbrock's 5089 23-degree E-Street heads are designed for entry-level street performance for the budget-minded customer. They are rated for peak of 5,500 rpm and maximum valve lift of 0.550 inch. (Photo Courtesy Edelbrock)

Edelbrock's 60715 RPM heads feature 23-degree valves, 70-cc combustion chambers, and are designed for use with hydraulic roller cams with a maximum lift of 0.575 inch. They require a minimum of a 4.000-inch bore and are rated for a powerband of 1,500 to 6,500 rpm. (Photo Courtesy Edelbrock)

Edelbrock's 60975 is a direct replacement for 302-, 327-, 350-, and 400-ci stock engines. Valve cover bolt holes are dual drilled to accept either perimeter or center bolt applications. (Photo Courtesy Edelbrock)

Edelbrock's 61209 E-CNC 225 heads offer 30 to 60 hp more than Performer RPM heads. Features include 23-degree valves, full-CNC machining and porting, 225-cc intake runner volume, 68-cc combustion chambers, and 2.100-inch intake valves. Intended for use with solid roller camshafts. (Photo Courtesy Edelbrock)

Edelbrock's 60637 Performer RPM heads are designed use in NHRA Stock/Super Stock applications and are offered bare. (Photo Courtesy Edelbrock)

Trick Flow Specialties

Trick Flow Specialties (TFS) offers both 23-degree and 18-degree aluminum heads in variations, including as-cast and fully CNC machined and ported.

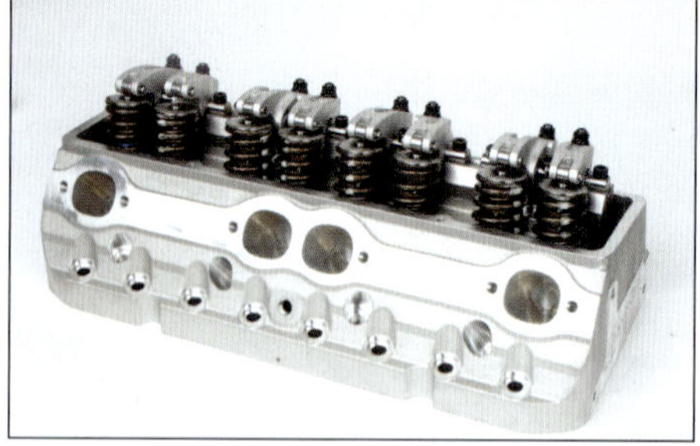

Trick Flow's Ultra 18-degree heads are fully assembled and are rated at 0.700-inch maximum lift. They require shaft-mounted offset rockers and an intake manifold that is designed for use with 18-degree heads.

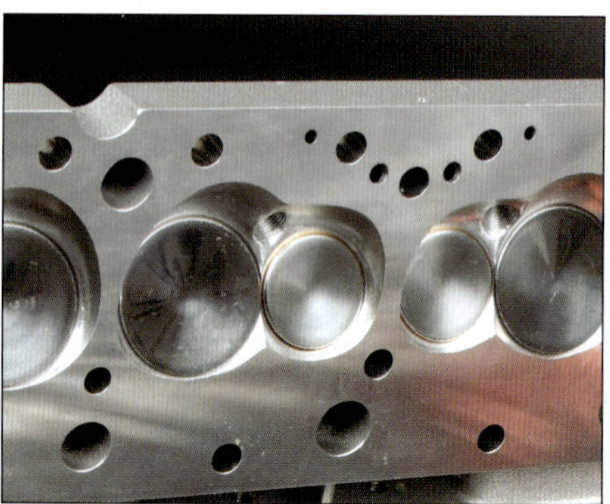

The Trick Flow Ultra 18-degree heads feature full CNC machining and porting with 2.150-inch intake valves and 64-cc chambers.

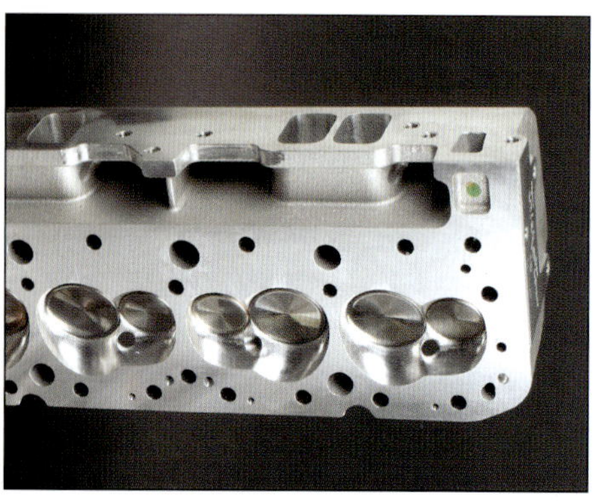

Trick Flow Ultra 18 250-cc, 18-Degree	
Part Number	3181T001-C01
Material	A356-T6 aluminum alloy
Intake port volume	250-cc competition ported
Intake port dimensions	1.350 inches x 2.200 inches
Intake seat material	Ductile iron
Intake valve	2.150 inch, 11/32-inch stem, 5.560-inch overall length
Combustion chamber volume	56-cc CNC profiled
Exhaust port volume	100-cc CNC ported
Exhaust port dimensions	1.760-inch x 1.460-inch oval
Exhaust seat material	Copper bronze alloy
Exhaust valve	1.600 inches, 11/32-inch stem, 5.570-inch overall length
Exhaust flange pattern	Standard GM 18-degree
Plug location	Angled, standard GM 18-degree
Spring pocket diameter	1.660 inches
Valve guide material	Manganese bronze
Seals	Viton fluoroelastomer
Locks	10-degree with recess for lash caps
Retainers	10-degree titanium, 1.550 inches
Valve soring ID locators	1.550-inch x 0.060-inch thick
Springs	1.560-inch OD double spring with dampers
	240 pounds at 2.000-inch installed height
	500 lbs/in rate
	0.700-inch max lift
Minimum bore diameter	4.155 inches

Requires shaft-style rockers with a 0.550-inch intake offset and a 0.220-inch exhaust offset. Also requires an intake manifold designed for 18-degree heads.

Due to the 18-degree valve layout, larger-diameter intake valves, and the exhaust valves positioned closer to the cylinder wall, the engine block must feature a minimum bore diameter of 4.155 inches.

Trick Flow offers a very wide range of small-block head formats of 23-degree heads with available intake runner volumes of 175, 195, 215, 230, and 250 cc. All heads are available bare or fully assembled.

A Trick Flow D-port 175-cc 23-degree street head is shown. Trick Flow offers a myriad of small-block head designs with intake runner volumes ranging from 175, 195, 215, 230, and 250 cc. Both 23- and 18-degree versions are offered. Shown here is DHC 175, which features 175-cc intake runners, 23-degree valves, 1.940 intake and 1.500 exhaust valves, and D-port exhaust ports. Ports are as cast. (Photo Courtesy Trick Flow)

Dart

Dart offers an incredible array of competition heads, about 22 in all, including 23-, 18-, 16-, 15-, 12.5-, 11-, and 9-degree versions. Sixteen variants of its 23-degree heads are offered. Complete specifications of an example of its 23-degree heads and one example of an 18-degree head is listed below.

Trick Flow's Super 23 heads feature a 23-degree valve layout, a 230-cc intake runner volume, 70-cc combustion chambers, D-port exhaust ports, and angled spark plugs. Assembled heads are rated at a maximum lift of 0.680 inch. These heads are CNC machined and CNC ported. (Photo Courtesy Trick Flow)

Dart PRO1 245-cc CNC 23-Degree	
Part number	1198116P
Material	RMR cast aluminum
Combustion chamber	66 cc (for 4.155-inch bore)
Intake valve diameter	2.100 inches
Intake port volume	245 cc
Intake port dimension	2.200 inches x 1.310 inches
Intake port location	Stock
Intake gasket	Fel-Pro 1206
Exhaust valve diameter	1.600 inches
Exhaust port volume	86 cc
Exhaust port dimensions	1.410 inches x 1.585 inches
Exhaust port location	Stock
Exhaust gasket	Fel-Pro 1405
Flow (intake)	325 cfm at 0.700 lift at 28 inches
Flow (exhaust)	244 cfm at 0.700 lift at 28 inches
Head bolts	Dart 66220011
Head studs	Dart 66120011
Manifold	Dart single plane 42411000
Pistons	Most aftermarket 23-degree pistons
Pushrod length	Stock 7.800 + 0.100 inch (always measure)
Pushrod guide plate	Shaft mount only, 0.150-inch offset
Retainers	Titanium, 10 degree

Dart PRO1 245-cc CNC 23-Degree *(Continued)*	
Part number	**1198116P**
Spark plug	Angle, 0.750 reach, gasketed
Spring pockets	1.550-inch OD (0.030-inch deeper max)
Valve springs	1.550-inch OD (215 pounds at 1.900-inch/0.690-inch max)
Valve length	5.015 inches (+0.100)
Valve stem diameter	0.3415 (11/32)
Valve train	0.150-inch offset intake (shaft mount only)
Valve guides	0.439-inch OD, manganese bronze
Valve guide length	2.100 inches
Valve guide clearance	0.0014 to 0.002 inch
Valve guide spacing	1.890 inches (moved 0.030-inch from stock)
Valve seats	Powdered metal, 0.006-inch press
Valve seat dimensions	Intake 2.160 x 1.810 x 0.350 inch; Exhaust 1.650 x 1.350 x 0.350 inch
Valve seat angles	Intake 32–45–60–70–80 deg; Exhaust 37–45-degree radius
Torque	Head bolts 70 ft-lbs; rocker studs 55 ft-lbs; manifold 35 ft-lbs
Weight	28 pounds (assembled)

Dart's 23-degree Pro1 is also offered bare or fully assembled. Exhaust ports are in the standard location and offer 86-cc volume. Heads feature angled spark plug ports.

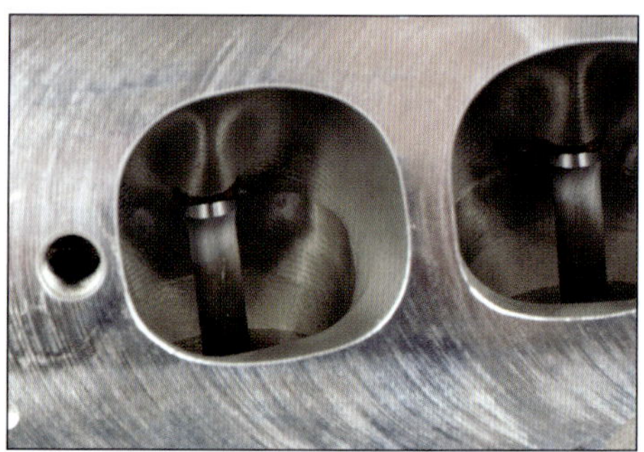

Pro1 23-degree heads feature CNC intake and exhaust ports.

Pro1 23-degree intake ports are featured in the standard location. Port volume is 245 cc. Always measure for pushrods, but these heads are designed to accept stock-length 7.800-inch pushrods.

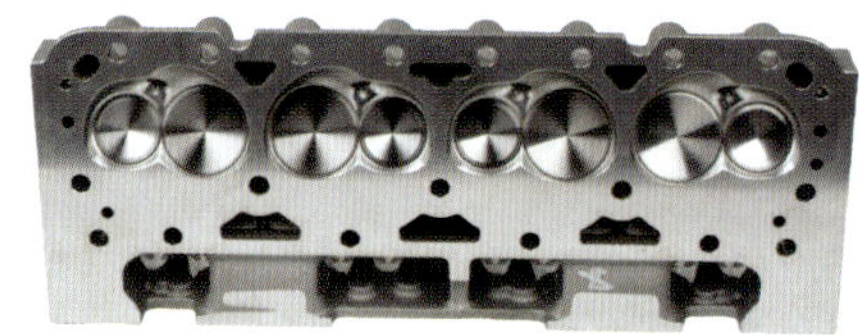

Pro1 23-degree combustion chambers provide 66 cc of volume. These heads require a block with a minimum bore size of 4.155 inches.

Pro1 intake valves are 2.100 inches. Exhaust valves are 1.600 inches. Chambers are CNC machined for precise volume and chamber-to-chamber consistency.

Dart PRO1 245-cc 18 Degrees	
Part Number	**11992133**
Material	RMR cast aluminum
Intake valve diameter	2.150 or 2.180 inches
Intake port volume	245 cc
Intake port dimensions	2.150 x 1.290 inches
Intake port location	Raised, 5-degree intake face (stock 10-degree)
Intake gasket	Mr. Gasket 143
Exhaust valve diameter	1.600 or 1.625 inches
Exhaust port volume	108 cc
Exhaust port dimensions	1.740-inch W x 1.500-inch H
Exhaust port location	Raised and spread port (GM and Stahl spread pattern)
Exhaust gasket	Dart 65222000
Flow (intake)	371 cfm at 0.750 lift at 28 inches
Flow (exhaust)	261 cfm at 0.750 lift at 28 inches
Lifter	180 offset lifters required
Manifold	42711000 only
Pistons	Most 18-degree aftermarket pistons
Retainers	Titanium 10 degree
Spark plug	Angled, 0.750 reach, gasketed
Spring cups	1.550-inch ID locator
Spring pockets	1.550 OD (0.030 deeper max)
Valve springs	1.550 OD, 215 lbs at 1.950 inches, 0.680-inch lift max
	1.550 OD, 235 lbs at 1.950 inches, 0.750-inch lift max
Heads studs	Dart 66110012
Valve angles	18 degrees
Valve length	5.550-inch (+0.600), 0.250-inch tip
Valve stem diameter	0.3415 (11/32 or 5/16)
Valvetrain	Jesel 0.550-inch intake offset/0.220 exhaust offset, or T&D intake offset 0.550/exhaust offset 0.170 inch
Valve guides	1/2-inch OD manganese bronze (cut for 0.530-inch PC seals)
Valve guide length	2.250 inches
Valve guide clearance	0.0014–0.0020 inch
Valve guide spacing	1.935 inches
Valve seats	Ductile iron or copper infiltrated

Dart PRO1 245-cc 18 Degrees *(Continued)*	
Part Number	**11992133**
Valve seat dimensions	Intake 2.250 x 1.850 x 0.375; Exhaust 1.680 x 1.350 x 0.375-inch
Valve seat angles	Intake 38–45–60–70–80; Exhaust 38–45 radius
Torque	Head stud nuts 7/16: 70 ft-lbs; 3/8: 50 ft-lbs; manifold 35 ft-lbs
Weight	32 pounds assembled
Note: Fuel injection down nozzle bosses provided	

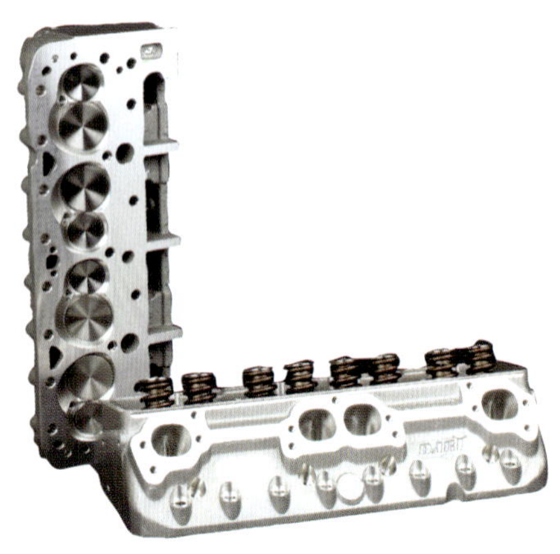

Dart 18-degree Pro1 heads feature 66-cc combustion chambers, available with either 2.150- or 2.180-inch intake valves, and 1.600- or 1.625-inch exhaust valves. The 0.750-inch lift is the maximum rating.

Dart 18-degree Pro1 cylinder heads offer intake port volume of 245 cc with 5-degree raised intake ports. Exhaust ports are raised and spread to the General Motors or Stahl pattern. Intake flow is 371 cfm at 0.750-inch lift. Exhaust flow is 261 cfm at 0.750-inch lift.

Dart's 18-degree Pro1 cylinder head features raised and spread exhaust ports and multiple header bolt hole patterns.

The 18-degree heads are clearly identified for the valve angle.

Dart 18-degree Pro1 245-cc intake ports are raised rectangular with a 5-degree intake face.

The Dart 18-degree Pro1 cylinder head is available with either 2.150- or 2.180-inch intake valves and 1.600- or 1.625-inch exhaust valves.

The 18-degree Dart's combustion chambers are CNC machined, providing 66 cc of volume.

Dart Aluminum Race Series 12.5-Degree 14400000C bare (14472010 CNC)

The 12.5-degree head features 38-cc combustion chambers and a 296-cc intake runner volume, accepting either 2.150- or 2.180-inch intake valves. Exhaust ports are spread bore. Combustion chambers are available in either 42 or 33 cc if titanium valves are used. The head requires 0.180-inch offset lifters and T&D 2127 shaft rockers. Intake ports are raised 5 degrees. Fuel injection down nozzle bosses are provided. Intake flow is 385 cfm at 0.800-inch lift. The head accepts Dart's 18-degree intake manifold.

Dart 11-Degree Little Chief 14600000 Bare or Assembled

These unique heads take advantage of the big-block Chevy Big Chief head features that are packaged for small-block applications. They were designed to accommodate full-race alcohol, nitrous, turbocharger, or supercharger applications for 8,000 or higher rpm. Features include canted valves; semi-hemi combustion chambers in 34-, 36-, or 50-cc volumes; Pro Stock–style oval ports; and they will accept 2.180- or 2.230-inch intake valves. They also include raised intake ports 2.000 inches from the deck, exhaust ports raised 2.900 inches from the deck,

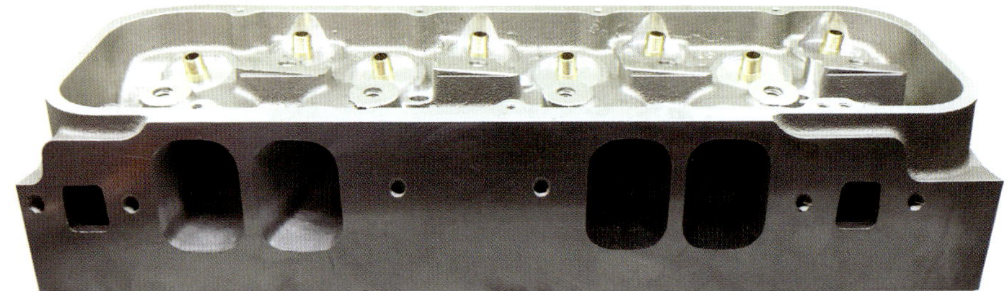

Dart Race Series 12.5-degree cylinder heads provide intake flow of 385 cfm at 0.800-inch valve lift. (Photo Courtesy Dart)

Dart's 11-degree Little Chief heads feature round exhaust ports with port spacing similar to big-block Big Chief heads. Both intake and exhaust ports are raised. They are available with an intake runner volume of 275, 315, or 330 cc, and with chamber volumes of 34, 36, or 50 cc. They require a minimum bore size of 4.155 inch and they require the use of Jesel rockers with individual stands. (Photo Courtesy Dart)

Dart's 11-degree Little Chief heads feature oval intake ports. The exhaust ports are raised 2.900 inches from the deck. (Photo Courtesy Dart)

This is an example of Dart's 12.5-degree CNC exhaust ports. There are 38-cc combustion chambers and a 296-cc intake runner volume with spread-bore exhaust ports. Both 42- or 33-cc combustion chambers are available. Intake ports are raised 5 degrees. Fuel injection down nozzle bosses are provided. (Photo Courtesy Dart)

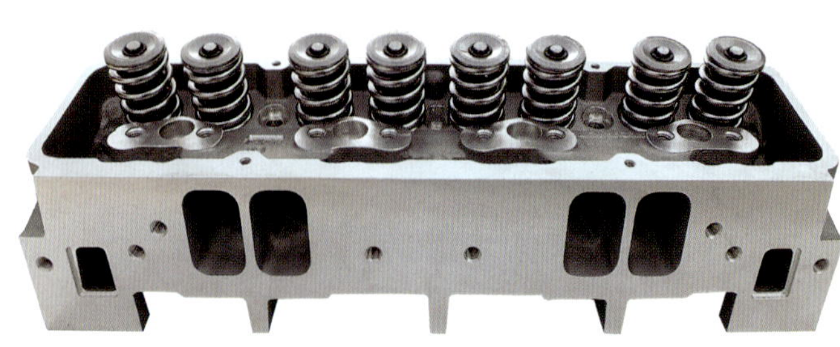

Dart 16-degree competition head. (Photo Courtesy Dart)

and splayed 11-degree valves. They require Jesel rockers with individual stands and a minimum bore of 4.155 inches. They are available with a 275-, 315-, or 330-cc intake runner volume.

Dart 15-Degree 14300000C (Bare) or 14372010 (Full CNC)

These heads are intended for 7,000 or higher rpm, the combustion chambers are 48 cc, and the intake runners are 284 cc.

Dart 16-Degree 14200000C (Bare) or 14272010 (Full CNC)

These heads are designed for 7,000 or higher rpm and are great for nitrous use. Combustion chambers are 47 cc and intake runners are 268 cc. They will accommodate 2.150- or 2.180-inch intake valves.

Dart 9-Degree 14500000C (for 4.400-inch Bore Spacing) or 145000001C (for 4.500-inch Bore Spacing)

These cylinder heads are rated for 7,000 and higher rpm. Features include raised intake and exhaust ports, expanded water jackets, bosses for down nozzles, and raised rails for rocker geometry clearance. Optimal valve angle and intake port positioning achieve maximum potential air/

Dart's 9-degree head is shown. The intake ports are rectangular. The flange for valve covers is taller, allowing the use of shorter valve covers. Provisions were made to use extra head bolts for improved sealing. (Photo Courtesy Dart)

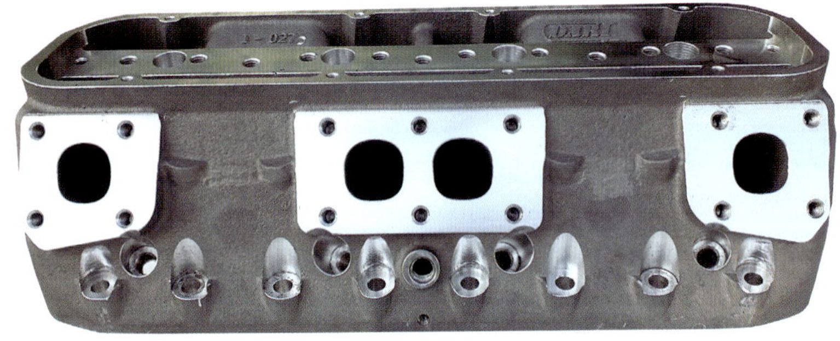

Dart's 9-degree heads configured for 4.400-inch bore spacing feature a unique 6-bolt exhaust flange for cylinders 3–5 and 4–6 and were designed to work with widely available 13-degree exhaust headers. (Photo Courtesy Dart)

fuel flow around the circumference of the valves with a mirrored valve configuration, offering superior throttle response due to even distribution between the runners.

The heads are cast from virgin 355-T61 alloy for strength. Combustion chambers as small as 38 cc are offered. Heads designed for 4.400-inch bore spacing use 2.200 intake and 1.625-inch exhaust valves, while the 4.500-inch bore

spacing versions use 2.230 intake and 1.625-inch exhaust valves.

Dart also offers a 15-degree head that features a 284-cc intake runner volume, 48-cc combustion chambers, and 2.150- or 2.180-inch intake valves and 1.6- or 1.625-inch exhaust valves. The heads also require the Dart intake manifold (301-42711000). The 15-degree heads, with their smaller combustion chambers, allow for a higher compression ratio.

Brodix

Brodix cylinder heads are offered in a wide range of valve angles, chamber sizes, port volumes, and unique heads for specific aftermarket race blocks. Variants include valve angles of 10-, 11-, 12-, 13-, 18-, and 23-degree valves. Series include the IK Series, Dragon Slayer Series, Track 1 Series, Head Hunter, 11X Series 23-degree, 18-degree C Series, and more. Within each series are variants in terms of combustion chamber and port volumes.

DS225 Dragon Slayer

Touted as having performance improvements over stock heads, the DS225 heads feature a 225-cc intake runner port volume, standard 23-degree valves, 2.080-inch intake valves, and 7/16-inch rocker studs. They accept all standard components, including the intake manifold, headers, and rockers. The flow rating is 300 cfm at 0.600-inch valve lift.

KC 13

The KC 13 head features a 13-degree valve angle, raised intake ports with a 5-degree intake face angle, a 283-cc intake port volume, 2.180-inch intake valves, 1.625-inch exhaust valves, interlocking valve seats, an angled spark plug configuration, tight 47-cc combustion chambers, standard/Stahl header flange, and requires 0.180-inch offset lifters. Open spring pressure is 550 pounds rated for maximum lift of 0.700 inch. It is designed for use with solid roller cams.

Brodix BD1010

The Brodix BD1010 race heads feature symmetrical intake and exhaust ports with massive 311-cc exhaust ports. They are 100-percent CNC machined from virgin A-356 aluminum. These heads eliminate the Siamese center exhaust port design for big-block-style exhaust flow.

BD4510 cylinder heads are 12-degree heads designed for blocks that feature a 4.500-inch bore spacing for cylinder bore diameters of 4.250 inches. The features include bosses that can be drilled for down nozzles.

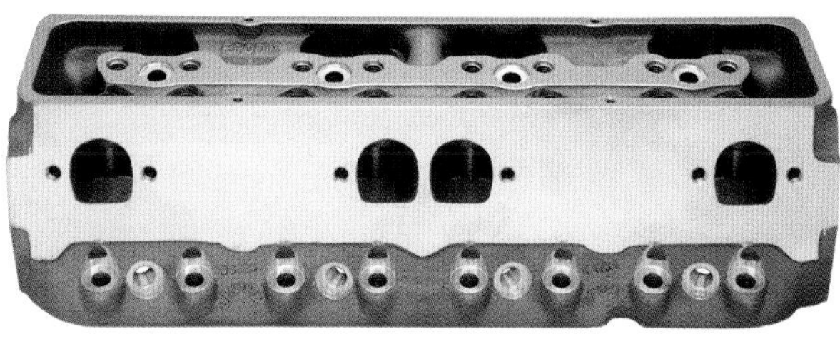

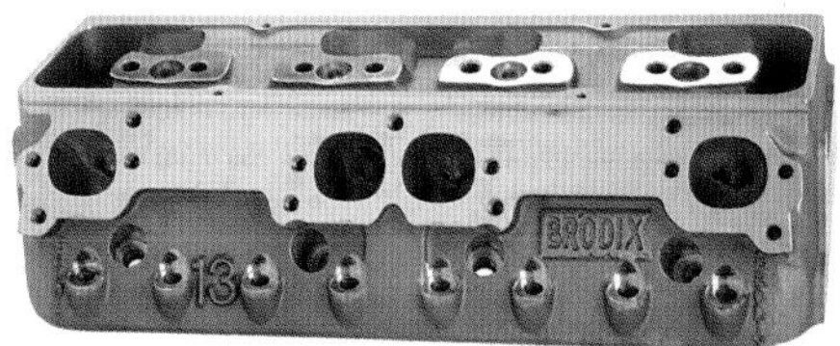

Brodix DS 225 Series street/strip heads, also known as Dragon Slayer heads, are 100 percent CNC machined direct-replacement heads. They feature a 23-degree valve angle, 225-cc intake port volume, and 2.080-inch intake and 1.600-inch exhaust valves. They flow 300 cfm at 0.600-inch lift and accepts all standard components, such as 7/16-inch rocker studs, rockers, etc. (Photo Courtesy Brodix)

The Brodix KC 13 heads boast a 13-degree valve angle. A shaft rocker system with 85/134 spacing is required. Chambers are 47 cc and intake port volume is 283 cc. (Photo Courtesy Brodix)

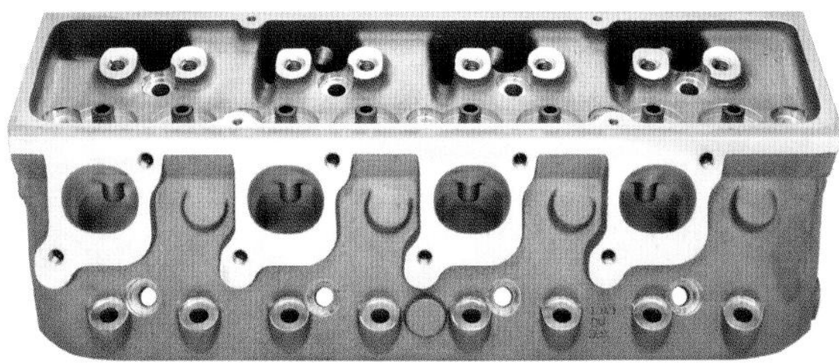

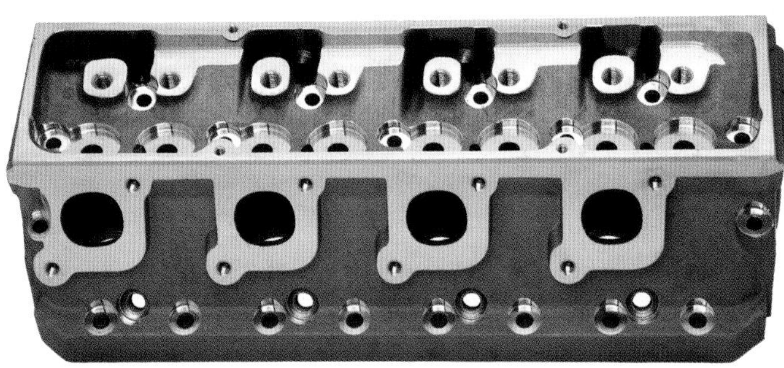

Brodix BD1010 heads are available with valve angles of 10, 12, or 13 degrees. Features include symmetrical intake and exhaust ports, line-of-sight intake ports, 2.230-inch intake and 1.600-inch exhaust valves, and 311-cc exhaust ports. They are rated to flow over 410 cfm. (Photo Courtesy Brodix)

Brodix BD4510 cylinder heads are designed for use in big-bore small-block applications for 4.250-inch bores with bore spacing of 4.500 inches. The valve angles are 12 degrees. (Photo Courtesy Brodix)

Air Flow Research

Air Flow Research (AFR) offers a full range of small-block heads for street and full-competition, including 23-, 18-, 15-, and 13.5-degree versions with a wide range of intake runner volumes in both bare and fully assembled models. Intake runner volumes range from 190 cc up to the whopping 305-cc runners found in the 13.5-degree heads.

AFR Eliminator PRO

AFR recently debuted its new pro-racing 15-degree Eliminator Pro cylinder heads offered in 285-cc or 305-cc intake runner volumes. The 13.5-degree version features 325-cc runners designed for drags, sprints, and late models and is based on the Brodix GB2300 casting. Initially based on the GM 18-degree head, the 15-degree 285-cc version features lightweight 2.150-inch intake valves and 1.600-inch exhaust valves in stainless or titanium. It has a 50-degree seat angle, chrome-moly retainers, and copper seats for titanium valves. It also flows 400 or more cfm at 0.700-inch lift. The 305-cc version features 2.200-inch intake and 1.600-inch exhaust valves with a 55-degree seat angle. The 13.5-degree head flows 450 cfm at 800 or

AFR's 15-degree head is pictured. (Photo Courtesy AFR)

Pictured is AFR's 245-cc, 23-degree fully assembled head. (Photo Courtesy AFR)

AFR's competition heads feature 100 percent CNC porting. (Photo Courtesy AFR)

higher lift and is good up to 0.800-inch lift. The 13.5-degree head features 2.235-inch intake and 1.595-inch exhaust valves.

World Products

World Products offers cast-iron heads in its Motown 220 and Sportsman II versions. The Motown 220 heads are offered in either 50- or 64-cc combustion chambers with a 220-cc intake volume. Both the intake and exhaust ports are at the standard locations. The intake valves are 2.080 inches and exhaust valves are 1.600 inches. Assembled heads are available with either 1.440- or 1.550-inch

springs and have a maximum lift rating at 0.600 inch. They are designed for use with 383 or larger displacement. Combustion chambers and ports are not CNC machined.

The Sportsman II heads, also as-cast iron, offer thick port walls that provide plenty of room for custom porting. The combustion chambers are 64 cc and intake runner volume is 200 cc. The intake valves are 2.020 inches and the exhaust valves are 1.600 inches. Intake and exhaust ports are at the standard locations. Straight or angled spark plug ports are offered. These heads will accept either perimeter or center bolt valve covers. They are not CNC'd.

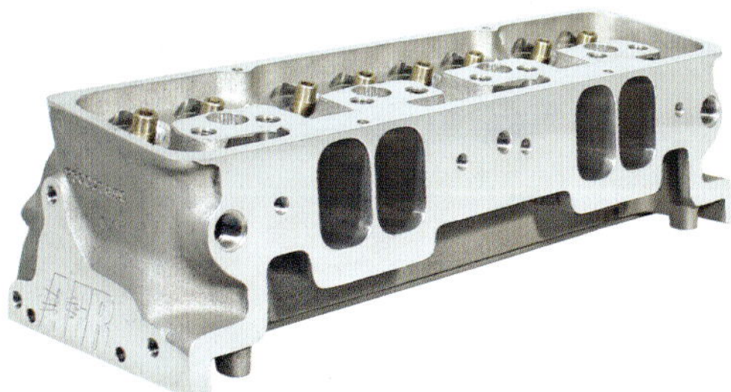

AFR'S 13.5-degree competition head. The 13- and 13.5-degree heads from all brands are currently very popular in Sprint car applications. (Photo Courtesy AFR)

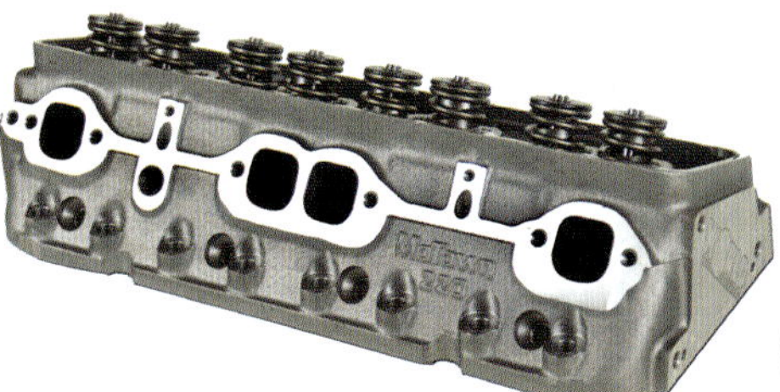

World Products Motown 220 heads are as-cast iron with standard intake and exhaust port locations. Intake port volume is 200 cc. Assembled heads are rated at a maximum 0.600-inch valve lift. (Photo Courtesy World Products)

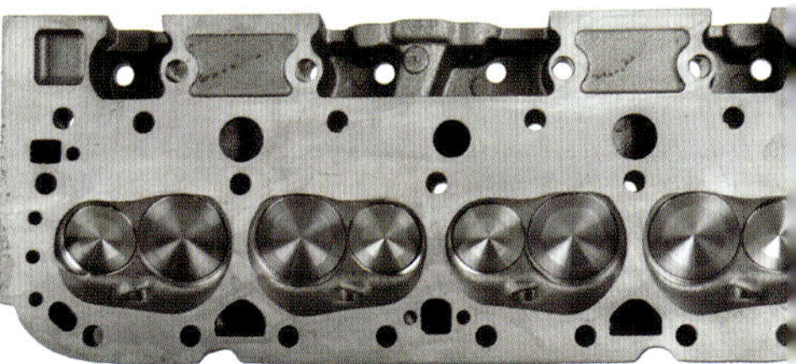

The Motown 220 cylinder heads are offered in either 50- or 64-cc combustion chambers and are ideal where iron heads are mandated. (Photo Courtesy World Products)

The Sportsman II heads are as-cast iron with plenty of extra wall thickness at the ports for custom porting. Combustion chambers are 64 cc and intake ports are 200 cc. Available with a straight or angled spark plug design, they will accept perimeter or center-bolt valve covers. (Photo Courtesy World Products)

Racing Head Service

Racing Head Service (RHS), a division of Competition Cams, offers several small-block heads in cast aluminum.

12055-02 Pro Action

These cylinder heads are the same as the 12055, but they are compatible with a hydraulic roller camshaft.

12060-02 Pro Action

This head is the same as 12060, with the exception that it was designed for hydraulic roller cams up to 0.600-inch lift. It is available with 64- or 72-cc combustion chambers.

12080 Pro Elite

Pro Elite heads are fully CNC machined with CNC porting. Features include extra thick decks and refined water jackets, and they are designed for use with 383- to 422-ci engines.

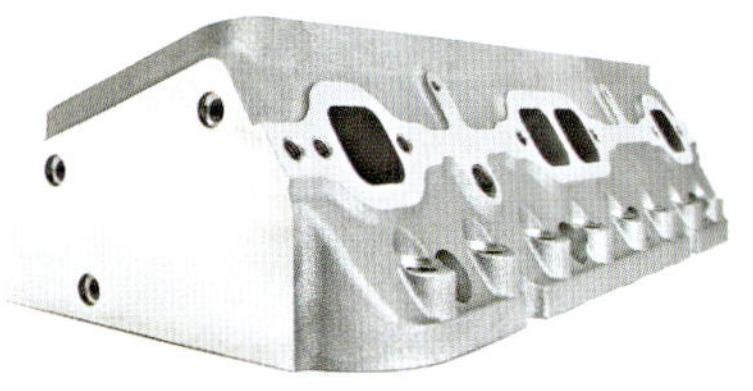

RHS Pro Action heads feature cast-aluminum construction, 23-degree valves, a 235-cc intake runner volume, and are available with 64- or 72-cc combustion chambers and straight spark plug ports. Variations are available to accommodate either flat tappet or roller cam applications. (Photo Courtesy RHS)

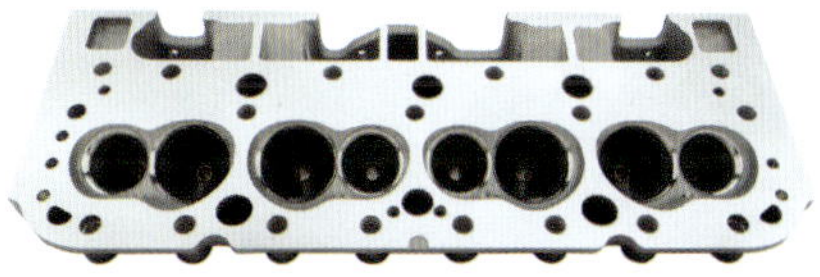

RHS Pro Action 23-degree heads (part number 12055) are compatible with flat tappet, solid, or hydraulic applications. They feature a 200-cc intake volume, 64-cc combustion chambers, 2.020-inch intake valves, and angled spark plugs.

RHS Pro Action 23-degree heads (part number 12055-02) are designed for use with hydraulic roller camshafts. (Photo Courtesy RHS)

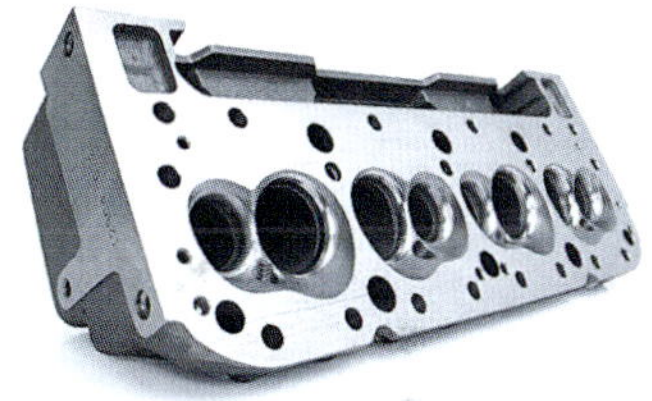

RHS also offers its Pro Elite aluminum heads that feature full CNC finishing and porting. The intake runner volume is 228 cc and exhaust volume is 82 cc. They are designed for use with 383- to 422-ci engines. (Photo Courtesy RHS)

12055 Pro Action	
Valve angle	23 degrees
Intake runner volume	200 cc
Combustion chamber volume	64 cc
Spark plug ports	Angled
Valve sizes	2.020 intake; 1.6 exhaust
Camshaft compatibility	Flat tappet solid or hydraulic

12060 Pro Action	
Valve angle	23 degrees
Combustion chamber	64 or 72 cc
Camshaft compatibility	Flat tappet solid or hydraulic
Intake runner volume	235 cc
Valve sizes	2.020 intake; 1.6 exhaust
Max lift	0.560 inch (also offered in 180, 200, 220 cc)
Spark plug ports	Straight
Accepts standard rockers	

12080 Pro Elite	
Intake runner volume	228 cc
Exhaust runner volume	82 cc
Valve angle	23 degrees
Valve sizes	2.050 + 0.100 intake; 1.6 + 0.100 exhaust
Combustion chamber volume	69 cc
Spark plug ports	Angled

ADVANCEMENTS IN CAMSHAFT DESIGN AND TECHNOLOGY

It should be no surprise that camshaft applications available today for the small-block Chevy include your choice of hydraulic flat tappet, hydraulic roller, mechanical (solid) flat tappet, and mechanical roller cams. For all-out performance, mechanical roller cams allow the use of the most aggressive profiles and accommodate higher spring pressures. As camshaft technology becomes more sophisticated, thanks to the ongoing research and development by the leading cam makers, Generation I small-block Chevy builders have an incredible number of camshaft choices today. Even though the engine platform originally debuted in the 1950s, and in spite of later-generation platforms, such as the LS and new LT designs, the small-block Chevy platform remains as popular, perhaps even more popular today.

Roller Cam Advantages

There's absolutely nothing wrong with sticking with a flat tappet cam and lifter setup. Cam makers continue to evolve and improve both flat tappet and roller designs in the pursuit of performance. While flat tappet cams continue to be used with great success, roller cams, in conjunction with roller lifters, offer superior durability with less frictional wear as opposed to flat tappet cams. Since the lifter rollers glide over the lobes as opposed to flat tappet cams, where lifters rub against the cam lobes, moving to a roller setup allows the use of more aggressive cam profiles.

Roller lifters can handle much more abrupt transitions from the bare circle to the ramp to the lobe peak and can hold the lifter at its maximum lift for a longer period of time. Another advantage, although it has nothing to do with performance, is interchangeability. With a flat tappet setup, the lifters wear-mate to their respective lobes. During a rebuild or freshening, the lifters must be kept in order relative to their respective lobes and positions in the engine. With a roller setup, the lifter positions can be

Roller cam lobes allow the use of more aggressive profiles. As opposed to a flat tappet cam, where the lobes are slightly tapered to provide flat tappet lifter rotation, roller cam lobes are straight because roller lifters operate on a fixed plane where they do not rotate within their bores. Rollers dramatically reduce friction because the lifter rollers glide on the lobes.

mixed up. Also, the existing lifters can still be used when changing to a different roller cam.

Camshaft technology has evolved and advanced appreciably from the old days. Not only do we now have access to the advantages of roller cam designs but we also have access to lobe ramp shapes, special-firing-order cams, asymmetric cams and dual-pattern cams, as well as superior camshaft core materials and surface treatments.

Roller camshafts require that the cam is not allowed to walk fore/aft at any appreciable amount to keep the footprint of the roller lifter bearings centered on the lobes. To accomplish this, the cam must be limited in its ability to move forward. A thrust button may be installed to the cam nose, which will contact the rear of the timing cover. In the case of a belt-driven cam setup, a retainer plate sandwiches between the cam sprocket's hub and cam with select spacer shims installed to achieve the desired amount of thrust. With a roller cam setup, cam thrust play should be kept to about 0.006 inch.

Camshaft Patterns to Compensate for Intake Manifold Runners

Traditionally, cams are made with the intake and exhaust lobes featuring the same lift and duration. Then came dual-pattern cams with a different lift and duration for the intake and exhaust lobes. For example, a dual-pattern cam might feature intake lobes with 260 degrees of duration, while the exhaust lobes have 270 degrees of duration. A dual-pattern camshaft is ground to bias the duration of either the intake or exhaust lobe.

If the build features a cam belt drive system, camshaft walk/thrust is dialed in with the selective use of shims located between the cam and the hub.

This is an example of spacer shim installed to the cam nose before installing the belt drive hub.

Once the shim(s) have been installed during test fitting, a dial indicator is used to check cam thrust. Again, a roller cam thrust movement should be limited to about 0.006 inch.

Roller cams are typically made from billet steel to better accommodate higher spring pressures.

For example, if an engine is restricted on the exhaust side (compared to the intake side), the camshaft maker might try to compensate by grinding in more lift and/or duration on the exhaust lobe.

Taking this evolution further, while the advent of dual-pattern cams provided cam makers with the ability to produce a different grind for the intake and exhaust lobes, a four-pattern cam addresses the inherent uneven air and fuel flow through the small-block Chevy's intake manifold to pick up a bit more horsepower.

In a typical 4-barrel-style intake manifold, the inboard cylinder runners are shorter than the outboard cylinder runners, resulting in about a 10-percent flow difference. The outboard runners, involving cylinders 1, 7, 2, and 8, are longer than the inboard cylinder runners for cylinders 3, 5, 4, and 6. Since air flows easily through different-length runners, fuel tends to run at a relatively diminished pace in comparison. At low RPM, the outboard cylinders tend to run leaner, while at higher RPM, the inboard cylinders tend to run leaner. To compensate for this, a four-pattern camshaft may feature the same lift and duration on the inboard cylinders. For the outboard cylinders, lift closing is delayed by 2 degrees and a bit more duration is added to provide the outboard cylinders with a tad more air.

This approach, depending on other variables, generally adds 5 to 20 hp. This was first employed by NASCAR Cup engine builders to address the uneven air/fuel distribution between inboard and outboard cylinders, and the concept is now offered by some cam makers for the public.

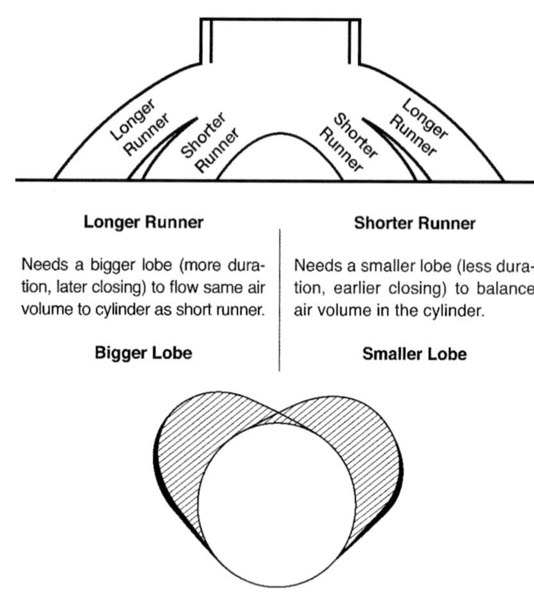

Longer Runner	Shorter Runner
Needs a bigger lobe (more duration, later closing) to flow same air volume to cylinder as short runner.	Needs a smaller lobe (less duration, earlier closing) to balance air volume in the cylinder.

Symmetrical Versus Asymmetrical Camshafts

A symmetrical camshaft features the ramp profile of the opening and closing ramps on a lobe as identical, resulting in opening and closing rates that are the same. This is the traditional approach that was used for decades. Due to the popular use of roller cams and today's CNC machining, asymmetrical camshafts were developed wherein the opening and closing lobe ramps are not identical. This is done in an attempt to achieve an opening ramp profile that provides a higher velocity and a closing ramp profile that offers a lower velocity. This allows the exhaust valve to close more gently compared to the intake valve, which opens quicker. This aids in reducing stress to the valve springs.

The decision to provide an asymmetric design and the specific opening and closing ramp speed is based on engineering research to optimize engine performance in specific engine applications. This is just one example of the technological improvements or evolution that continues to develop, even for the long-held performance

This illustration shows a dual-pattern cam profile, which is often used to compensate for airflow restrictions. For example, if an engine is restricted on the exhaust side (compared to the intake side), the camshaft maker might try to compensate by grinding in more lift and/or duration on the exhaust lobe. (Photo Courtesy Comp Cams)

standard that is the small-block Chevy. Things have come a long way since the early days.

Surface Finishing Technology

When camshafts are machined during the manufacturing process, the grinding process leaves microscopic peaks and valleys on the surfaces. While you want valleys to aid in oil retention, you want to minimize peaks that reduce the surface load bearing area. By rounding off and reducing these peaks, an increased bearing surface is created by spreading the load area. Currently, there are two successful methods that help to achieve this.

To achieve a super smooth finish that retains surface finish valleys for oil retention while leaving plateau-finished peaks for surface loading, a process known as REM

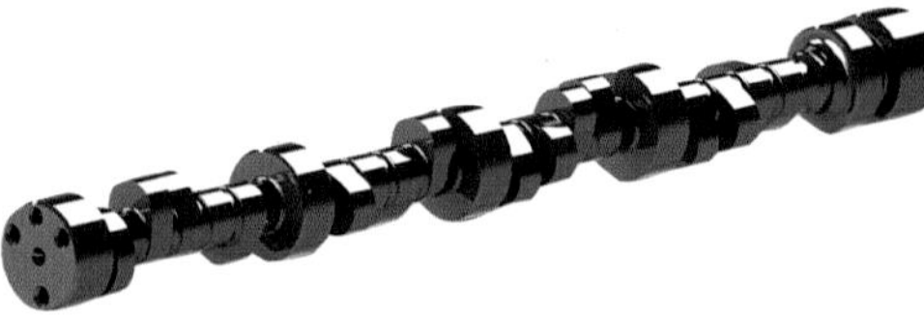

Here is an example of a polished cam that features Comp's MSE surface finish. REM finishing or MSE finishing reduces the microscopic peaks that result from the grinding process and creates more surface area on journals and lobes, which more evenly spreads load forces. (Photo Courtesy Comp Cams)

isotropic finishing is available. In essence, this finishing process produces a smoother, slicker finish and removes any microscopic sharp edges in the peaks that were left from machining.

This is a chemically accelerated two-step process. A chemical interacts with the surface that produces a one-micron film. This is followed by a tumble-polishing process using ceramic media that burnishes the surface, which is followed by a mild alkaline wash to remove the chemical film. The result is a finish that resembles that of polished chrome. Lifters glide over the lobes with greater ease and the cam journals glide within the bearings with less friction, while maintaining the necessary oil film for lubrication. This finishing treatment is offered by some cam manufacturers and is also available through various finishing services.

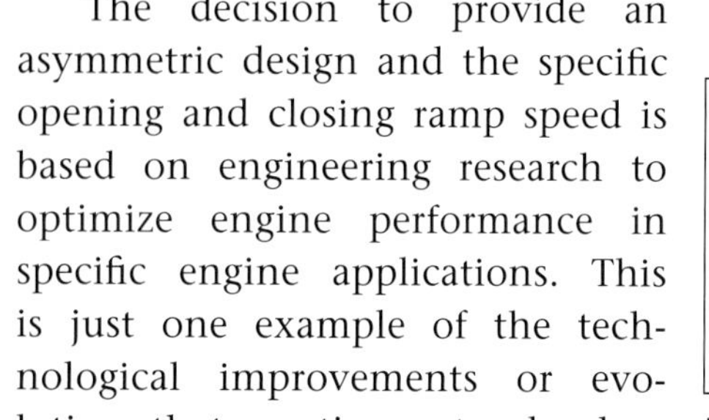

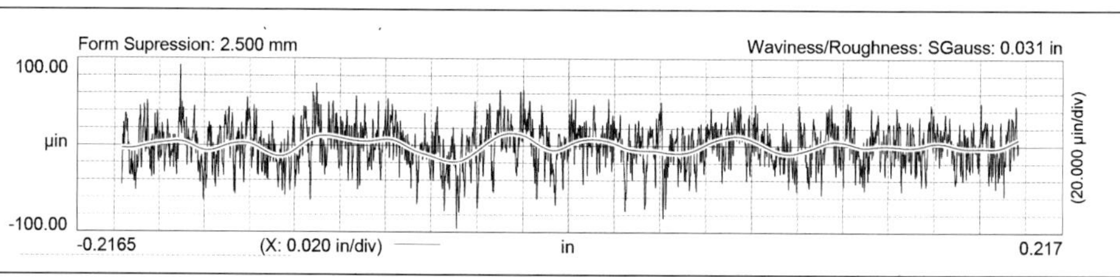

This is an example of a roughness average/waviness chart after the surface finish is ground. (Photo Courtesy Comp Cams)

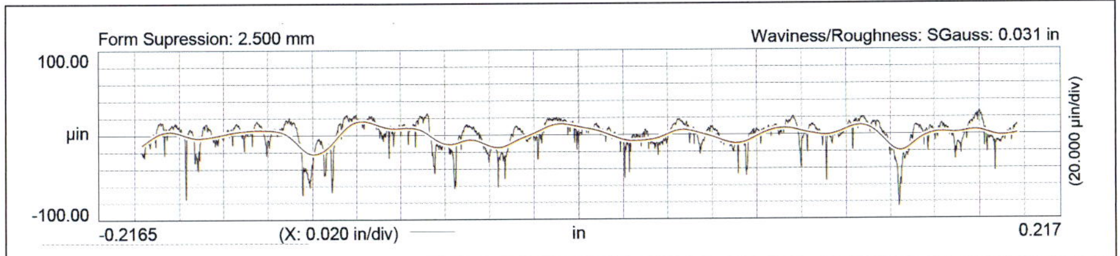

The same surface is shown after belt polishing. Notice how the roughness average has improved. (Photo Courtesy Comp Cams)

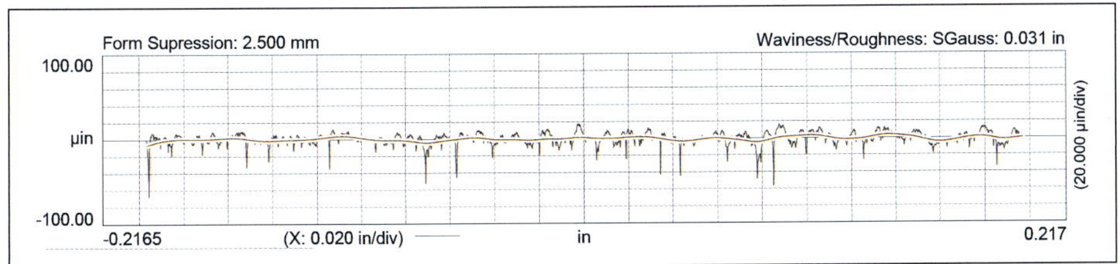

This shows the same surface after MSE finishing. The roughness average is drastically improved, reducing surface finish peaks, and improving waviness. (Photo Courtesy Comp Cams)

From left to right, a microscopic view of surface area is shown from initial grinding, which provides about 18–36 percent of surface area for load; after belt polishing, which shows that surface area increased to about 20–50 percent; and after MSE finishing, which shows surface area increased to 76–99 percent, providing maximum load-bearing surface area. (Photo Courtesy Comp Cams)

Another method currently used by Comp Cams is their Micro Surface Enhancement (MSE), which, unlike the REM system, does not use a chemical treatment as part of the process. Rather, the initial grinding uses a carbon fiber–based grinding hub that initially provides a more uniform surface, initially reducing the difference in the peaks and valleys and reducing the possibility of overall surface waviness. This is followed by the kinetic-based energy process of micropolishing. This also results in a highly polished appearance but avoids the possibility of surface annealing that may result from an acid-chemical pre-treatment.

While either system produces a visually appealing high-polish appearance, this is simply a byproduct of the actual goal, which is to minimize surface finish peaks. By drastically minimizing microscopic surface finish peaks, the bearing surface is maximized. This results in reduced stress by more evenly spreading the bearing load at both cam journal bearing areas, lifter load contact at the lobes, and superior distributor gear engagement.

Perhaps to make this more understandable, similarities may be drawn by considering plateau finishing cylinder bores. When cylinder bores are final-honed to size using honing stones, this leaves microscopic peaks and valleys. By following this with plateau honing brushes, the peaks are reduced while maintaining the valleys needed for oil retention. This results in providing a greater load bearing area for the rings, allowing the rings to seat more quickly and to reduce frictional heat by increasing the load bearing area.

Lobe Separation Angles

A camshaft's lobe separation angle (LSA) has more to do with performance than you might first think. As LSA becomes tighter with lobe angles closer together, this decreases piston-to-valve clearance, increases maximum torque, and places the torque curve in a lower RPM range. However, this results in a more narrow powerband.

A tighter LSA helps increase cylinder pressure (since the transition time between the valve opening and closing is smaller), and also increases the chance of detonation due to higher cylinder pressure and increased compression. A tighter LSA also reduces engine vacuum and idle quality.

Conversely, as we widen the lobe separation angle, this has the opposite effects. Piston-to-valve clearance increases, we gain higher engine vacuum, and we face less chance of detonation. A wider LSA tends to produce a wider powerband, reducing maximum torque, but it raises torque to a higher RPM range. Generally speaking, a tight LSA is better for bottom-end torque, whereas a wider LSA is better for higher-RPM running.

Base Circle Diameter

Some builders prefer to use a smaller 0.900-inch base circle to improve connecting rod–to–cam lobe clearance. However, a reduced base circle moves the lifter farther down in its bore with the possibility of moving the lifter's oil feed passages below the lifter oil gallery feeds. If you're concerned with rod-to-cam interference, remember that many aftermarket blocks are available with a raised cam tunnel that moves the cam farther away from the rods.

Special Firing-Order Camshafts

In certain racing applications, as in drag racing and long-distance competition, a special firing order (SFO) camshaft can be used as a tuning aid, allowing the competition engine builder to further address combustion heat and crankshaft harmonic issues. Why change firing order? This is done to create a smoother-running engine, more even fuel distribution, and to eliminate hot spots that occur when two companion cylinders fire in succession, which occurs with the normal firing order when cylinders 5 and 7 fire in succession.

Cams are now available in SFO for the small-block Gen I engine, which was born out of experimentation by a few race engine builders with the practice incorporated by General Motors during development of the Gen 3 LS platform, wherein the automaker adopted a special firing order that swapped cylinders 4/7 and 2/3. While smoothing out engine firing harmonics and reducing deflection on the crankshaft and the main bearings, we have the potential for freeing up additional horsepower. In a V-8 configuration, a 4/7 swap theoretically reduces crankshaft torsional vibration for smoother dampening and potentially more power.

The normal small-block Chevy has a firing order of 1-8-4-3-6-5-7-2. By swapping 4 and 7 to create a new firing order of 1-8-7-3-6-5-4-2, some builders claim to gain an additional 5 to 10 hp.

To achieve a special firing order, a specially designed camshaft is required. Thanks to the use of computer design and CNC machining capabilities, cam makers have the ability to produce such cams in a relatively short period of time.

While the firing order can be changed via a custom camshaft for engines that use a single-plane carb-style intake manifold, if the engine is direct-port injected, individual cylinders can be commanded richer/leaner via the engine controller. So, firing order changes may not be as beneficial in an injected engine because fuel is delivered on an individual-cylinder basis.

The 4/7 firing order moves the hot spot from the 5/7 cylinders up to the 4/2 cylinders. Because the water pump is mounted up front, the front pair is easier to cool as opposed to the rear pair.

Firing order changes can benefit bearing life, especially when you consider when two cylinders on the same rod pin fire in succession. When we swap firing positions, this moves the opposing forces on the rod pin toward the rear of the engine, allowing the drivetrain to absorb more of the harmonics.

Examples of different firing orders are shown. From top to bottom is a 7-4 swap, a 7-4/3-2 swap, and the standard firing order.

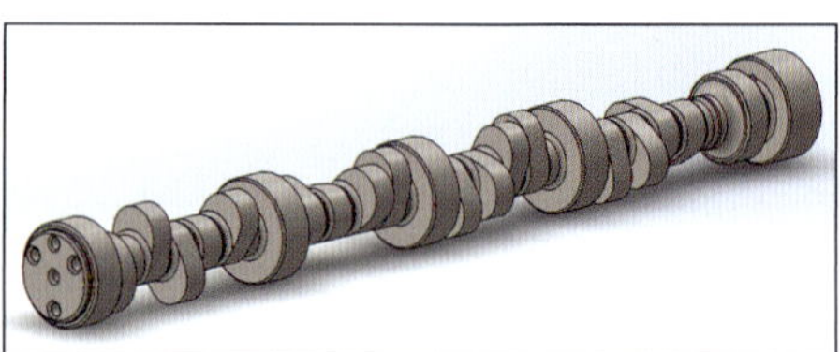

An example of a standard firing order cam is shown. (CAD Drawing Courtesy Comp Cams)

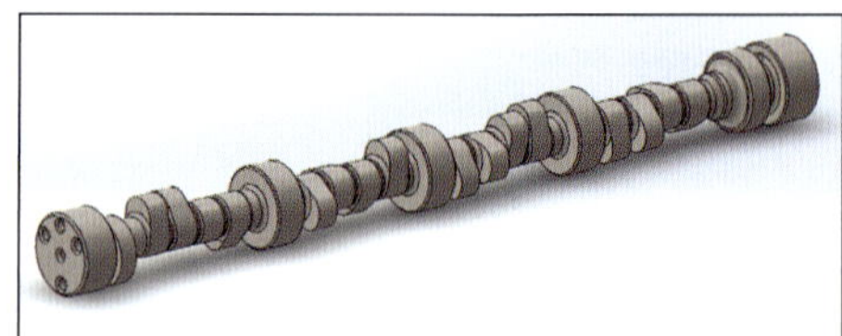

This is an example of a 4-7 swap firing order cam. (CAD Drawing Courtesy Comp Cams)

Camshaft Needle Bearings

Traditionally, cam bearings are interference-fit cast multilayer babbit-style bearings. However, many competition engines feature needle bearings. The advantages of moving to needle bearings in the cam bores include less friction at the cam journals and a more precise maintaining of the camshaft centerline during engine operation.

A conventional babbit cam bearing features an oil hole, allowing oil to lubricate the cam journal. The oil clearance between the cam journal and the bearing is filled with oil so that during camshaft rotation the cam journals ride on a film of oil, which is just like the rod and main bearings.

A camshaft needle roller bearing allows the cam to ride directly on the bearings. Oil splash is sufficient for lubrication, and the needle bearing housing blocks off the cam tunnel oil passages, so there is a slight reduction of oil temperature (at least in theory).

To install camshaft bore needle bearings, the cam's bore must be increased in diameter (usually by about 0.040 inch or so) to result in about a 0.002-inch interference fit for the bearings. This must be done on an alignment boring fixture (or in a CNC machine).

The use of needle bearings requires the use of a camshaft with larger-diameter journals (a larger diameter core). This results in a beefier cam core that is less prone to flexing, which is great when using ultra-high-pressure valve springs.

The downside to needle bearings is that the labor/machining cost to modify a block to accept needle roller bearings is roughly $600 to $700. Aftermarket race blocks are available already machined for needle bearings. You must also run a steel billet camshaft with needle bearings, which raises the cost more. A potential glitch is that the use of needle bearings may promote valvetrain harmonics as opposed to the use of cast babbit cam bearings, where the cam journals ride on an oil film that helps to reduce harmonics.

If you want the ultimate product and don't mind paying the price, needle cam bearings are the way to go. If you're simply building a strong street engine where continuous high engine speed isn't a factor, it's a waste of money.

Camshaft needle roller bearings are commonly available in sizes ranging from 50-mm ID with 58-mm OD to 55-mm ID with 63-mm OD. If you move to needle bearings, you must order a camshaft that has the appropriate-diameter journals.

With all of that said, the move to needle roller cam bearings is not needed for street applications or any application where the engine will not be torn down and inspected on a routine basis. Needle roller cam bearings cannot be installed in the traditional manner of cast bearings, where the bearings are tapped into place using a cam bearing installer tool and a hammer. Rather, cam roller bearings must be carefully drawn into place using a special tool that eliminates the application of hammering/shock installation. In many aftermarket race blocks, the block is designed for the use of roller cam bearings, where special stopper bolts are installed from the lifter valley, one on each side of the cam bearing location, to prevent the cam bearing from moving fore or aft during engine operation.

Choosing the Correct Distributor Gear

There are four different types of commonly used distributor gears, including composite, bronze, cast iron, and melonized steel. Using a distributor gear that's incompatible with the type of material used for the camshaft gear can result in quick destruction of the distributor gear and/or the cam gear, sending debris throughout the engine. Ideally, the distributor gear should be made of a softer material than the gear on the cam to prevent cam gear wear. It's important to know what type of material your camshaft gear is made

Cam needle bearings provide reduced friction but are intended for competition engines that will be inspected and rebuilt routinely.

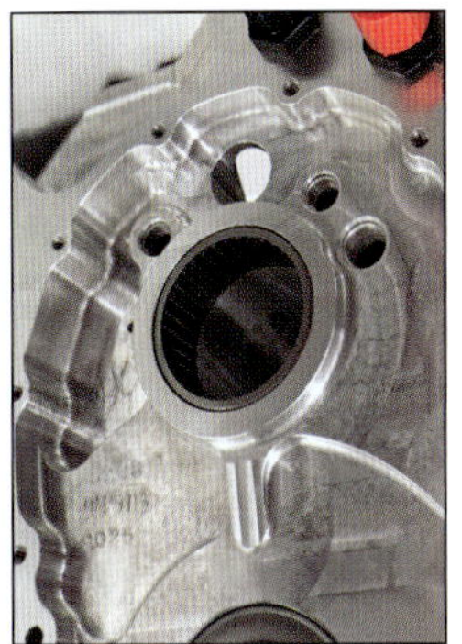

Needle bearings must be carefully drawn into their bores, as opposed to tapping them in place with a conventional cam bearing installation tool.

Some aftermarket racing blocks feature a non-press-fit for cam needle bearings for easy service. The lifter valley will feature thread holes at each side of each bearing location for the use of stopper plugs, as shown in this Brodix aluminum block, to prevent the bearings from walking.

from. When in doubt, contact the maker of your cam for a recommendation for distributor gear material. This is a critical aspect that some folks overlook.

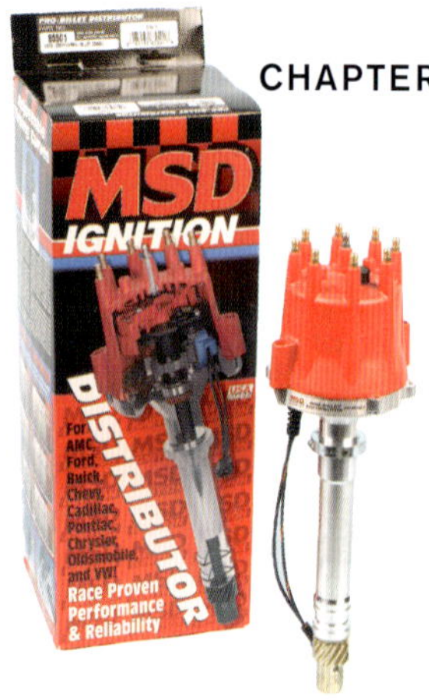

Composite Gears

Advancements in polymer chemistry have now made it possible to use this material for distributor gear applications. Composite, or poly, gears consist of super strong polymer. While the thought of using a "plastic" gear might sound like a crazy idea, this material actually does offer acceptable performance and durability. Composite gears are compatible with all camshaft gears. Poly gears are lightweight as well. Yes, they cost a bit more than other types, but they're durable and safe to use with any cam gear. Poly gears are compatible with cams that feature a cast-iron gear, ductile iron gear, or billet steel.

Bronze Gears

Bronze gears are machined from an extruded aluminum bronze alloy with a 5 percent nickel content. Bronze gears are relatively soft and won't damage the cam gear while conforming well to the cam gear. Bronze gears are commonly used with steel billet roller cams. The only downside to a bronze gear is its service life, as it will eventually wear and is considered somewhat sacrificial. Bronze is fine for a race engine that will be periodically disassembled and inspected along with gear replacement, but it is perhaps not the best choice for a street engine that will see lots of miles and never be torn down. Supposedly, poly gears offer about a 300-percent longer service life than bronze gears. Bronze is compatible with a billet steel roller cam but should be avoided if the cam has a cast- or ductile-iron gear.

Cast-Iron Gears

Cast-iron gears are, as the name implies, made of cast iron. However, they are made in a manner where the outer layer is solidified and the

When you're in doubt regarding distributor gear to cam compatibility for a roller cam, simply swap out the original gear with a bronze or composite gear.

Bronze distributor gears or composite gears are suitable choices for steel billet roller cams. Bronze gears should be checked for wear periodically. Depending on the application and type of use, for racing applications, check after every race or every couple of races. For street applications, it's a good idea to check every 10,000 miles or so.

When test fitting, it's a good idea to paint the gear with machinist dye (Prussian blue, Dykem blue, etc.). Install the distributor, rotate the crank a few turns, and remove the distributor to check gear engagement. If the distributor features an adjustable height collar, you can move the distributor up or down to achieve a perfect mesh.

core is left as molten iron. Cast-iron distributor gears are compatible with cam gears that are made of the same material. Cast-iron gears are suitable for hydraulic and solid flat tappet camshafts as long as the cam has a cast-iron gear.

Melonized Steel Gears

This material is commonly used by original equipment manufacturers. Steel gears feature the hardest material that is used for distributor gears and are intended for a long life in a mild stock engine. While they may be harder, melonized distributor gears are heat treated for durability but offer a relatively slick surface that makes them compatible with most cams.

Check for Runout

All camshafts, whether new or used, should be checked for runout before installation, simply to confirm that the cam is straight. A cam with excessive runout can result in cam bearing clearance issues and bearing damage, erratic valve opening and closing rates, and erratic timing.

Rest the cam on clean V-blocks and set up a dial indicator at the cam's center journal. After preloading the dial indicator plunger by about 0.050 inch, adjust the gauge to zero. Rotate the cam slowly and observe it for runout. Ideally, there should be zero runout with a bit less than about 0.001-inch runout considered allowable. Any more runout than that indicates the cam is bent or the center journal was ground out of round and the cam should be replaced.

Especially when inspecting a used cam, it's always a good idea to check for runout to see if the cam has deflected. With the cam resting on clean V-blocks, position a dial indicator at the center journal. After preloading the dial indicator by about 0.050 inch, the gauge is zeroed and the cam is slowly rotated, measuring runout. The maximum allowable runout should be less than 0.001 inch.

INDUCTION

Feeding the small-block Chevy with air and fuel offers all of the approaches imaginable, including naturally aspirated carburetion, central fuel injection, multi-port injection, and turbocharged or supercharged systems. Of special note is the viability of easy conversion from traditional carburetion to central fuel injection, where a simple carb-type mounting offers the added efficiency of built-in injectors. Here, we'll provide an overview.

Manifolds

Not surprisingly, a wide range of intake manifold designs are readily available due to the popularity of the small-block Chevy platform. Whether you want to run a single 2-barrel or 4-barrel carburetor setup, multiple 2-barrels, down draft or side draft carbs, central fuel injection or multi-port fuel injection, you have plenty of choices. Examples of intake manifold manufacturers catering to the small-block Chevy include Holley, Edelbrock, Weiand, Pro-Filer Performance Products, Wilson Manifolds, AFR, Brodix, Trick Flow Specialties, Borla Induction, Inglese, and FAST.

Carbureted dual-plane versus single-plane manifolds differ in the way the cylinders are fed. A dual-plane (commonly known as a 180-degree style) features a split plenum with each side feeding four cylinders. Each plenum connects to every other runner in the firing order. Dual-plane styles are typically better at producing peak torque at lower RPM ranges, and single-plane manifolds feature an open plenum that feeds all eight cylinders for better airflow at higher RPM. Depending on your choice of heads and cam, vehicle weight, etc., either style may work best for a given application. Single-plane manifolds generally work better with more aggressive cams. Dual-plane manifolds tend to pull fuel out of the carb boosters quicker and may offer better off-idle response.

In days of old, choices of intake manifolds were generally limited to cast aluminum dual-plane, single-plane, low-rise and high-rise tunnel ram styles. Today, we're blessed with a vast array of ever-evolving designs with improved airflow characteristics designed for carburetor, fuel injection, nitrous, flat tappet or roller cams, and various configurations that maximize low-end or high-end horsepower and torque. In addition to cast-aluminum, fabricated sheet metal intake manifolds constructed of TIG-welded aluminum are available as well.

Even though later-model engine platforms, such as the LS series, have garnered widespread popularity, manifold makers continue to support and innovate superior designs for the venerable Gen I small-block plat-

Who doesn't love the looks of a set of downdraft 8-stack Webers on an Inglese manifold? Weber setups are offered in both carb and EFI packages. (Photo Courtesy Comp Cams/Inglese)

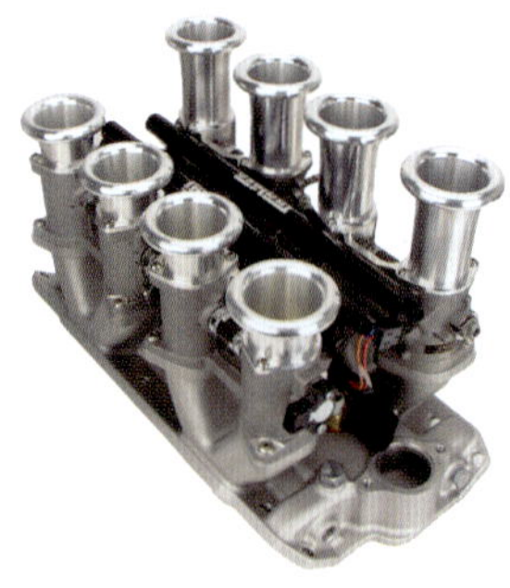

Inglese/Weber setups are also available as EFI systems with fuel rails tucked between the stacks. Depending on the injector size, these are rated as handling up to 1,000 hp. Velocity stacks are available in short or tall sizes. (Photo Courtesy Comp Cams/Inglese)

Pure sex appeal. Notice the injectors are positioned on the inboard side of each manifold runner, giving the outward appearance of old-school Weber carbs. (Photo Courtesy Comp Cams/Inglese)

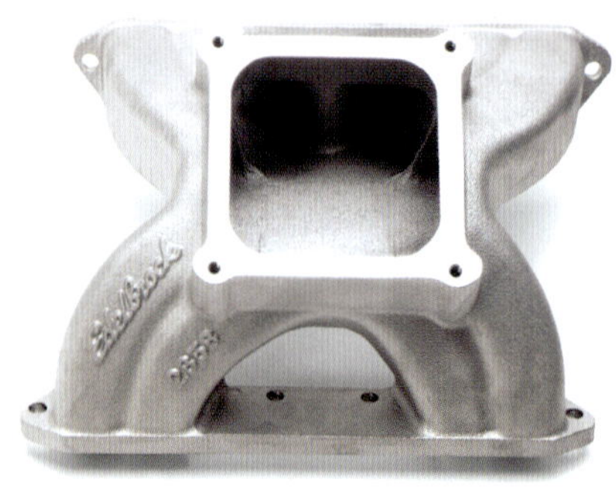

This is an example of a single-plane intake manifold from Edelbrock (part number 2858), where coolant crossover is not used. (Photo Courtesy Edelbrock)

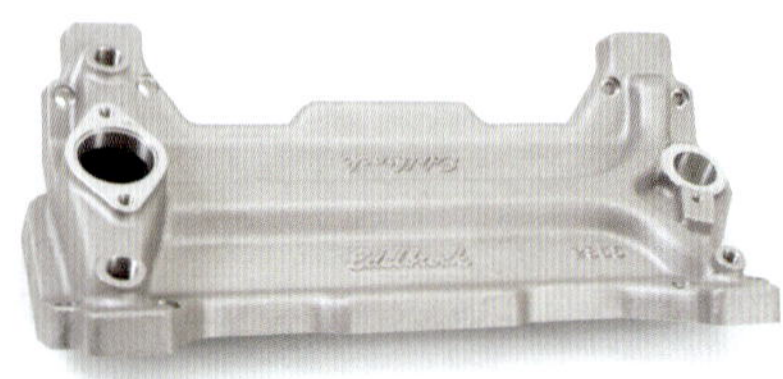

The valley cover (part number 2856) is used in conjunction with the 2858 manifold. This covers the lifter valley, removing engine heat from the underside of the manifold. (Photo Courtesy Edelbrock)

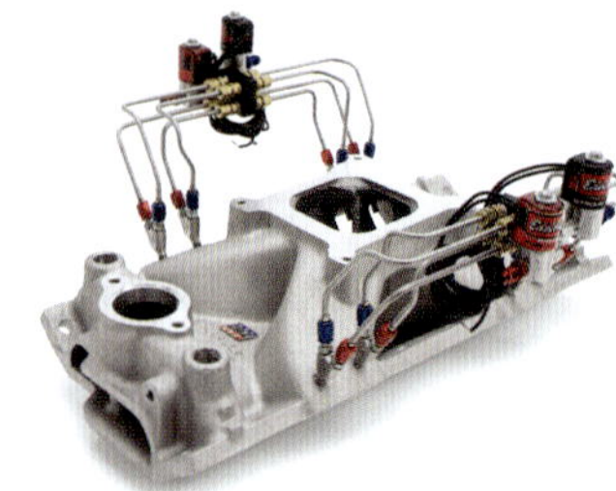

Nitrous injection system applications vary in terms of design and location of the nitrous injection. This example is Edelbrock's air gap manifold (part number 72975) with a nitrous injection system included. (Photo Courtesy Edelbrock)

Want to go old-school? Edelbrock still offers a setup with three 2-barrel Stromberg carbs for that cool tri-power look. (Photo Courtesy Edelbrock)

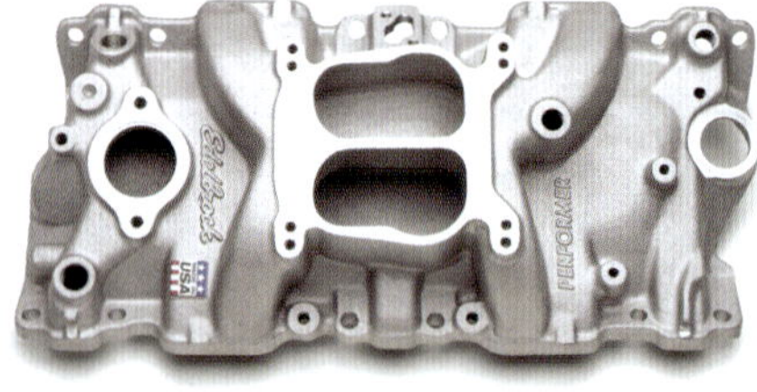

Dual-plane manifolds, referred to as 180-degree manifolds, typically offer low-end torque. (Photo Courtesy Edelbrock)

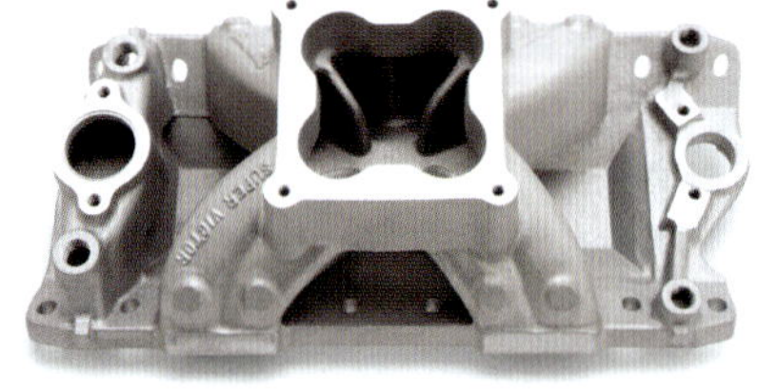

Single-plane manifolds are typically better suited for providing power and torque at a higher RPM band. (Photo Courtesy Edelbrock)

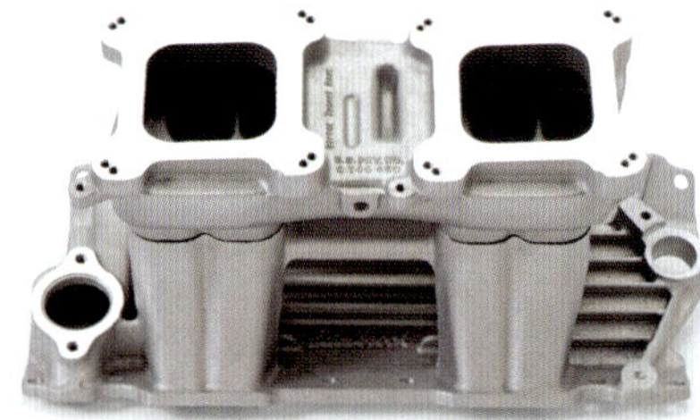

High-rise dual-quad manifolds continue to be available. For a high-RPM gulp of air and fuel, it's hard to resist. (Photo Courtesy Edelbrock)

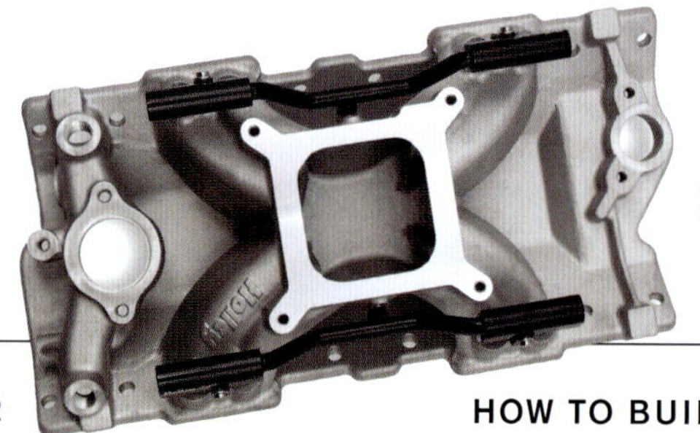

This example of a 4-barrel intake with multi-port injectors and rails was designed for use with a throttle body. (Photo Courtesy Holley)

A high-rise intake with dual carbs is a real eye-catcher and can offer more power as long as the engine build can justify the use of this setup. For visual bragging rights on a carbureted naturally aspirated engine, it's hard to beat.

While perhaps not practical for street or hood-restrictive applications, tall velocity stacks provide a cool old-school appearance.

form. In essence, regardless of your performance requirement in terms of appearance and/or function, you're covered. The aftermarket industry has no plans to phase out offerings for the beloved small-block.

Selecting Carburetor Size

The following is an excerpt from my book *Holly Carburetors: How to Rebuild* that is available from CarTech. Carburetor size (cubic feet per minute [CFM] capability) needs to be selected with a host of variables in mind, not only for the engine itself but also for the vehicle, drivetrain and how the vehicle is to be used. If the vehicle is equipped with an automatic transmission, for example, consider the torque converter stall speed. This will represent the lowest engine RPM at which wide open throttle will be applied. If the vehicle is equipped with a manual transmission, consider the lowest engine RPM that is expected to be used at wide open throttle.

The relationship between the lowest engine RPM expected to be used at wide open throttle and engine displacement will roughly determine what carburetor size should be most appropriate. Citing the Holley sample graph shown here, draw a line from the minimum engine RPM at wide open throttle (the value range seen at the far left) through the value line for engine displacement. Continue

this line to the carburetor size value range at the far right. In the example shown, if the minimum RPM at which you expect to use wide open throttle is about 1,350 rpm and the engine size is 350 ci, the maximum suggested carburetor size is just a tick below 700 cfm. In this case, a 650 to 700 cfm carb should be adequate.

The vehicle's weight and axle ratio needs to be factored into the selection as well. A heavier vehicle and/or a numerically lower axle ratio typically prefers a carburetor size on the smaller side, while a lighter vehicle and/or a higher axle ratio prefers a larger carburetor size. In the chart example shown below, a lighter car (such as a Mustang or Camaro) equipped with a numerically higher axle ratio may require a slightly larger carb along the lines of 700 to 750 cfm. Bear in mind that this applies when selecting a carburetor with mechanical secondary operation. If the plan is to use a vacuum secondary carb, you can always move up a bit in CFM because the secondary operation will be enabled according to engine demand.

The carburetor must be matched to the application. While it may

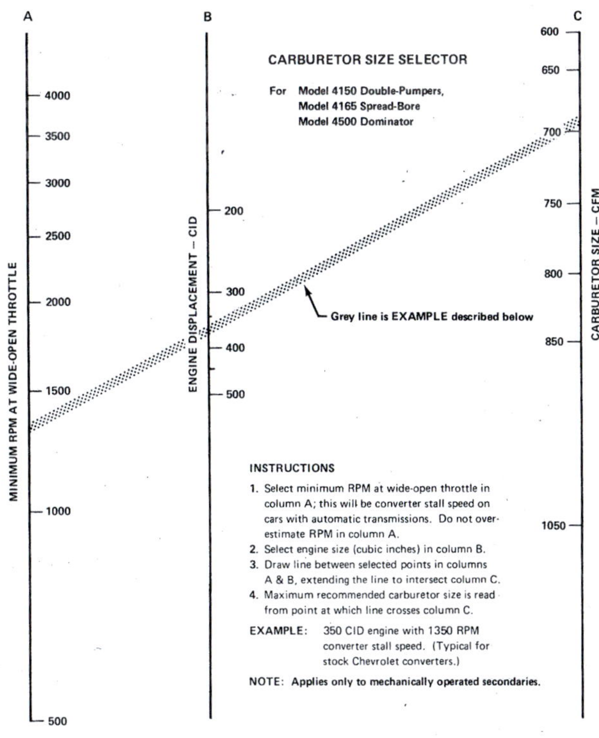

This chart can aid in selecting carburetor size. By drawing a line that intersects your minimum engine RPM at wide open throttle and the engine displacement size, you get an approximate idea of what size carburetor is appropriate. Use this as a baseline because vehicle weight, axle ratio, and vehicle use need to be considered as well. (Photo Courtesy Holley)

be tempting to purchase a larger carburetor based on the theory that bigger must be better, keep in mind that if the carb size is too large, absolute top-end power might improve, but off-the-line and cruising mid-range acceleration can suffer (bogging). If you err on the side of caution by choosing a slightly smaller carb, a bit of top end power may be sacrificed, but low-end and mid-range acceleration will improve.

A formula to use as a base reference follows. Bear in mind that this formula assumes that the engine operates at 100-percent efficiency, which doesn't happen in the real world.

Carburetor CFM = half the engine size x maximum RPM / 1,728.

This formula considers engine displacement divided by two because a 4-cycle engine intakes once with each crank revolution. The number 1,728 divides into maximum engine RPM because this is the factor used to convert cubic inches (CI) into cubic feet (CFM).

Another way to view this formula is:

Carburetor CFM = Engine CI x Max RPM / 3456.

$$\text{Carburetor CFM} = \frac{\text{Engine CI x Max RPM}}{3456}$$

An example of using this formula (again, based on 100-percent engine efficiency) would be as follows: Let's say that the engine features 455 ci, and the maximum expected engine speed will be 6,000 rpm.

455 x 6000 = 2,730,000

2,730,000 / 3456 = 789.93 cfm

In this example, it appears that this engine would prefer a carburetor size closest to 800 cfm. Since most engines (assuming the engine is properly built and is operating at its best) have a volumetric efficiency in the 80 to 95 percent range, we assume that a slightly smaller carb, in the range of 650- to 750-cfm range would be a more realistic choice for this engine.

Before you try to determine the ideal carburetor size for a given application, have an idea of the engine's volumetric efficiency. Volumetric efficiency (VE) is an indication of the engine's ability to breathe. The better the engine breathes, the higher the VE. This is expressed as a ratio of the air mass (weight of the air) that the engine intakes, compared to the air mass that the engine's displacement would theoretically ingest if there were no losses. VE will be fairly low at idle and will increase (and vary) according to engine speed. VE should be considered according to the engine RPM at which the engine will realistically operate.

Assuming that the engine is not worn out, has been assembled correctly, and that it has no operating problems, a typical low-performance engine may have in the range of 70 to 80 percent VE at the engine's maximum torque level. A typical high-performance engine that offers increased breathing may have a VE in the range of 80 to 85 percent at maximum torque. A top-level racing engine may have a VE in the range of 90 to 95 percent at maximum torque RPM. The variables of engine parameters, including tuning the intake and exhaust systems, cylinder head porting, the camshaft profile, etc., all work in combination to increase volumetric efficiency. Holley's carb selection charts are based on 100-percent VE.

So, if the chart indicates that the best size is, say, 700 cfm, but the engine features around 85-percent VE, in theory, a better choice for that engine might be a carb size of 600 cfm.

Forced induction, supercharging for example, usually requires about 40 to 50 percent more carburetor size capacity compared to a naturally aspirated engine. Note: Holley now offers a line of carburetors specifically designed for supercharged applications.

Charts and formulas aside, consider moving to a bigger carb when displacement increases, higher RPMs are to be used, engine compression is higher, mechanical ignition advance increases, higher-ratio drive gears are used, and as vehicle weight is decreased. A smaller carb suits conditions where engine compression is low, the vehicle is heavier, the torque converter stall speed (on an automatic transmission) is very low, and the drive gear ratio is numerically lower.

Also, keep in mind that a given carb (or carb tuning) used during an engine dyno session won't necessarily perform the same when the engine is in the vehicle. The engine dyno run is merely a starting point. Additional tuning and possibly a move to a different carburetor is potentially necessary once the vehicle is on the track or road.

E85 Fuel

Are you thinking of switching to E85 fuel? E85 is a mix of gasoline and 85-percent ethanol. The advantages, aside from the cleaner emissions output, is that the engine temperature will drop slightly. E85 is essentially 105-octane fuel and slightly cheaper than high-dollar race gas. The big advantage is that E85 allows you to run more timing, which yields more power gains.

To experience the full power benefit of ethanol-based fuels, you'll need to increase the fuel flow. The disadvantage is that despite having a higher octane rating, E85 has a lower overall energy density than pure gasoline fuel. Pure gasoline contains approximately 125,000 BTUs per gallon, while E85 contains approximately 84,000. So, you'll use more E85 as mile-per-gallon economy will suffer. Be aware that to run E85 with a carburetor, you need a carb that is designed to use this fuel both in terms of carb calibration and internal components and seals that are compatible with the greater ratio of ethanol.

EFI

There are old-school and new-school hot rodders, and there's nothing wrong with either mindset. Traditionalists prefer carburetors for a number of reasons. They're less costly than a fuel injection system, they provide a more traditional appearance, and there's no need for computer management and the associated wiring. On the other hand, a fuel injection system provides perhaps greater efficiency and allows easier and often more precise tuning.

Depending on the owner's view, either system is more favorable. It all depends on individual taste. Electronic fuel injection systems vary in terms of approach. A central EFI throttle body may be mounted in exactly the same way as a carburetor with built-in fuel injectors, providing a unit that handles both air and fuel delivery. Another option is multi-port injection with one injector installed in the intake manifold at each cylinder location, coupled with a carb-style-mounting of an air throttle body. This provides both the efficiency of a fuel injection system with the somewhat similar appearance of a carburetor, dual carbs, or 8-stack downdraft Weber-style throttle bodies on a dedicated manifold.

If you're dealing with a carb-style intake manifold designed to accept a single or dual 4150-style carb, you have two choices for EFI: an EFI throttle body unit that incorporates air and fuel in one unit, such as MSD's Atomic, or Holley's Terminator or Sniper line, which features a throttle body that mounts as a carb but includes built-in injectors. Or, you can install an air throttle body in place of a carb to a manifold that features eight injector ports at the runners.

An alternative is a tune-port plenum EFI with multi-port injection that accepts a front-mounted throttle body, such as Edelbrock's part number 2019. The choices are extensive. Regardless of the setup you want, there's a system available.

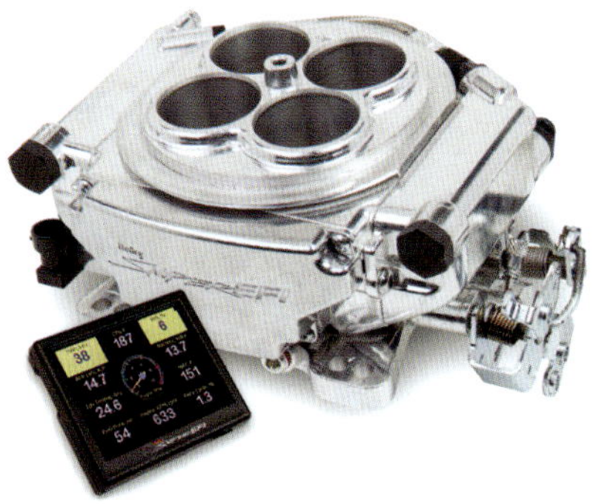

Holley's Super Sniper, also called the "turbo Sniper" throttle body EFI unit, is designed for use with forced induction as a blow-through carb option. It is rated to handle up to 1,200 hp. This also includes a built-in nitrous injection controller.

This is Holley's Terminator EFI. The unit features built-in injectors that are hidden from view under what looks like fuel bowls so you can maintain the appearance of a carb with the benefits of fuel injection.

Holley's Sniper EFI is shown. This approach is becoming increasingly popular, providing an easy swap from carburetion to fuel injection. The unit mounts just like a carb but has built-in injectors to create a central throttle body fuel injection platform. Designed to fit a 4150-flange manifold, it features a built-in ECU, so no additional control boxes are needed. It is rated at supporting up to 650 hp with four 100-pound injectors. The unit is self-learning as you drive, or the tune can be programmed.

Here is an example of a tune-port injection manifold that accepts a front-mounted air throttle body. (Photo Courtesy Edelbrock)

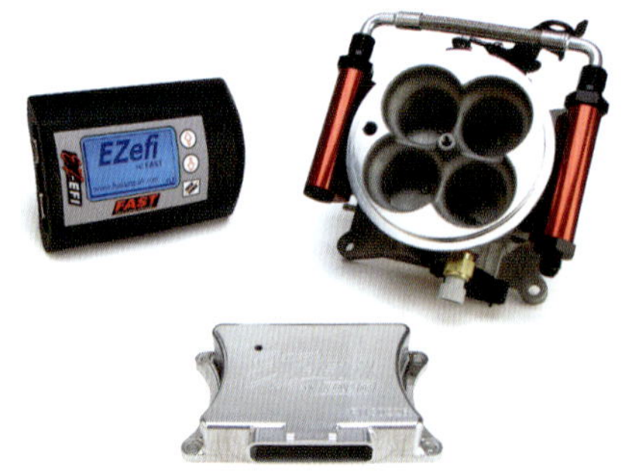

FAST's EZ-EFI throttle body features external fuel rails, built-in injectors, an ECU, and a programmer. (Photo Courtesy FAST)

Here is another example of a central EFI unit. The FAST EZ-EFI mounts like a carb and features faux fuel bowl covers that hide the injectors.

This bottom view of the FAST EFI reveals the four built-in injectors.

While the complete installation kit for the FAST EZ-EFI may look daunting at first glance, the installation is actually quite simple.

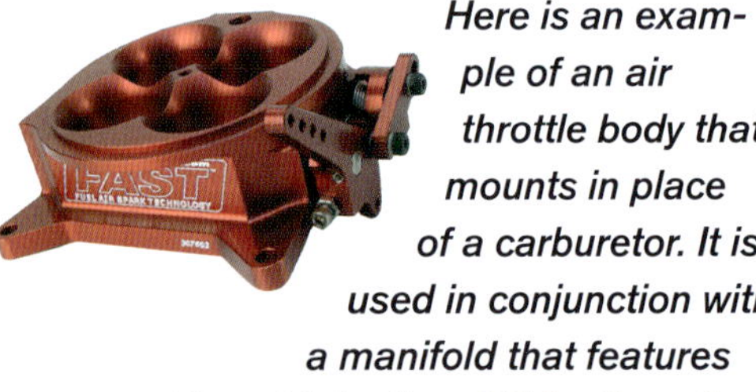

Here is an example of an air throttle body that mounts in place of a carburetor. It is used in conjunction with a manifold that features multi-port injection. CFM ratings from about 1,300 to over 2,000 are available in either 4150- and 4500-style flange designs. Since fuel delivery is accomplished by injector size and duration, the throttle body size can be larger than that of a carb, allowing great blow-through for forced induction. Many air throttle bodies include a throttle position sensor (TPS), idle air control (IAC), and air temperature sensor. (Photo Courtesy FAST)

The FAST XFI fuel injection kit provides everything that is needed, including the manifold, air throttle body, injectors, distributor, and all of the wiring and hardware. (Photo Courtesy FAST)

This wet-style EZ-EFI throttle body by FAST mounts the same way as a 4-barrel carb. It has a pair of injectors mounted on the front and rear with external feed rails. (Photo Courtesy FAST)

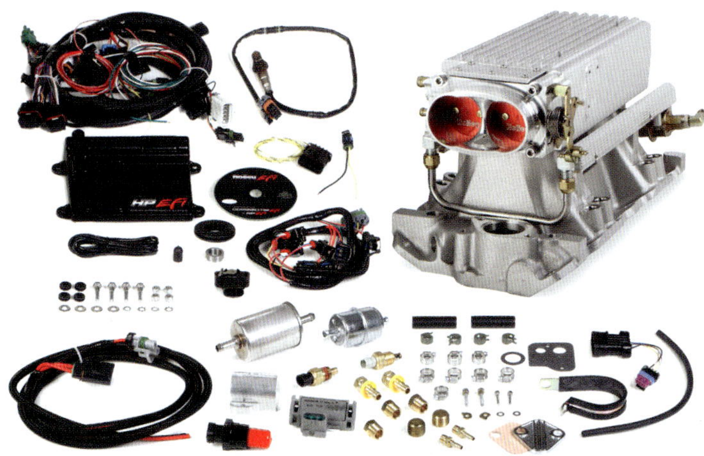

Pictured is a complete tune-port injection system from Holley with everything needed for installation. (Photo Courtesy Holley)

EFI Throttle Body

CFM ratings of throttle bodies can be confusing at first if you're accustomed to choosing carburetors based on CFM. When researching the various throttle bodies and EFI systems, it is clear that their CFM ratings are huge compared to those of carburetors. Typically, performance aftermarket EFI throttle bodies are rated at 1,000, 1,200, 1,375, and even 2,000 cfm. Looking at those numbers with a carburetor mentality, those ratings will at first seem way off the charts. Here's what you need to understand: while a carburetor moves both fuel and air (and must be sized according to engine size and horsepower), an EFI throttle body only moves air, essentially serving as an air door. Fuel delivery is controlled by the electronically operated injectors.

EFI throttle bodies are sized larger (again, strictly in terms of available airflow) to provide greater latitude for a range of air delivery requirements. The engine will only pull enough air through the throttle body as it needs. If you place a 1,000-cfm throttle body on a mild small-block engine, the engine may only need to pull, say, 600 cfm. A wild big-block 500-ci engine with healthy heads and a wild cam may require, say, 1,000 cfm. The same size of throttle body can handle this wide range because, again, the throttle body only serves as a door through which the required amount of air can pass.

It may take a while for this understanding to sink in. Just remember not to compare CFM ratings on an equal basis between carburetors and EFI throttle bodies. Just because a throttle body is rated at 1,375 cfm does not mean that the engine will be forced to accept this volume of air. The throttle body simply makes this amount of air available if the engine needs it. The engine will only draw the amount of air that it needs. Fuel delivery is handled as a separate, controlled issue.

Fuel Pressure

EFI systems require high fuel pressure and low volume, which is the opposite of a high-volume/low-pressure carburetor setup. The high pressure is maintained in the lines and fuel rails. When injectors are signaled to open, the constant pressure is already there to be dispersed. System pumps will vary. In general, the operating pressure for typical applications will likely run in the 30 to 90 psi range. However, some systems, depending on the specific application, may run as little as 19- to 24-pound injectors. A special EFI fuel pressure regulator is also required with a high-pressure inline fuel filter, which is all included in a complete EFI system. EFI also requires a fuel return line, which may or may not be included in your specific kit.

Note: Fuel filters must be high-pressure rated with a minimum burst strength of 100 psi. Don't use just any inline filter; make sure that it's designed for high-pressure applications.

Fuel Injectors: Low Impedance Versus High Impedance

High-impedance resistance injectors (about 10–16 ohms) and low-impedance resistance injectors (about 1.5–4 ohms) are available. Which type do you need? Generally speaking, if you're running an OEM engine control unit (ECU), you need high-impedance injectors. These feature a somewhat slower response time. If you're running a performance aftermarket ECU, you need low-impedance injectors that react quicker. If you run low-impedance injectors with an OEM computer, you run the risk if damaging the OEM ECU.

Most injectors that feature high flow rates are the low-impedance type. Low-impedance injectors offer a faster opening response time and generate less heat. They are generally preferred for aftermarket performance systems, although this can vary depending on the specific aftermarket system.

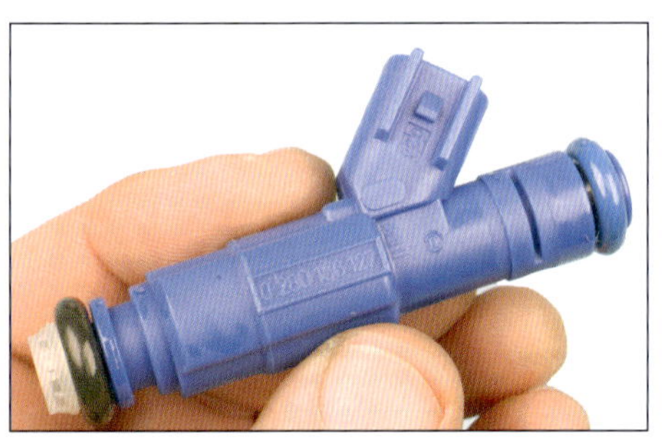

An EV6-style injector is shown. This style is popular due to its slim profile.

This is an example of an EV1-style injector. This is often referred to generically as a Ford-style injector.

Generic Rule of Thumb for BSFC	
Naturally aspirated engines	0.4 to 0.5
Engines with nitrous injection	0.5 to 0.6
Forced induction (turbo or supercharger)	0.6 to 0.7
For engines running methanol, double the BSFC number	

Choosing Injector Size

Based on your engine's anticipated horsepower and the engine's Brake Specific Fuel Consumption (BSFC) efficiency number, you can target the appropriate-sized injector. BSFC represents the amount of fuel that the engine will consume divided by its power output (how many pounds of fuel will be used per HP produced in an hour).

$$\text{Injector size} = \text{engine HP} \times \text{BSFC} / \text{No. of cylinders} \times 0.8$$

Example: A 500-hp V-8 with high compression has:

$$500 \text{ hp} \times 0.50 / 8 \times 0.8 = 39 \text{ lbs}$$

Theoretically, this application calls for a 39-pound injector. This is merely a starting point. Depending on the system and as the result of tuning, a larger injector may be required.

Bigger isn't always better. If too large of an injector is selected, throttle response may suffer and you'll waste fuel. Low-impedance injectors are available up to 160 lb/hr, so don't simply jump to a bigger injector because it sounds like a good idea. Remember, injectors alone don't make power; the system must be tuned with the most efficient-sized injector for the specific application.

Aftermarket performance systems will provide the appropriate-sized injector for your specific application. Since injector range varies depending on the anticipated horsepower, it's important to select the proper system part number to match your needs or contact the manufacturer for a recommendation.

Commonly used fuel injectors include the EV1 and EV6 body styles. The EV1 is the fat style, which is often generically called the Ford style. The EV6 features a skinnier profile and a different connector (such as the EV6-style injectors used in newer Fords and in GM LS engines). The thinner-profile EV6 is available in different lengths, so between the lower O-ring diameter and overall length differences, you can really get confused if you're piecing together an MPFI system without knowing what you're doing. For that very reason, it's best to simply purchase a complete system, where the injectors (in addition to impedance and flow rate) are already matched to fit your intake manifold, fuel rail and harness setup.

8-Cylinder Injector Application Chart

Chart courtesy Fuel Air Spark Technology (FAST). Note that part numbers shown here refer to specific FAST injector numbers. Note: N/A refers to naturally aspirated with no forced induction.

Injector Size (lb/hr)	8-Cylinder Set Number	N/A Peak HP	Supercharged Peak HP	Turbo Peak HP
24	302408	346	288	276
36	303608	518	432	415
42	304208	605	504	484
55	305508	792	660	634
60	306008	864	720	691
65	306508	936	780	749
83	308308	1195	996	956
95	309508	1368	1140	1094
160	3016008	2304	1920	1843
All ratings shown here are based on a reference constant of 45-psi fuel system pressure.				

Remember that the injector itself does not make power. Choose the injector size based on realistic engine output. When in doubt, it's usually best to go with the next larger size.

Forced Induction

Forced induction generates increased airflow and pressure. Mixed with the appropriate fuel ratio, you get increased power. That's no secret. Superchargers, or "blowers," provide not only power increases by packing in more air (accompanied by the appropriate ratio of fuel) but also just plain look cool with a big blower housing sticking up out of the hood, topped off with dual carbs or dual EFI throttle bodies.

Whenever you're considering adding boost to an engine via supercharging or turbocharging, bear in mind that you're introducing increased dynamic compression and heat to the pistons. For that reason, depending on the anticipated power output and amount of boost level, forged pistons are highly recommended. In addition, consider taking advantage of piston dome surface treatments, such as hard anodizing and/or ceramic thermal barrier coatings. This helps to protect the piston and increase thermal energy by deflecting combustion heat away from the pistons instead of allowing heat to be absorbed into the pistons.

Whether you opt for supercharging or turbocharging, combustion pressure will increase. Beyond about 6 or 8 psi of boost, the engine experiences increased stress, so upgrading the bottom end is something to take seriously. For pistons, stick with forged. Consider going with strong

forged steel connecting rods and a forged steel crank. While OEM-level hypereutectic pistons and a cast crank and rods may suffice, the more boost, the more stress the engine will experience. For supercharging, depending on the amount of boost, pay attention to the compression ratio. Start with the compression ratio in the 8:1 to 9:1 range because compression will increase as boost is applied. Turbocharged applications often use compression ratios in the 9.5:1 to 11:1 range.

Rather than delving into the specifics of turbochargers and superchargers, we'll discuss currently available components and systems offered for small-block applications as manufacturers continue to develop these applications for this engine format.

Turbo manufacturers include BorgWarner, Weiand, Comp Turbo Technology, Inc., Garrett, Precision Turbo & Engine, Edelbrock, Hypermax Engineering, and Turbonetics, to name a few. Examples of supercharger sources include Edelbrock, Eaton, Magnuson, ProCharger, Sprintex, Supercharger Systems, The Blower Shop, Vortech, and Whipple Superchargers.

A naturally aspirated engine uses available (ambient) air to enter the engine, mix with fuel, and ignite in the combustion chamber. A forced induction system (a supercharger

A number of firms offer turbochargers. Shown here is an STS turbo by Holley. Turbos are available in a wide variety of sizes to accommodate any single or twin setup.

BorgWarner offers a wide range of turbo sizes to suit any application.

or turbocharger) does just what the term implies: it forces additional air into the combustion chamber. When the air is mixed with the appropriate ratio of fuel, higher cylinder pressure is created and referred to as boost, which makes more power. While the space isn't available to delve into great detail, a few informational tidbits will hopefully help you to better understand the basics.

For ease of installation, complete turbo kits are offered. Intercooler and turbo plumbing requires fabrication to suit specific applications. (Photo Courtesy Edelbrock)

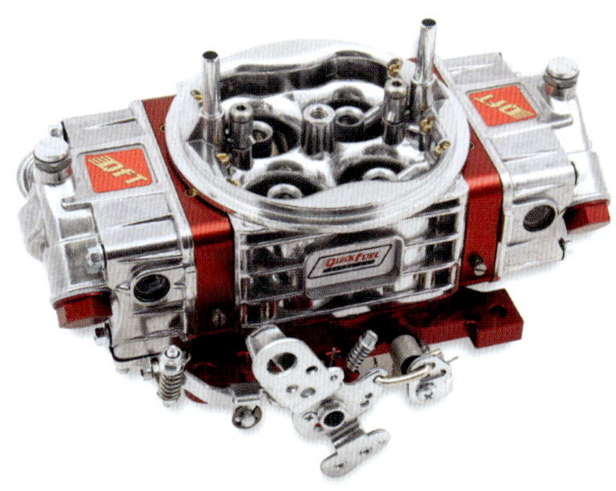

Carburetors specifically designed for supercharger applications are available, including blow through and draw-through designs with enhanced metering and air-flow, eliminating airflow restrictions. They are available in sizes from 650 to 1,050 cfm. (Photo Courtesy Holley)

This is a supercharger setup for a small-block Chevy. Edelbrock's 1552 E-Force supercharger features a Roots-style blower that is rated at a 500-hp capability. It is designed for use with a long-style water pump. (Photo Courtesy Edelbrock)

Supercharger Basics

The three types of superchargers (also known as blowers) in common use today include the Roots type, centrifugal, and the screw type. The Roots type is the least complex, functioning as an air pump. Instead of compressing air inside the unit, pressurization takes place in the manifold and combustion chambers. It's referred to as external air compression.

Centrifugal and screw-type superchargers compress air inside the supercharger (internal compression), pushing the compressed air into the intake and combustion areas. A centrifugal unit mechanically functions much the same as a turbocharger, using an internal impeller. Instead of being driven by exhaust gas (as with a turbo), a centrifugal supercharger impeller is driven mechanically with a drive belt. The screw-type supercharger features two inter-meshing spiral rotors. If you're familiar with a twin-screw shop air compressor, it's easy to understand this style. The two rotors progressively compress the air as they spin and as air passes through the spiral teeth. Because of the precision tolerances required in the manufacturing process, screw-type superchargers tend to be more expensive. Regardless of the style, a supercharger (and a turbocharger as well) packs more air into the cylinders, effectively forcing the air into the cylinders. This allows and demands a more-dense fuel/air charge. Igniting a higher-pressure/more-dense charge makes more power.

Blower Size and Speed

The engine displacement and driven speed of the blower directly affects boost. If the blower is driven at a constant speed ratio (between the crank and blower), a larger-displacement blower will produce more boost than a smaller blower on the same engine. As engine displacement increases, for example, going from a stock-displacement 350 engine to a 421 stroker, boost is reduced if the blower is driven at the same speed. If engine displacement is reduced and the blower runs at the same speed, boost is increased. If the blower runs at a higher speed, boost is increased. At a lower blower speed, boost is reduced.

This is a very basic overview, but typically you should choose a smaller blower size for smaller displacement and a larger blower size for bigger displacement engines. Drive pulleys can be selected with either a larger or smaller diameter to make the blower run slower or faster to tune boost for the given engine. For instance, a larger blower on a small-block can be tuned by driving the blower at a slower speed to keep the boost level down to a point where you avoid detonation. However, running the blower too slow can reduce boost if the blower isn't running fast enough to compress the air sufficiently. If you run too-small of a blower for a given displacement engine, the blower speed would need to increase, possibly to the point of becoming inefficient. Running at too high of a speed can create excessively heated intake air, which would ruin the air density. In other words, pay attention both to blower size and the speed at which it's driven.

Whether using a turbo or supercharger, incorporating a form of adjustable pressure-release valve (blow-off/pop-off) offers a safety margin, allowing the release of a preset amount of pressure to avoid over-boosting. Again, lots of variables are involved here. Talk to your forced induction supplier for recommendations based on your specific setup. The two types of valves included here include a wastegate (WG) and a blow-off valve (BOV).

In the simplest of terms, a WG regulates pressure on the exhaust side, while a BOV regulates pressure at the intake side. The BOV is usually positioned on the feed pipe between the turbo and the intercooler. When the throttle is lifted, the BOV prevents forced air from being packed into the engine when decreasing RPM. The WG regulates the amount of boost from the turbo to prevent over-boosting. Both are required.

If the plan is to use a carburetor with a forced induction system, carbs designed for forced induction are available as draw-through and blow-through designs. In short, a draw-through setup places the carb before the compressor, which allows the compressor to pull air and fuel through the carb. A blow-through setup places the carb after the compressor with the carb being pressurized by the compressor. Makers such as Holley/Quick Fuel Technology offer both carb designs.

Fuel System

Often, customers tend to ignore the fuel system, which needs to be adjusted to accommodate the forced induction in terms of the fuel line diameter and richening via jets, injectors, ECM reprogramming, etc. When using forced induction (when boost is applied), more fuel will be needed because it always takes more fuel to make more power. Plan on tuning with a richer mixture. Retarding ignition timing also allows the use of more boost. We're speaking in broad generalities here, so talk to the supercharger/turbocharger manufacturer and plan to spend some time tuning both fuel and spark.

To optimize the use of forced induction, ideally the engine will likely prefer a lobe separation angle (LSA) in the moderate to wide range, probably around 112 to 114 degrees. It's best to consult with a cam maker for a recommendation, and you'll need all of your engine specs and forced induction information before you call.

Also, when running a supercharger, it's generally recommended to use a spark plug that is one heat range colder than stock. A spark plug gap of 0.035 inch is common.

Compression Ratio

Static compression ratio (CR) refers to the compression ratio of your engine without forced induction. Final compression ratio (FCR) refers to the compression that you'll have when full boost is applied.

The formula for calculating FCR is as follows:

$$(Boost / 14.7) + 1 \times Static\ CR = Final\ Compression\ Ratio\ (FCR)$$

Here's an example of a compression ratio reference chart that explains how static compression is affected by various forced induction boost levels.

Note that the higher the final compression ratio is, the higher the octane rating of the fuel needs to be to prevent detonation. Final compression ratios above 12.4:1 are not recommended for use with premium pump gasoline. The far-left column indicates the static compression ratio. The numbers under the various boost pressures indicate the dynamic compression ratio.

Final Compression Ratios									
CR	Boost (PSI)								
	2	4	6	8	10	12	14	16	18
6.5	7.4	8.3	9.2	10.0	10.9	11.8	12.7	13.6	14.5
7.0	8.0	8.9	9.9	10.8	11.8	12.7	13.6	14.5	15.3
7.5	8.5	9.5	10.6	11.6	12.6	13.6	14.6	15.7	16.7
8.0	9.1	10.2	11.3	12.4	13.4	14.5	15.6	16.7	17.8
8.5	9.7	10.8	12.0	13.1	14.3	15.4	16.6	17.8	18.9
9.0	10.2	11.4	12.7	13.9	15.1	16.3	17.6	18.8	20.0
9.5	10.8	12.1	13.4	14.7	16.0	17.3	18.5	19.8	21.1
10.0	11.4	12.7	14.1	15.4	16.8	18.2	19.5	20.9	22.2
10.5	11.9	13.4	14.8	16.2	17.6	19.1	20.5	21.9	23.4
11.0	12.5	14.0	15.5	17.0	18.5	20.0	21.5	22.9	24.5

Upgrading the Engine to Accommodate the New-Found Power

As noted earlier, it's important to consider the strength of the rotating and reciprocating components and how they'll hold up to increased boost. Remember that any forced induction system will increase cylinder pressure. The extent of this increase may dictate the need to also upgrade stress-related internal components.

While today's commonly used OEM hypereutectic pistons and powder metal connecting rods are certainly adequate for daily and even spirited driving, when we're talking about increasing horsepower levels up to about the 450-plus-hp range and beyond, we're starting to take risks in terms of durability. If the plan is to boost the induction system and pack in a tighter air/fuel mix, seriously consider upgrading to forged pistons that are designed to work with forced induction (possibly with a thicker dome area and a hardness treatment to protect ring lands) and forged connecting rods. By the same token (and granted, this is a debatable area in terms of horsepower levels), consideration should also be given to upgrading to a forged crankshaft in place of a stock cast crank.

Yes, upgrading the engine will add to the expense (parts, machine shop labor), but would you rather spend a fraction of what the engine is worth for upgrading, or do nothing and experience the "thrill" of watching your stock engine hand-grenade, resulting in the expense and hassle of replacing the entire long block?

I'm certainly not suggesting that the installation of any supercharger or turbocharger system will destroy your engine. That would be ludicrous. The point I'm trying to make is to pay attention and consider the big picture: the existing engine's limitations and the potential need for a few component upgrades. Again, it boils down to the existing engine's components and the level of the power increase that is being planned.

Fuel Injection Tech

Obviously, the subject of fuel injection encompasses a wide range of topics. The discussion here is limited to the understanding and selection of fuel injectors with a sidebar note regarding camshaft duration and lobe centerline with regards to a fuel injection setup.

Injector Selection

As with selecting the proper size carburetor for a specific engine application, when it comes to choosing injectors sizes, bigger is not always better. A too-small injector won't be able to deliver enough fuel, which can result in both drivability issues and lean engine damage. With injectors that are too large, idle and low-RPM operation will suffer, as injector pulse width (the amount of time the injector is open) will be too low.

It's important to understand that simply moving to a larger injector won't add horsepower unless the engine demands have exceeded the capacity of the original

Upgrades to Consider for Durability

Depending on the existing engine type/age/condition, there's much more to this subject than we have room to discuss in this book, but the primary areas of potential concern are pointed out here.

- Pistons (switch to forged aluminum in place of hypereutectic)
- Lower compression (where needed) to accommodate added amount of boost
- Specialty coatings (thermal barrier and antifriction)
- Moly-coated bearings (rods and mains)
- Forged steel connecting rods
- Upgraded connecting rod bolts (for example, using ARP bolts that offer higher tensile strength
- Forged steel crankshaft
- Double-keyed crank snout
- Steel/high-performance crank damper
- Cylinder head gaskets. Take advantage of today's MLS gaskets.
- Cylinder head studs instead of bolts
- Forged or billet steel main caps
- Higher-strength main cap studs or bolts
- Upgrade to stainless steel valves and/or Inconel for exhaust valves)
- Appropriate rate valve springs based on camshaft profile
- Full-roller rocker arms
- Cooling system (make sure the existing cooling system is clean and functions properly, and address the potential need for a more-efficient water pump and radiator, especially if using an intercooler) ■

injectors. Changing to larger injectors in an otherwise unmodified engine won't increase horsepower. The injector size needs to match or support the engine's fuel requirements.

Before purchasing injectors, consider the brake-specific fuel consumption (BSFC) and injector duty cycle. BSFC represents the amount of fuel (in pounds) the engine will consume per horsepower per hour.

The following are general guidelines when choosing a BSFC number:

Supercharged or turbocharged engines run at richer air/fuel ratios that raise the BSFC number, requiring larger injectors for the same horsepower compared to naturally aspirated engines.

The duty cycle is the maximum amount of time that the injectors will remain open at a certain horsepower level. Generally, injectors should not be open for more than 90 percent of engine operating time. Commonly, duty cycle will be about 80 percent. If an injector were to run at 100-percent duty cycle, it could overheat and fail. A 100-percent duty cycle rating is considered a theoretical baseline. More realistically, no more than a 90-percent duty cycle should be considered.

When calculating injector size, round up to the next nearest size required. For example, if you determine that you need 26 lb/hr injectors and have a choice between 24 lb/hr and 30 lb/hr injectors, choose the 30 lb/hr injectors.

Basically, once you select the size of injector, you'll be in the ballpark. To tune, adjust the injector duty cycle (via the ECU), in essence, to richen or lean.

BSFC Numbers	
Low- to medium-performance street engine	0.50–0.50
Performance engine with good cylinder heads	0.45–0.50
Race engine with very efficient cylinder heads	0.38–0.45
Supercharged engines	0.55–0.60
Turbocharged engines	0.60–0.65

Formula for Determining Injector Size

Injector size = (engine HP at flywheel x BSFC) / (number of injectors x duty cycle)

Injector size is based on flow rate (lbs per hour).

Examples:

8-cylinder 400-hp engine

Injector size = (400 hp x 0.5 BSFC) / (8 injectors x 0.9 duty cycle) = 27.7 lb/hr

8-cylinder 600-hp supercharged engine

Injector size = (600 hp x 0.57 BSFC) / (8 injectors x 0.9 duty cycle) = 47.5 lb/hr

Sample Injector HP Rates					
Injector Size	Max HP at Given BSFC (With Pump at 43.5 psi)				
	0.4 BSFC	0.45 BSFC	0.50 BSFC	0.55 BSFC	0.60 BSFC
14	280	250	225	203	186
19	380	337	304	276	253
24	480	426	384	349	320
30	600	533	480	436	400
36	720	640	576	523	480
42	840	746	672	610	560
50	1000	888	800	727	666
55	1100	977	880	800	733
65	1300	1155	1040	945	866
75	1500	1333	1200	1090	1000

Formula for Determining Injector Size *(Continued)*

Sample Injector HP Rates *(Continued)*

Injector Size	Max HP at Given BSFC (With Pump at 43.5 psi)				
	0.4 BSFC	0.45 BSFC	0.50 BSFC	0.55 BSFC	0.60 BSFC
85	1700	1511	1360	1236	1133
95	1900	1688	1520	1381	1266

NOTE: This general-reference chart represents operation at 43.5 fuel psi, and at a theoretical 100-percent duty cycle. Raising fuel pressure will increase maximum horsepower capability. (Reference Chart Courtesy Holley)

Reference Chart, Based on Common 80-Percent Duty Cycle

HP	0.45 BSFC	0.50 BSFC	0.55 BSFC	0.60 BSFC
300	21.09	23.40	25.78	28.12
400	28.12	31.25	34.37	37.50
500	35.15	39.06	42.96	46.87
600	42.18	46.87	51.56	56.25
700	49.20	54.68	60.00	65.60
800	56.25	62.50	68.75	75.00
900	63.28	70.31	77.34	84.37
1000	70.31	78.12	85.93	93.75

Cross-reference HP and BSFC to find injector size.

How Much HP Will an Injector Support?

((Injector flow rate in lb/hr x Number of injectors) / BSFC) x maximum duty cycle

Example: If you have a 44 lb/hr injector on a V-8 that will make 0.50 BSFC, and you want a maximum of 85-percent duty cycle, here is the result:

$$44 \times 8 = 352$$
$$352 / 0.50 = 704$$
$$704 \times 0.85 = 598.4 \text{ HP}$$

Note: These injector flow rates are based on 43.5 psi fuel pressure. If you change fuel pressure, you'll need to know the new flow rate to use the above formula.

Formula for Injector Flow Versus Pressure

(Square root (new pressure/old pressure)) x old pressure

If new pressure is 60 psi and old pressure is 43.5 psi with 44 lb/hr injectors,

$$60 / 43.5 = 1.378$$
The square root of 1.378 = 1.174
$$1.174 \times 44 \text{ lb/hr} = 51.7 \text{ lb/hr}$$

This new flow rate would then allow the following HP calculation:

$$((51.7 \times 8) / 0.50) \times 0.85 = 703 \text{ hp}$$

Boosting fuel pressure requires larger injectors to achieve higher horsepower. ■

Injector Impedance

Fuel injectors are designed to operate at either low or high impedance, which is generally dictated by the ECU. Although, some aftermarket controllers allow the use of either type. From an OEM standpoint, most late-model systems are designed to use high-impedance injectors because they run cooler and are less prone to overheating and are theoretically more reliable, which is not to say that low-impedance injectors are unreliable. If the plan is to use an OEM ECU, the drivers in the ECU are likely designed to handle high-impedance injectors. If using an aftermarket ECU that's programmable, you'll be able to use low-impedance injectors. Note: Failure to use high-impedance injectors with an OEM EFI computer will damage the computer, so pay attention!

If you're wondering about the impedance of your injectors, this is easy to check. Using a multimeter, run a resistance check between the two injector terminals. If resistance is in the range of 0.5 to 6 ohms, it's a low-impedance injector. If it is in the 12- to 16-ohm range, it's a high-impedance injector.

Low-impedance injectors (also called "peak and hold" injectors) feature a resistance of about 0.5 to 6 ohms and require about 4 to 6 amps of power to initially open. Then, they require about 2 to 3 amps to stay open. The performance advantage: Low-impedance injectors provide a quicker trigger time, so the injector is more responsive to opening and closing quicker.

High-impedance injectors (also called "saturated" injectors) feature a resistance of about 12 to 16 ohms and require only about 1 to 1.5 amps to open and maintain injector operation. High-impedance injectors use this current during the entire time of operation, but because of the lower current, less heat is generated in the injector, which increases its reliability. The downside is that a high-impedance injector provides a slightly slower trigger time compared to a low-impedance injector (because there is less initial current to open the injector).

Note that both EV1- and EV6-style injectors are available in both low- and high-impedance versions. The EV1 injector is the early, wider body style, and the EV6 (and more recent EV14 upgrade) features a thin, pencil-style body. In terms of performance, the EV6 (and EV14) supposedly provide a superior fuel spray pattern, plus the one-piece body construction eliminates body leakage). As far as spray patterns are concerned, various aftermarket performance injectors feature superior spray patterns in either style.

As was mentioned earlier, using an OEM controller requires using the impedance that the controller was designed to handle, which is usually high impedance. If you plan to use an aftermarket controller, you have options and can use either high- or low-impedance injectors. If you have a choice, low-impedance injectors are usually preferred for performance upgrades due to their quicker trigger times.

Injector Harness Adapters

If you mess around with an OEM wiring harness but plan to change the injector style, bear in mind that different-style harness connector issues can drive you nuts. Basically, two different styles of connectors are popular: the older-style Jetronic/Minitimer and the newer-style USCAR (United States Council for Automotive Research). The Jetronic/Minitimer connector, which is on the injector itself, is rectangular in shape with two blade-type terminals. One terminal is switched 12V, and the other terminal is ground.

The USCAR style is square with radiused corners, and it features two smaller pin terminals. Typically, EV1 injectors (the large style) feature the Jetronic/Minitimer–style connector, and the EV6 injector (the thin pencil style) uses the USCAR-style connector. However, EV6 injectors are available with either style of connector. If you face a mismatch of the harness connector to the injector, it's not a problem. Luckily, harness connector adapters are readily available to plug just about any OEM harness to any style of EV1 or EV6 injector that features either Minitimer or USCAR-style connections (Minitimer-to-USCAR and USCAR-to-Minitimer). Two such sources include FiveoMotorsport and FAST.

Injector Physical Dimensions

If you've messed around with EFI, you already know that a multitude of injector dimensions come into play, specifically when retrofitting a system. Injectors vary in terms of overall height, seat-to-seat height, manifold O-ring OD, and fuel rail O-ring OD. This is one of the reasons to choose a prepackaged system designed for specific applications (engine type, intake manifold brand/model, fuel rail). If you're piecing the system together, plan to spend a bit of time in terms of selecting injectors that will both seal and that will physically accommodate your fuel rails.

The subject of fuel injector selection can be quite daunting to engine builders who are not seasoned tuners of electronically controlled fuel injected engines.

One thing to remember: just because an injector physically fits the application, that doesn't mean that it will perform properly. Injectors must be selected based not only on the injector's own pressure rating but also in conjunction with the system flow pressure, which takes into account the fuel pump, the intake manifold volume, etc.

ROCKERS AND LIFTERS

In this chapter, the focus is on aftermarket full-roller components, including roller lifters and full-roller rocker arms, each of which offer substantial performance advantages over old-school flat tappets and ball-pivot/friction-tip rocker arms. While roller systems are certainly nothing new, it should come as no surprise that the performance aftermarket industry has made and continues to make substantial advances in rocker arms and lifters in terms of materials, design, performance, and durability. They just keep getting better. Happily, so many more choices are available today compared to only a few years ago, thanks to the continuing efforts by leading manufacturers. Rather than being complacent with established and successful designs that have been around for years, aftermarket development never stops, even with regard to the mainstay and venerable small-block Chevy engine platform.

means of valve control and stability as opposed to factory rockers that feature a friction-laden pivot and rubbing friction between the rocker and the valve. A full-roller rocker may be stud mounted to the head or pivots on a rocker arm shaft, wherein the shaft is bolted to the cylinder head with the rocker bearing pivoting on the secured shaft. The reduction of friction should be obvious. Full-roller rockers available for small-block Chevy applications include forged or billet aluminum or tempered steel in a variety of shapes, weights, and arm ratios.

For applications involving 18-degree or shallower valve angles and the use of larger-diameter valves, it's common to require the use of offset rocker arms to maintain the rocker arm alignment to both valves and pushrods. The required rocker arm offsets are determined by the specific cylinder head manufacturer. For example, a set of Trick Flow 18-degree heads require an exhaust rocker arm offset of 0.220 inch and an intake rocker arm offset of 0.550 inch when using Jesel rocker arms. The cylinder head manufacturer will usually

Note the rocker arm valve tip to pushrod offset on these Jesel roller rockers that are mounted to an 18-degree cylinder head. The intake (left) shows a noticeable offset, which is readily visible by the staggered position of the ends. The exhaust rocker's shaft bore angle provides a slight offset with the valve tip roller angled to align in plane with the valve tip.

Roller Rockers

This refers to rockers that feature both a needle bearing trunnion pivot and a roller wheel for valve tip contact. Full-roller rocker arms reduce friction and provide a more accurate

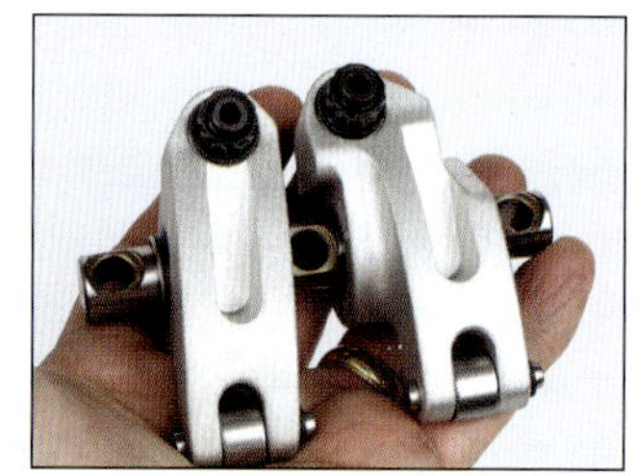

This is an example of the offset rockers required for use with an 18-degree cylinder head, where the intake rocker is offset by 0.550 inch and the exhaust rocker is offset by 0.220 inch. Depending on the brand and model of cylinder head, valve placement and the need for rocker offsets can vary, so adhere to the cylinder head maker's recommendations.

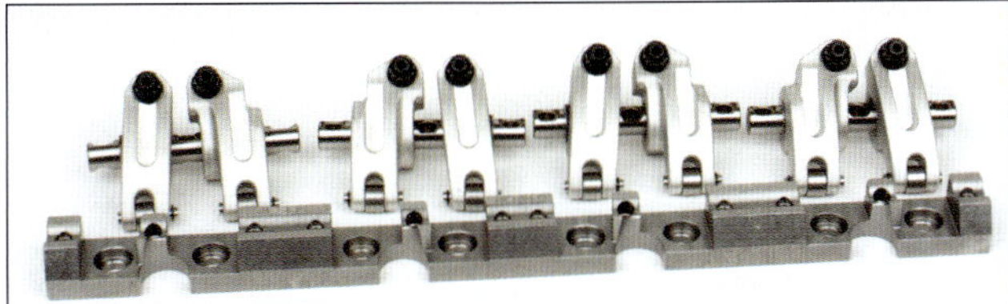

Depending on the specific cylinder heads, shaft-mounted roller rockers may require stands that accept the rocker arm shafts and hold all the arms in plane and at the specified height required for proper rocker arm geometry. The stands bolt directly to the heads.

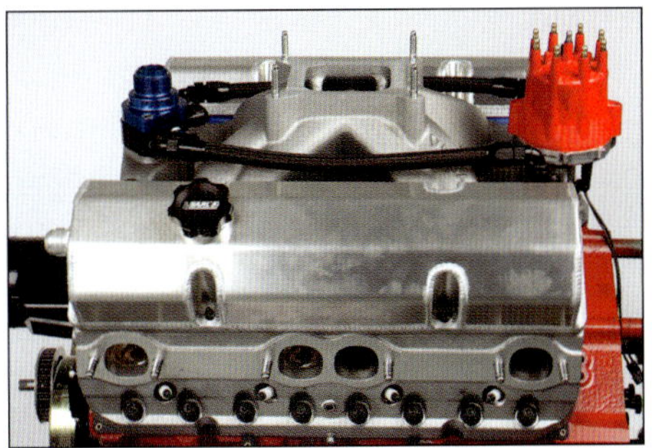

When offset rocker arms are used due to the valve angle and valve size, wider valve covers are needed. Since the inboard and outboard walls are spaced farther apart to provide rocker arm clearance, the perimeter bolt flange is covered. Recessed bolt hole pockets are featured to allow attachment to the heads, as seen on these Moroso aluminum fabricated valve covers.

recommend one or more specific rocker arm brands as well as offsets to properly fit their heads.

One aspect to bear in mind deals with potential valve cover clearance issues because beefier aluminum rockers may not accommodate standard OEM-style valve covers. Taller aftermarket valve covers are readily available, so this isn't an issue of great concern. Just make sure to check for clearance. When dealing with heads that feature shallower valve angles than the traditional 23-degree valve angle, offset rockers are required, which place additional clearance restrictions relative to the valve covers at the inboard/intake sides of the covers. In this case, wider valve covers, often referred to as "sheet metal" or "welded" covers are used due to the common construction style. These covers feature wider-spaced walls, which places the walls beyond the bolt hole flange lips of the head. As a result, the covers feature recessed/pocketed bolt hole locations that accommodate the wider walls while still bolting directly into the cylinder head holes.

Shaft-Mounted Rockers

Performance rocker arms are available as stud mount or shaft mount. In the early days, stud-mount rockers pivoted via a ball and socket design. As higher performance requirements were needed, aluminum and steel rockers that pivoted on a roller bearing became available. As development progressed, a roller bearing was added to the rocker's valve tip.

With more-aggressive cams, higher engine speeds, and increased loads, stiffer materials were employed and various geometric rocker arm shapes were developed. The next step in the evolution was to offer shaft-mounted rockers. Instead of each rocker pivoting at a single stud, a horizontal shaft serves as the fulcrum point, which greatly increases both mounting stiffness and valvetrain stability. Since the rockers pivot on a common shaft, this prevents the rockers from individually wiggling around the axis of the valve, which results in superior rocker-to-valve and rocker-to-pushrod stability.

Stability is optimized because the rockers can only pivot on their shafts and can't dance/move laterally across the valve tips. Also, since each shaft secures to the head with multiple bolts, this provides a more stable and strong mounting platform that is ideal for high engine speeds and loads.

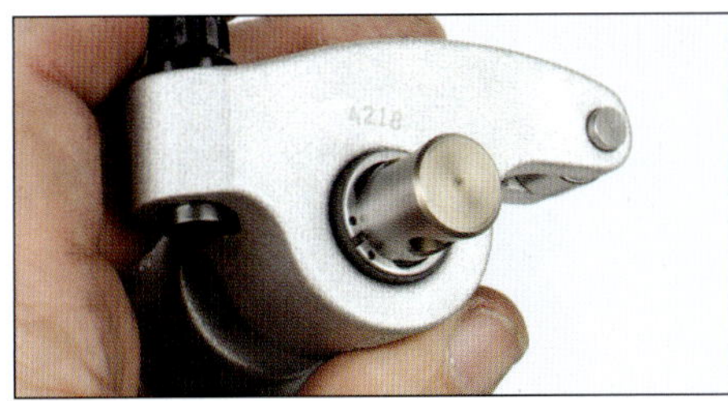

Rocker arm shaft axles are hardened steel riding on precision needle bearings. Note the circlip that secures the axle in place, which makes the rocker arm rebuildable.

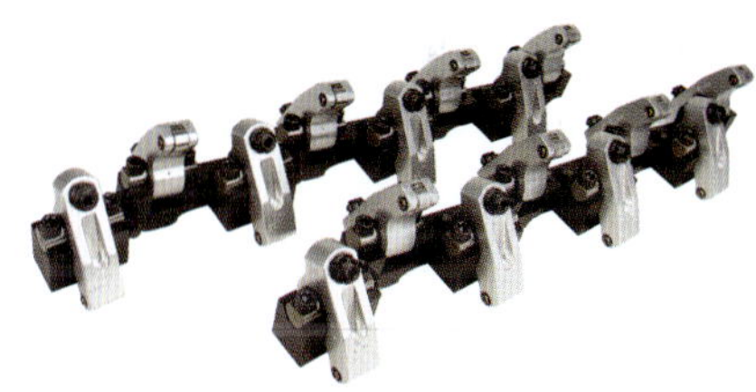

While stud-mount rockers are used successfully in a myriad of builds, moving to a shaft-mount system increases system rigidity and rocker operating precision. (Photo Courtesy Comp Cams)

Rocker Arm Materials

Performance roller rocker arms, depending on the manufacturer and the series or types offered, may consist of precision-cast stainless steel, forged or extruded aluminum, chrome-moly steel, or other steel alloy materials. Aluminum roller rocker arms require a thicker design than steel; although they are lighter, they tend to be bulkier, which in some cases can cause interference issues with the valve covers and some heads. Steel rockers can be made thinner to approach the lighter weight of aluminum. Although generally heavier, they can be designed to achieve the same moment of inertia as aluminum.

The bottom line is that these are generalities that really don't amount to much of a concern. The goal is to use rockers that suit the specific application. The higher the spring pressure, the stronger the rocker and its mounting platform needs to be. For all-around performance and racing use, aluminum rockers are available for just about anything you plan to build. If you plan to run endurance races where high 8,000- to 9,000-rpm use will be constant, high-strength steel may be the better choice. Again, the big variable is the manufacturer and series of rockers that each maker offers because some are stout and full-bodied, some are lightened and feature strengthening ribs, and the quality and design of bearings and trunnions can differ.

All-aluminum rockers are not equal, nor are all steel rockers equal. The bottom line is that if you choose rockers made by a seasoned and reputable maker, the chances are good that they'll have what you need. Just stay away from low-priced offshore rockers. Saving up for a few extra months to buy the best parts beats having a few rockers fail during a high-RPM run.

Specifically designed for sustained high-RPM use in the 9,000-rpm range with gear changes as experienced in pro endurance racing, ultra-strong shaft-mount steel rockers that offer minimal deflection are available as an alternative to aluminum. Pictured are Jesel's Pro Steel rockers, featuring a high-strength steel alloy, heat treating, and REM isotropic super finish. (Photo Courtesy Jesel)

If you had the chance to tour a high-end rocker arm manufacturing facility, you would be astonished at the level of precision CNC machining and quality control that takes place. Shown here is one of the many computer-controlled machining stations in Jesel's plant.

In an effort to further reduce weight, steel rocker arms are available in designs that remove unneeded material where it can be sacrificed while maintaining strength. Shown here is a Jesel rocker arm during early initial production where side material has been CNC milled.

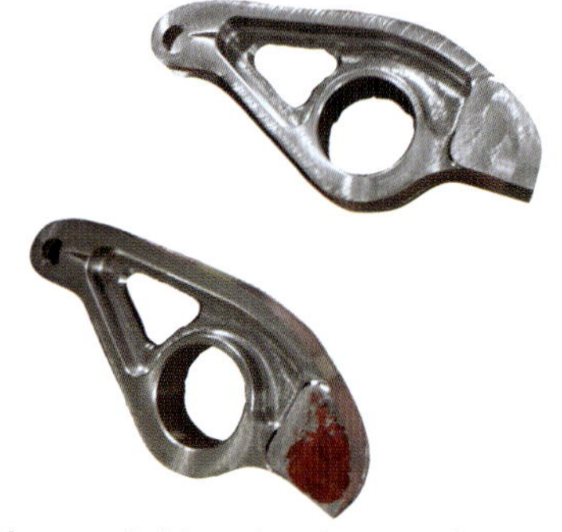

Further weight reduction on these arms was done by skeletonizing them to remove additional mass. This will be followed by burnishing to removed sharp edges and heat treating to improve strength.

Pictured is a chrome-moly stud-mount steel rocker with lightening reliefs. The example shown here is Comp's Ultimate Pro Magnum roller rocker. (Photo Courtesy Comp Cams)

This is an example of a forged aluminum stud-mount roller rocker. Shown here is Comp Cams' Ultra Gold ARC Series in 1.5:1 ratio. (Photo Courtesy Comp Cams)

Rocker Arm Ratio

What is rocker arm ratio? Simply put, it is the comparison of two pivot-point distances: the distance between the centerline of the rocker arm pivot (the trunnion bearing, where the rocker rides on its shaft or stud pivot) and the centerline of the rocker arm's roller tip (where it meets the valve stem tip) compared to the distance from the pivot centerline to the pushrod cup. The distance between the pivot centerline and the pushrod cup centerline is referred to as distance X. The distance from the pivot centerline and the roller tip is distance Y. Distance Y is also referred to as the rocker arm's pivot length (more on that later). The ratio is determined by dividing distance Y by distance X.

For example, if distance X (pivot center to pushrod cup center) is 1.000 inch, and distance Y (pivot center to roller tip center) is 1.500 inches, Y divided by X is 1.500 inches, so this rocker arm has a ratio of 1.5:1. Another example is if Y = 1.620 inches and X = 1.010 inches, the ratio would be 1.6039:1. These are simply arbitrary dimensions used only as examples.

So, what changes when increasing the ratio? The distance from the rocker arm pivot to the roller valve tip does not change. This is a fixed distance that is referred to as the pivot length to suit the specific cylinder head since the location of the valve stem can't be changed. When the ratio is increased, the distance from the rocker arm pivot to the pushrod adjuster cup (X) is the dimension that changes, decreasing the length of the X dimension. This slightly changes the angle of the pushrod, moving the upper end of the pushrod outboard closer to the valve spring.

Increasing rocker arm ratio is a simple means of increasing effective valve lift. By knowing the camshaft's lobe lift, multiply the lobe lift by the rocker arm ratio to determine effective valve lift. If the lobe lift on the cam is 0.432-inch, using a small-block Chevy standard arm ratio of 1.5:1, 0.432-inch x 1.5 produces a 0.648-inch valve lift. If the arm ratio is increased to 1.6:1, by multiplying 0.432-inch x 1.6:1, we increase valve lift to 0.6912 inch. So, rather than changing the cam, we can cheat by changing to a higher-ratio rocker arm.

The change in lift can also be determined by referring to the cam's published valve lift. Divide the known valve lift by the existing rocker arm ratio to reveal the camshaft's lobe lift. Then, multiply the lobe lift by the proposed higher rocker arm ratio to determine the new valve lift. For example, if the known valve lift is 0.500 inch and the existing rocker arms have a ratio of 1.5, 0.500 divided by 1.5 shows a cam lobe lift of 0.333 inch. If you're considering moving to a 1.6:1 rocker arm, multiply the 0.333 lobe lift by 1.6, which results in a new valve lift of 0.5328 inch.

The majority of aftermarket performance roller rocker arms are stamped or laser etched to identify the ratio, so there's no need to actually measure the rocker arm. Although, hand measuring the arm's two pivot distances using a dial caliper will provide an approximate ratio.

So, instead of buying a higher-lift camshaft, increasing the rocker arm ratio allows you to obtain a greater valve lift. However, there are other factors to consider. Since the higher-ratio rocker arm is longer, there is the potential risk of increased valve guide wear if pushrod length isn't considered. Altering arm ratio will potentially require a different pushrod length, otherwise the rocker arm may need to be raised or lowered to achieve proper geometry. So, as with any valvetrain setup, it's important to measure for the proper pushrod length.

Never assume the pushrod length. Always measure, rather than assuming that the stock pushrod length will provide the correct geometry. Another element to consider is the valve spring. Since the higher-ratio rocker arm will open the valves farther, stiffer valve springs or springs that provide additional coil clearance may be needed to avoid spring bind under full lift because an increase in the rocker arm ratio will compress the spring further during the full valve open event.

Aluminum rockers tend to be beefier than steel rockers to provide the needed strength. To change from stock-type rockers to a fatter aluminum rocker, you may run into rocker arm-to-valve-cover clearance issues, so be sure to check this. If you already have beefy aftermarket lifters and adequate valve cover clearance but are simply changing ratios, you likely won't have an issue in terms of valve cover clearance. If needed, buying taller valve covers is a small price to pay for the performance and durability advantages of stronger and more robust roller rockers.

Even though roller-tipped rocker arms induce less friction at the valve stem tip, attention must be paid to the valve material. If a softer valve material, such as titanium, is featured, a harder surface is required at the valve tip to avoid high spring pressure forcing the rocker arm wheel from digging into the valve. While some titanium valves feature a hard coating, the common practice involves the use of hard steel lash caps. Lash caps are available in various thicknesses to allow fine-tuning of the pushrod length. If lash caps are to be installed, they must be in place during pushrod length measuring.

When determining the pushrod length, as well as shaft-mounted rockers that feature bolt-on stands, install light checking springs, tag the valve tips (or lash caps) with a marker, and slowly rotate the crank and cam, turning the crank a full 360-degrees. Remove the rockers and inspect the witness mark made by the roller tip, which is the rocker sweep pattern. The witness mark should be narrow and centered on the valve tip. If the mark is biased toward the intake side of the head, the pushrod is too short or the rocker arm stand needs to be lowered. If the witness mark is biased toward the exhaust side, the pushrod is too long or the rocker arm stand needs to be raised using shims. On shaft-mount rocker systems that feature a mounting stand, rocker stand height will influence the rocker arm to valve sweep location.

Lifters

Again, the focus is on roller valvetrains, which includes roller lifters. The use of roller camshafts and lifters reduces lobe contact friction and allows the use of more aggressive camshafts. Roller lifters (and cams designed for roller lifters) offer distinct advantages over flat tappet designs. The obvious advantage lies in the reduced friction between the lifters and cam lobes. A flat tappet lifter rubs against the cam lobe, while a roller lifter glides across the lobe as the roller wheel rotates.

In terms of camshaft break-in, while a flat tappet cam requires a specific break-in period to allow the lifters to properly rotate in their bores to mate the two surfaces and avoid a dig-in of the lobe to the lifter, a roller lifter setup essentially requires no lengthy break-in period, providing that the lifter is properly lubricated.

On the subject of lubrication, pay attention to the lifter maker's oil recommendations. Some manufacturers specify a certain viscosity based on their lifter design. Some makers, depending on the specific lifter model, may recommend the use of 5W30 or 10W30, etc. and to avoid anything heavier than 40W. Just pay attention to their recommendations before adding your lube juice. Lighter-viscosity oil may be needed to suit smaller oil passages and tighter clearance tolerances.

Hardened lash caps provide protection for titanium valves by preventing wear on the softer titanium material. Lash caps are also available in varying thicknesses and can be used to alter the valve stem's overall height when fine-tuning the rocker arm geometry in combination with the pushrod length. If the lash caps are to be installed, they must be in place when measuring for the pushrod length.

When checking the rocker arm's installed height and checking the pushrod's length, paint the valve tip with a marker. With the rocker and pushrod installed, rotate the crank and cam to create a rocker arm sweep witness mark. The witness mark where the rocker arm roller wheel sweeps across the valve should be narrow and centered. If the mark is biased inward toward the intake side of the head, the pushrod is too short. If the mark is biased outside toward the exhaust, the pushrod is too long.

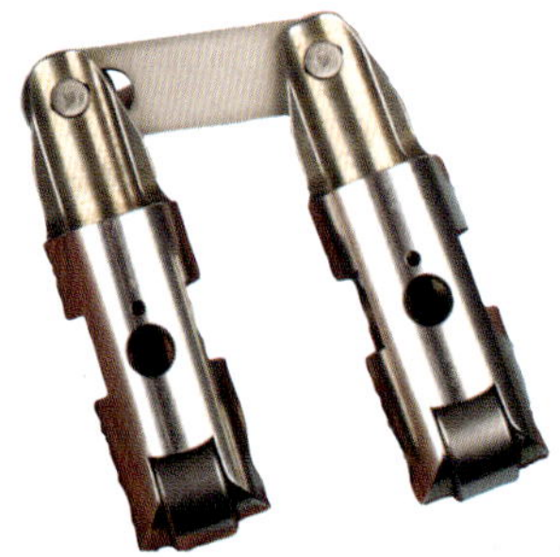

The location of oil feed holes on hydraulic and solid lifter bodies must align with the oil galleries within the lifter bore to ensure adequate oil delivery. During test fitting, always check this while slowly rotating the camshaft and observing the oil hole location from cam base circle to peak lobe movement.

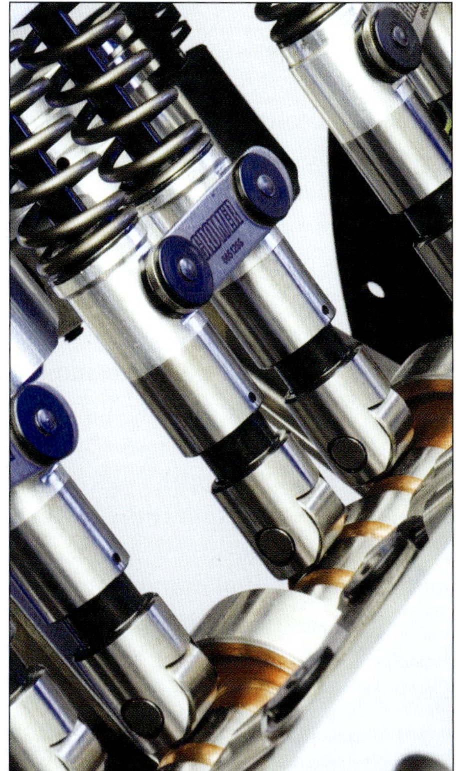

Today's roller cams/lifters provide not only greatly reduced friction compared to flat-tappet designs but also allow more aggressive cam profiles. (Photo Courtesy Crower)

All high-quality roller rocker arm manufacturers use high-strength steel trunnions and needle bearings to provide durable and stable rocker arm motion, such as found on this Harland Sharp rocker. While bearings are pre-lubed during assembly, it's still a good idea to soak new rockers in 30W oil before installation to insure initial lubrication.

While aluminum provides reduced weight compared to steel, aluminum arms require more mass to provide the required strength. In an effort to further reduce weight, various manufacturers provide material removal in areas where strength is not compromised. The example shown here is Harland Sharp's Diamond series with material chamfer cut on the edges to reduce weight by as much as 100 grams.

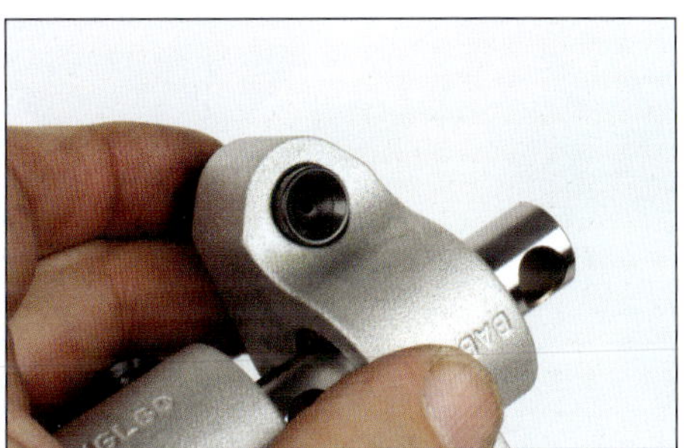

Pushrod cups are hard steel and coated for lubricity.

Note the slight undercut relief under the valve tip on this Jesel aluminum rocker. This provides additional clearance for the valve spring retainer.

However, the frictional reduction that rollers offer is only one aspect of the advantage that roller cams and lifters offer. Roller lifters provide increased acceleration and lifter velocity. Because a roller lifter doesn't dig into the lobe during operation, the cam lobe lift curve can be broader without the need to increase lift or the need to increase duration. Granted, roller setups are more pricey, but the performance gains and potentially longer lobe life make the move to roller setups well worth it.

Many of today's aftermarket engine blocks feature taller lifter bores. Using a standard-height lifter requires notching the lifter bore for pushrod clearance. To address this, aftermarket lifter manufacturers, such as Jesel, Crower, Crane Cams, Comp Cams, Morel Lifters, Isky Racing Cams, etc., offer 0.300-inch taller lifters, eliminating the need to notch the top of the lifter bores.

In the past, the use of flat tappet solid lifters may have required the addition of oil restrictors to limit the amount of oil being pushed to the lifters, pushrods, rockers, and valve springs. However, many of today's aftermarket engine blocks and solid roller lifters are designed to supply a generous amount of oil to the valvetrain with lifter makers often cautioning against the use of restrictors. Pay close attention to the instructions provided by the lifter maker. Roller lifters require a generous amount of oil being delivered to the roller needle bearings or roller wheel bronze bushing, depending on the design. Starving the roller bearings or bushing can lead to a quick death of the roller's bearing assembly.

Roller lifter wheels are precision-machined steel to exacting tolerances, which is followed by burnishing to remove any sharp edges and heat treating.

Speaking of roller lifters, some are designed with a series of needle bearings that provide the rotational performance of the roller wheel, while some lifters feature a specially formulated high-hardness bronze alloy bushing. The reason that some lifter makers now offer bronze-bushed wheels is to eliminate the potential catastrophic damage that might occur if the needle bearings were to break loose. This type of failure can send needle bearings scattered through the engine.

Any failure of the roller wheel's location can destroy the camshaft in quick order. Whether you opt for lifters that feature needle bearings or bushings, sticking with established manufacturers that have a track record of making components that provide performance and endurance is key. As with any critical engine component, if you plan on pounding the engine, avoid bargain-basement roller lifters. The golden rule: if you want to play, you gotta pay.

When dealing with cylinder heads that feature shallower valve angles than the traditional 23-degree angle, rocker arms often require an offset to accommodate the relocated valves due to both the angle and increased valve diameter. As a result, lifter pushrod cups often need to feature an offset to provide the proper alignment from the rocker to the pushrod to the lifter. Offset pushrod cups feature the cup moved from the center of the lifter to 180 degrees right or left, depending on the individual cylinder location. Offset lifter pairs may feature a centered cup at the exhaust lifter and an offset cup at the intake lifter or offsets at both lifters. Various combinations are available to suit specific aftermarket cylinder heads.

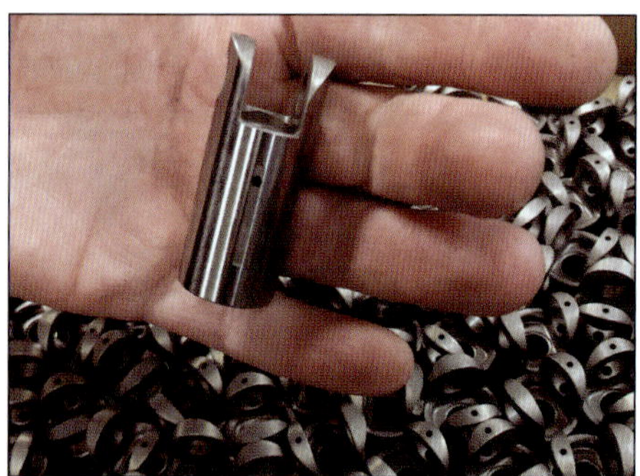

As an example of quality control, lifter wheels are checked on tightly calibrated go-no-go gauges to ensure dimensional accuracy. This photo was taken at Jesel's factory.

High-quality roller lifter bodies are CNC machined from alloy steel and undergo multiple steps of dimensional inspection, burnishing, heat treating, surface coating treatments, and hand-fitting during assembly. Ultra-smooth and durable REM finishing is also offered by certain manufacturers.

One side of the bronze axle bushing is threaded; it is secured and installed with a spanner wrench. This also makes the bushing serviceable.

Several roller lifter makers offer needle-less bronze axle bushings, which eliminates the need for needle bearings. Shown here is an example of Morel's Black Mamba roller lifter.

Roller lifter wheels are designed to create an oil wedge between the wheel and cam lobe for superior lubrication.

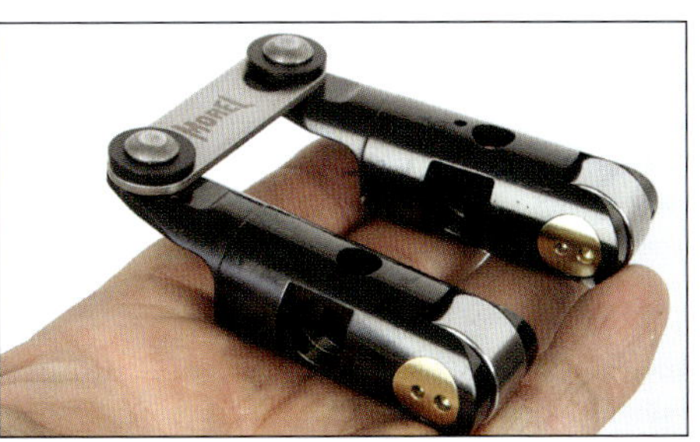

Short-bodied lifters are available for weight savings with the ear length maintained to provide link-bar clearance above the block's lifter bores.

Offset lifters accommodate cylinder heads that feature relocated valves, such as with 18-degree-and-shallower valve degree heads that require offset rockers. Note that the intake pushrod cup in this linked pair of lifters is offset compared to the centered exhaust lifter cup. Depending on the specific

cylinder head, the valve angle, and the valve size, offset cups may be required in intake or both intake and exhaust locations.

Taller lifters are available to accommodate blocks that feature 0.300-inch-taller lifter bosses.

This is an example of a normal linked pair of roller lifters for a 23-degree head, where both intake and exhaust pushrod cups are centered in the lifter bodies.

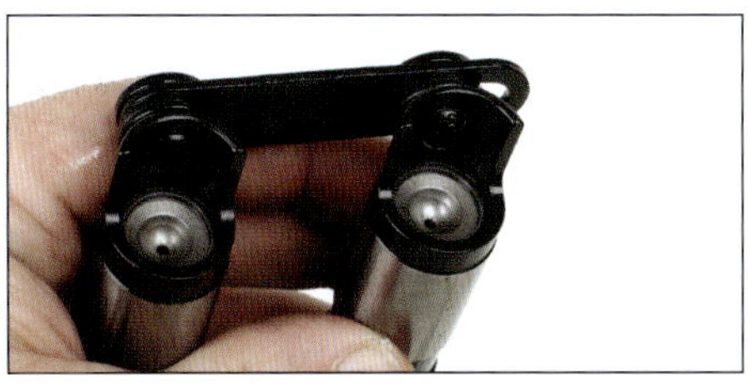

Pushrod pocket depths can vary among lifter designs, which directly affects the required pushrod length. Always measure the pushrod length when test fitting. It may sound basic, but never assume that a standard length is appropriate.

Today's roller lifters are offered with a variety of body and roller wheel diameters. For small-block Chevy applications, commonly available body diameters include the "standard" 0.842, 0.847, 0.903, 0.904 inch, etc. Lifter diameters can vary among manufacturers. Regardless of whether you plan to use an OEM block or an aftermarket block, it's critical to measure the lifter bores and correct them as needed to achieve proper oil clearance for the specific lifters that have been selected. Always adhere to the lifter maker's clearance specifications, but in general terms, oil clearances of 0.0015 to 0.0018 inch are recommended. Don't assume any dimensions. Regardless of the lifter printed specs, measure the lifter body diameters before performing milling or honing of the lifter bores.

Roller lifter wheels are offered in a range of diameters in the range of 0.700 inch all the way up to a whopping 1.220 inches. A larger-diameter roller rotates slower and reduces the loads needed to open the valvetrain. Cam specs may need to be adjusted when using a larger-diameter roller due to an increase in duration. A larger-diameter roller may allow you to get more aggressive with your opening ramp design. Discuss your planned lifters' roller wheel diameter with your cam supplier to obtain the proper lobe design.

A range of roller lifter designs have been designed over the years, each with its own characteristics and advantages. First, understand that by design a roller lifter must not be allowed to rotate within its bore so that the roller wheel stays aligned with the cam lobe. While a flat tappet lifter is designed to rotate in its bore during operation to prevent the lifter from digging into the lobe, a roller

Aluminum rocker arms, such as the Harland Sharp rollers shown here, are available with pairs riding on common axles. This eliminates rocker wiggle, keeping the rockers in a precise operating plane at all times. The example shown here applies to an application where the lifters feature centered pushrod seats with both rockers in the same operating plane.

lifter must be guided in a fixed vertical plane to allow the roller wheel to rotate without skidding across the lobe. Several designs exist to accomplish this.

An OEM design may feature individual lifters that have opposing flat spots on the lifter body. To keep the lifters guided in the same plane, a double dog bone plate captures a pair of lifters, serving as a guide. The plate, somewhat resembling a double-ended open-end wrench, features flat internal surfaces that guide the flats on the lifter. The dog bones are held in place by a tempered sheet metal brace that is bolted to the block's lifter valley with fingers that hold down the center of each dog bone.

One of the very common approaches with aftermarket roller lifters involves a pair of lifters that are connected by a pivoting link bar. The bar holds the pair of lifters in plane, preventing each lifter from rotating in its bore. The link bars pivot on each lifter, allowing freedom of vertical lifter movement. The link bar length is designed to accommodate the engine style (SBC, BBC, etc.) in terms of lifter bore-to-bore spacing.

More recently developed designs include keyed lifters that require special bronze bushings. The bushings, which are interference fit to the parent bores, feature a male key (usually located in line with the roller axle, 90-degrees from the roller wheel rotational plane) that rides in a milled groove slot in the bronze bushing. This style requires no link bar because the keys maintain roller lifter alignment relative to the cam lobes. Naturally, the bronze bushings must be installed to the engine block to locate the vertical grooves to place the lifter roller wheels in plane with the cam lobes. This style eliminates the weight of the link bars, reducing valvetrain reciprocating mass. Manufacturers, such as Jesel, offer a special keyway bushing installer tool to achieve the correct bushing keyway position/alignment.

Another innovative design is the cartridge-style roller lifter. This unique approach features a bronze guide and lifter system that is easily serviceable, even trackside. Instead of a press-fit bronze guide, the parent bore is opened to accept a drop-in 1.312-inch-OD bushing. The bushing is secured to the block with an aluminum collet and a single screw. The collet engages to the outside of the bushing with a fine thread that allows for the bushing height location to be adjusted in increments of 0.0125 inch.

Once the height is established, a set screw prevents the installed

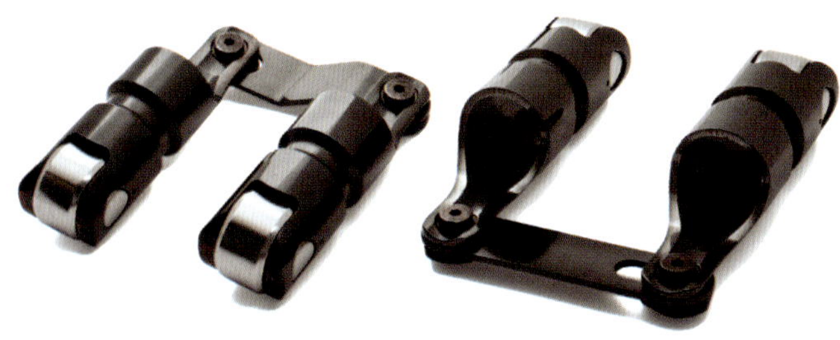

While a 0.842-inch-diameter lifter is considered to be the standard size for small-block Chevy applications, lifter makers offer a range of body diameters to suit specific needs. Jesel, for example, offers body diameters including 0.842, 0.875, 0.905, 0.937, and 1.00 inch with roller wheel diameters of 0.760, 0.820, 0.850, and 1.220 inch. Morel, as another example, offers 0.842-, 0.875-, 0.903-, and 0.936-inch bodies with wheel sizes of 0.700, 0.750, 0.810, and 0.850 inch. (Photo Courtesy Jesel)

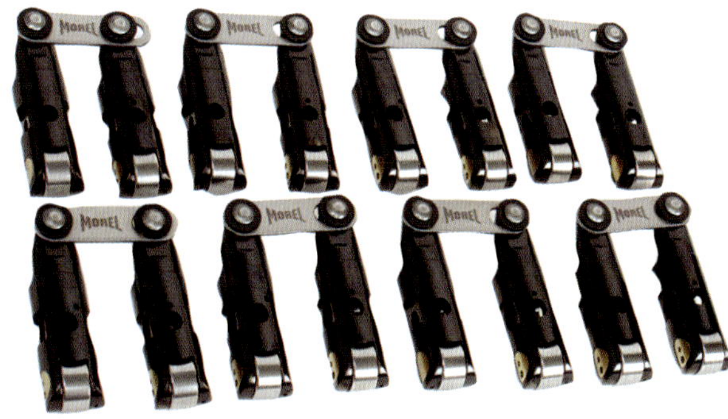

Mechanical/solid roller lifters are available in a variety of body diameters, roller wheel diameters, and structural designs. The example shown here is a set of Morel's Black Mamba lifters that are made from billet bodies and rated at 9,000 or more rpm. Features include a bronze axle diameter of 0.470 inch, DLC coating, and a 0.750-inch wheel. The lifters are recommended to accommodate valve spring seat pressures of 150 to 400 pounds and open pressure of 550 to 1,000 pounds.

bushing location from changing. The 1.000-inch diameter lifter drops into the bushing, guided by channels machined into the bushing. The distinct advantage of this style is its ease of service, since the bushings are easily removable when needed for block cleaning, bushing wear, or in the rare event of a lifter failure, eliminating the need to remove a press-in bushing and reinstall and hone a new bushing. To cite Jesel's cartridge roller lifters as an example, these lifters also feature a large 1.220-inch roller wheel, which reduces the pressure angle of the lifter.

A recent innovation/evolution is the cartridge roller lifter. This style of lifter is designed for purpose-built iron and aluminum high-pressure drag racing engine blocks that can accept the 1.312-inch OD bronze bushing. This multipiece, modular lifter system features a 1.00-inch roller lifter fitted with a huge 1.220-inch diameter roller wheel. The lifter body is keyed to run inside of a keyway bronze lifter bushing. The vertical key engagement prevents the roller lifter from rotating inside the bushing. The unique aspect of this system is the bushing, which hand-inserts into the block's lifter bore. A micro-threaded top and collet allows the bushing height to be adjusted in the lifter bore, while the aluminum collet features a bolt-through tab that secures the bushing in place. This allows the engine builder/racer to quickly replace lifters and bushings without the need to re-hone the lifter bores when servicing the engine between races. Once the block's lifter bores are sized to accept the bronze bushings (in the rare event of a lifter failure, or for purposes of cleaning the block), the lifter and bushing assemblies can easily be removed. Shown here is an example of Jesel's cartridge lifter assembly. (Photo Courtesy Jesel)

Roller lifter wheels must be kept in plane with the cam lobes for the wheels to rotate against the lobes. One method of maintaining this alignment involves the use of keyed lifters that feature a male key that rides through a female keyway in a special bronze lifter bushing that is press-fit to the block's lifter bores. Naturally, precise indexing of the keyway bushing is critical so that the lifter roller wheel engages the cam lobe properly. (Photo Courtesy Jesel)

View the male keys on these keyway lifters. Depending on the manufacturer, the lifter bodies may be DLC coated (a nano-composite diamond-like carbon treatment), which provides reduced friction, a hardened surface, and high corrosion protection. (Photo Courtesy Jesel)

Pistons

In this day and age, it should come as no surprise that pistons are available for purchase in any diameter, compression height, and dome configuration that can fit into OEM and aftermarket small-block Chevy blocks. Especially considering the common use of CNC machining, it's relatively easy to obtain the exact pistons that are required in terms of dimensional factors. Want to lower or increase the compression ratio? No problem. With the available flat-top, inverted-dome, and high-dome options available, the compression ratio can easily be tailored in combination with the cylinder head chamber volume to achieve as little or as much squeeze as desired.

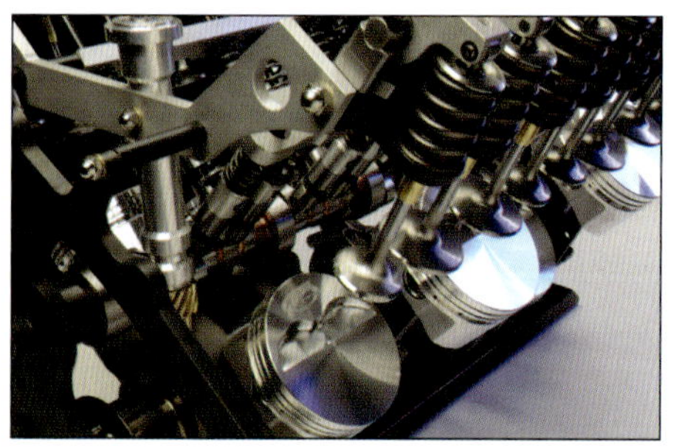

Selecting the right piston for the application is a key element for maximizing performance if you can achieve the desired compression ratio based on the cylinder head combustion chamber volume. (Photo Courtesy Crower)

Piston Skirts and Major/Minor Thrust

The piston experiences a major and minor thrust force at opposing sides of the piston skirts. The major thrust face is the side of the piston that receives the thrust on the power stroke. As viewed facing the front of the engine, if the crankshaft is rotating clockwise, the major thrust face is on the left side of the cylinders (the exhaust side of the passenger-side cylinders and the intake side of the driver-side cylinders). The minor thrust side experiences force on the compression stroke.

This difference in force at each side of the piston is caused in part by the operating angles of the connecting rod during its travel.

During the firing cycle, the load experienced on the major thrust side skirt can be as much as 10 times greater than the load experienced on the minor thrust side skirt. The difference in skirt loading will vary depending on several variables, such as crankshaft stroke, connecting rod length, and peak cylinder pressures.

Now, consider the piston skirt design as it relates to these thrust issues. The shape, area of mass, and weight of a piston's skirts play a major role in managing friction and in stabilizing the piston during TDC and BDC transitions. Asymmetric skirt designs have been developed to minimize weight and maximize efficiency. The major thrust side skirt is made larger compared to the use of a small minor thrust side skirt.

Left-bank and right-bank pistons can feature an asymmetric design. Note the difference is skirt width for major and minor thrust sides for each bank location. A left-bank/driver-side piston is seen at left; the right-bank/passenger-side piston is on the right.

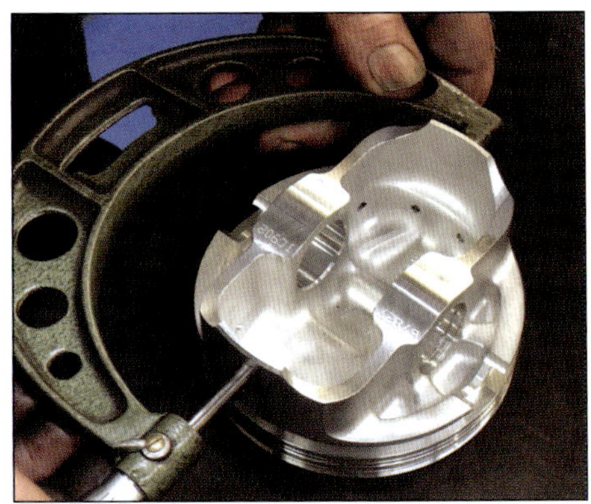

Piston skirts are not perfectly round; they are actually slightly barrel shaped. Each side of the piston experiences different levels of loading relative to the intake and exhaust sides of the cylinders. Skirt design plays a major role in accommodating these forces in terms of durability, performance, and piston weight.

The amount of surface area must accommodate the load while providing piston stability to minimize rocking relative to the pin axis as the piston moves down from TDC and back up from BDC.

Since asymmetric pistons are bank-specific, each piston is labeled for its right- or left-bank position. The dome may also feature a laser-etched arrow that indicates the piston's orientation toward the front of the engine.

Major Thrust Side

During the power stroke, as the piston begins to be forced down, it experiences resistance as it attempts to turn the crankshaft. As the load increases, the amount of resistance increases. During this resistance, the piston side load is forced to one side (the major thrust side), which places more force with subsequently increased friction and potential wear on the thrust side of the cylinder wall.

Before boring and honing cylinders, always measure the piston skirt diameter at the location specified by the piston maker. Measuring the skirt diameter higher or lower will result in an incorrect reference diameter relative to the required finished cylinder bore diameter.

If the piston dome features a reference dot or other mark denoting the side of the piston that must face towards the front of the engine, it's critical to install the piston with this mark facing the appropriate direction. The piston side loads on the major side tend to increase in a stroker engine and/or with forced induction/boosted pressures. The major thrust side will be at the exhaust side of the engine's passenger-side (right) bank and the intake side of the driver-side (left) bank.

A wider major thrust side skirt is featured on this asymmetric piston. Providing a wider skirt for the major thrust side provides the support and stability needed for the side of the piston that experiences the greater force load.

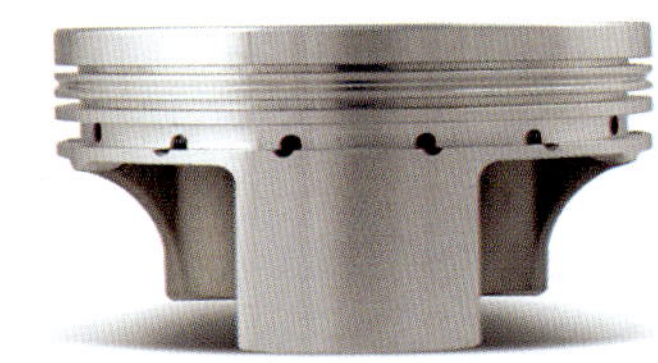

Shown here is the narrower minor thrust side of the same asymmetric piston. The small skirt that faces the minor thrust side provides stability but reduces mass where it's not needed.

Minor Thrust Side

The role of the minor thrust side is basically to provide piston stability as the major thrust side takes the brunt of the cylinder wall contact.

The piston's minor thrust side is directly opposite of the major thrust side. The minor thrust side is forced to the opposite side of the cylinder wall as it moves up on the compression stroke, due to the resistance generated by meeting the air/fuel mixture. Since the minor side experiences less thrust force, this allows the piston maker to use a more narrow skirt on the minor side, which reduces the piston's weight without sacrificing strength. Weight savings are in the 10-gram range.

Not all piston makers offer this asymmetric skirt design. However, JE Pistons offers it in their FSR (forged side relief) line. A reduced-width skirt area is featured on the minor thrust side, and the pin bosses are relieved at the outboard sides to allow the use of a shorter and lighter wrist pin.

The asymmetric design approach was initially developed for specific racing applications, but the concept has trickled down to street applications as well.

Some pistons are laser etched on the dome to indicate which side of the piston must face forward. This is a helpful reminder regarding valve locations or with asymmetric pistons.

Another benefit to the asymmetric approach with regard to the skirt mass and profile is increased piston ring sealing and ring stability. Basically, the dedicated major and minor thrust skirt design coupled with a slightly offset wrist pin directly addresses ring performance in addition to reduced wall friction.

While the concept of an asymmetrical piston design isn't new (supposedly General Motors came up with the idea back in the 1960s), the design only recently has been used in aftermarket performance production, beginning with limited custom race orders to the present day of broader offerings for street and racing applications.

Offset Pin

Asymmetric pistons also feature an offset wrist pin with the pin centerline biased from zero towards the major thrust side by about 0.020 inch. This slight offset tends to balance the piston to accommodate the difference in skirt mass and to compensate for and alter the effect of the rod angle, transferring a bit of force away from the major thrust side.

Match the Valve Angle

It's important to be aware of the cylinder head valve angles and the intake and exhaust valve diameters when ordering pistons, since the valve pockets/reliefs in the pistons must accommodate these factors. Since the valve angles may be 23, 18, 15, 13.5, 13, or 12 degrees, the valve reliefs in the piston domes must be able to accommodate the selected angles.

Modifications are often possible, depending on the combination. For example, if you're running 18-degree valves but have access to 23-degree pistons, the valve pockets may be milled to lay-back and match the 18-degree valve angle, assuming that the piston dome thickness allows this without compromising piston material strength. Obviously, it's best to simply order pistons with the appropriate valve pocket angles that your heads require.

Valve reliefs obviously need to provide the desired depth and radial clearance for the valves. Radial clearance, the distance from the edge of the valve to the radial relief cut, should provide a minimum of 0.050 inch at the intake valve and about 0.060 at the exhaust valve. The exhaust valve is closest to the piston at about 10 degrees BTDC. The intake valve is closest to the piston at about 10 degrees ATDC. Valve-to-piston depth clearance should be kept at a minimum of 0.080 inch at the intake valve and 0.100 inch at the exhaust valve. If clearance is too tight, there is potential valve-to-piston contact. Clearances that are excessive sacrifice compression. Note that if aluminum connecting rods are to be installed, increase the minimum valve-to-piston depth clearance by an additional 0.030 inch due to the anticipated thermal growth of the aluminum rod during operation.

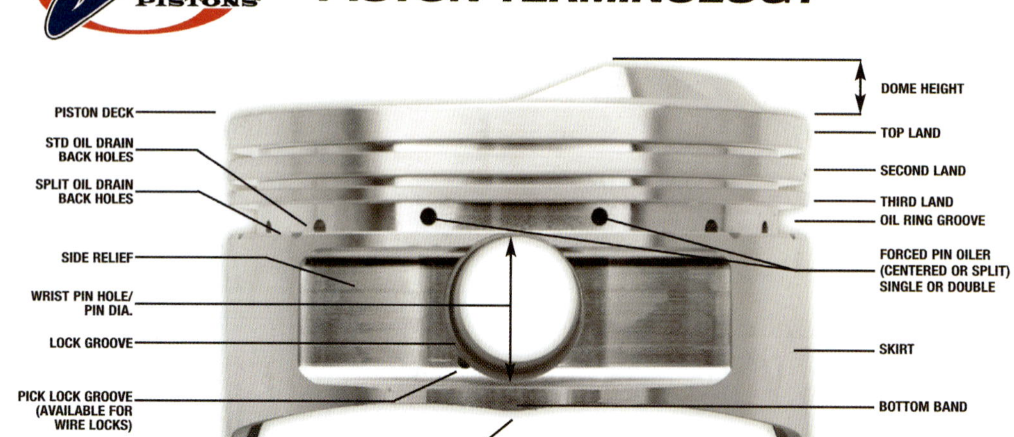

An overview of piston features and terminology is shown. (Photo Courtesy JE Pistons)

Examples of Piston Choices

Listing all available pistons for small-block Chevy applications by every maker, in every diameter, in every dome configuration, and in every cylinder head application would take more space than this book allows. The following are merely a few select examples of pistons offered by JE Pistons.

Variables obviously include the bore diameter, required displacement, crank stroke, rod length, piston CD (compression distance), piston dome volume, cylinder head combustion chamber volume, and the style of head in terms of valve angles and sizes. Rest assured that regardless of your needs, the leading piston makers either have what you need in stock or can cater to any custom order.

Examples For 23-Degree Heads (Hollow Dome)

CI	Bore	Stroke	Rod	Deck	CD	Compression		
						58 cc	64 cc	76 cc
377	4.000	3.750	6.000	9.000	1.125	14.8	13.5	11.5
381	4.020	3.750	6.000	9.000	1.125	14.9	13.6	11.6
383	4.030	3.750	6.000	9.000	1.125	15.0	13.6	11.6
384	4.035	3.750	6.000	9.000	1.125	15.0	13.7	11.6
385	4.040	3.750	6.000	9.000	1.125	15.1	13.7	11.6
388	4.060	3.750	6.000	9.000	1.125	15.2	13.8	11.7
352	4.000	3.500	6.000	9.000	1.250	14.5	13.1	11.1
355	4.020	3.500	6.000	9.000	1.250	14.6	13.2	11.2
357	4.030	3.500	6.000	9.000	1.250	14.7	13.3	11.3
358	4.035	3.500	6.000	9.000	1.250	14.7	13.4	11.3
359	4.040	3.500	6.000	9.000	1.250	14.8	13.4	11.3
362	4.060	3.500	6.000	9.000	1.250	14.9	13.5	11.4

Examples for Brodix 12–15 Degree (Raised Dome)

CI	Bore	Stroke	Rod	Deck	CD	Compression		
						50 cc	54 cc	58 cc
407	4.130	3.800	6.000	9.000	1.100	15.8	14.6	13.6
408	4.135	3.800	6.000	9.000	1.100	15.8	14.6	13.6
409	4.140	3.800	6.000	9.000	1.100	15.8	14.6	13.6
410	4.145	3.800	6.000	9.000	1.100	15.8	14.6	13.6
412	4.155	3.800	6.000	9.000	1.100	15.9	15.0	14.1

Examples for 400 23-Degree (Hollow Dome Vol 10.8)

CI	Bore	Stroke	Rod	Deck	CD	Compression		
						58 cc	64 cc	76 cc
428	4.125	4.000	6.000	9.000	1.000	16.5	15.0	12.7
432	4.145	4.000	6.000	9.000	1.000	16.6	15.1	12.7
434	4.155	4.000	6.000	9.000	1.000	16.7	15.2	12.9
436	4.165	4.000	6.000	9.000	1.000	16.8	15.2	12.9
440	4.185	4.000	6.000	9.000	1.000	16.9	15.3	13.0
414	4.129	3.875	6.000	9.000	1.062	16.0	14.6	12.4
417	4.130	3.875	6.000	9.000	1.062	16.0	14.6	12.4
418	4.145	3.875	6.000	9.000	1.062	16.1	14.7	12.5
420	4.155	3.875	6.000	9.000	1.062	16.1	14.7	12.5
422	4.165	3.875	6.000	9.000	1.062	16.2	14.8	12.6
426	4.185	3.875	6.000	9.000	1.062	16.3	14.9	12.7
406	4.125	3.800	6.000	9.000	1.100	15.7	14.3	12.2
410	4.145	3.800	6.000	9.000	1.100	15.8	14.4	12.3
414	4.165	3.800	6.000	9.000	1.100	16.0	14.6	12.5
401	4.129	3.750	6.000	9.000	1.125	15.5	14.3	12.0
409	4.165	3.750	6.000	9.000	1.125	16.3	14.8	12.5

Piston Dome Shape

Domes are available in several configurations, including flat tops with valve reliefs, inverted or "dished" domes where the center area is lowered, and high domes where positive height takes up more room in the combustions chamber. Depending on the desired compression ratio, the dome volume needs to interact with the cylinder head combustion chamber volume.

In general terms, a flat top is considered by many the best choice for a more even dispersion of flame travel and combustion efficiency. Inverted/dished domes are popular with forced induction because the additional boost pressure increases dynamic compression. High-dome or "pop-up" pistons may be needed to obtain the desired compression ratio due to a larger volume in the cylinder head combustion chamber. Considering the choices in chamber volume offered by

aftermarket heads, try to create a combination wherein a flat top or inverted dome can be used.

High-dome pistons tend to slow down the flame dispersion. With the right combination of flat-top pistons and head chambers that provide the desired compression, they are a better choice than dealing with high domes. If an increased compression ratio is desired using flat-top pistons, choose heads with the appropriate size of reduced combustion chamber volume.

Note that the pin bore is raised where it begins to intersect the oil ring groove. To retain a complete footprint support for the oil ring package, a separate support rail is needed. Install it after the piston has been assembled to the connecting rod and before the oil ring package is installed.

Raised-dome configurations reduce the piston volume, increasing the compression ratio. If a larger-volume combustion chamber is used, increasing the dome height provides a way to bump up compression. A better alternative is to select a head with a small chamber and use flat-top pistons, but often there is no choice, depending on the heads and your desired compression ratio.

The inverted/dished dome relieving in the center area increases volume and lowers compression ratio compared to a flat top.

If a part-numbered, off-the-shelf piston doesn't suit your needs, custom pistons CNC machined from billet blanks are readily available. This allows you to order exactly what you want in terms of bore diameter, compression distance, valve pocket location, depth, angle, and radial clearance, dome volume, and any additional features, such as oil drainback holes, accumulator grooves, etc. The example shown here is from Diamond Racing.

Coatings

Specific-application specialty coatings are certainly nothing new, but we're seeing increased applications to take advantage of what these coatings offer. With regard to pistons, this includes anti-friction skirt coatings that consist of various formulations depending on the piston maker or coating service, including but not limited to dry film moly or Grafal coating, ceramic-reinforced dry film that also decreases heat saturation.

The specific material used is usually proprietary to the coating service or piston maker with various terms or labels to describe them. Whatever terms applies, this is a thin coating applied to the skirts that provides a safety margin against skirt scuffing and enhances lubricity, reducing parasitic drag. It serves to protect both the skirts and the cylinder walls in the event that insufficient oil exists on the cylinder walls, at the major thrust sides, and during piston rock as the piston transitions to and from top dead center.

In addition, this slippery coating serves to retain an oil film, further enhancing lubrication and further protecting the cylinder walls. It's just a nice option that can do no harm but can add a level of protection. In the early days of the use of these coatings, they was only available through specialty coating services, such as Swain Tech Coatings, PolyDyn Performance Coatings, and Calico Coatings to name a few. Today, many piston makers offer skirt coating either as standard practice or as an option.

The other coating to consider is a ceramic thermal barrier coating that is applied to the dome. Offered in various grades or levels of performance, a thermal barrier coating does what the term implies: it reduces the amount of heat generated during combustion from soaking into the piston. This has several benefits. Since the piston absorbs less heat, the piston's diameter does not change as much during thermal cycles, helping to maintain a more consistent ring pressure against the cylinder walls. Also, heat that would have been transmitted into the piston is somewhat reflected and stays in the combustion chamber, providing greater combustion efficiency.

Using a ceramic thermal barrier coating on the piston domes in conjunction with the combustion chamber, valve faces, exhaust valve throat, and exhaust ports can in combination result in enough of a more-efficient burn to actually increase horsepower. Applications vary depending on other engine factors, but taking advantage of this thermal barrier approach may add as little as say, 2 hp or potentially as much as 15 hp more.

Just as moly skirt coatings have come of age, so has the use of thermal barrier coatings as many leading piston makers now offer this as an option. Especially for applications where cylinder pressures and temperatures are at extreme levels, such as with the use of nitrous injection, supercharging, or turbocharging, ceramic thermal barrier dome coatings can help pistons to withstand this additional abuse. Several coating service facilities and piston makers offer specially formulated ceramic coatings that are specifically designed for these applications.

Note that the piston's surfaces must be prepared to accept these coatings, and this is absolutely critical. I don't suggest applying a ceramic material yourself. If the surface is not properly treated and/or if the material is not applied under the correct temperature and procedures, it can separate and contaminate the engine, killing bearings and other friction-prone surfaces. If it has been decided to take advantage of thermal barrier coatings, get it done by the piston maker or send the pistons to an experienced and reputable service house.

Specialty coatings have grown in popularity, especially anti-friction skirt coatings and thermal barrier coatings for piston domes, particularly for high combustion pressure and forced induction applications. Again, while it is not mandatory for all engines, thermal barrier ceramic-based coatings reduce piston thermal soak, helping to reduce thermal expansion, and can result in enhanced combustion efficiency for added power.

Anti-friction skirt coatings have become much more commonly used as acceptance has increased. This dry film coating provides added insurance against skirt and cylinder wall scuffing in and when lubrication is minimal, such as with cold starts or short-term oil starvation. There is no downside to these skirt coatings. While it is not mandatory, it's always a good idea.

Anti-friction and thermal barrier coatings are now offered by most piston makers as options. If you decide to have your bare pistons coated after purchasing them, ship them to a service facility that specializes in applying these coatings. (Photo Courtesy Icon Pistons)

Another coating treatment area that relates to pistons is the wrist pin. A form of diamond-like carbon (DLC) referred to as casidium is a surface treatment that makes the pin smoother, slicker, harder, self-lubricating, more resilient to wear, and it prevents galling. This vacuum-based coating is applied by a process called plasma assisted chemical vapor deposition (PACVD).

The coating won't change the pin diameter enough to cause a fitment issue because it's only 80 to 160 millionths of an inch thick, so it's not enough of a change to measure with a micrometer. In those applications where the piston maker deems it necessary, some piston makers offer this along with their pistons. However, DLC can be applied by various surface treatment services, such as Anatech. Use of this treatment is common among NASCAR engine builders.

Yet another option involves hard anodizing to the top ring groove, which is subject to higher temperatures. In extreme power applications, the top rings may be subject to possible micro-welding at the groove edges. Hard anodizing the groove surfaces aids in eliminating this potential.

A number of aftermarket specialty coating services, both by piston makers and coating specialty facilities, are available if you opt to send your parts out on your own.

Piston Features and Options

Many aftermarket piston makers offer additional features to improve efficiency and performance either as standard on certain piston series or as an option. These include vertical gas ports, which are small vertical holes placed along the perimeter surface of the piston dome that allow combustion pressure to enter directly behind the top ring during the power stroke. This increases top ring sealing at the cylinder wall. Another option involves lateral gas ports, which are tiny slots milled into the roof of the top ring grooves, also allowing combustion pressure to push the top rings out against the cylinder wall. Vertical ports are popular for drag racing applications; lateral ports are often used for circle track use where engine speeds are held high for longer periods.

To reduce reciprocating weight, some aftermarket piston makers remove weight from the pin bosses and/or they window-mill mate-

Gas ports allow a slight pressure feed to the top ring to push the ring to the cylinder wall for superior ring sealing. This mod is popular in drag racing applications.

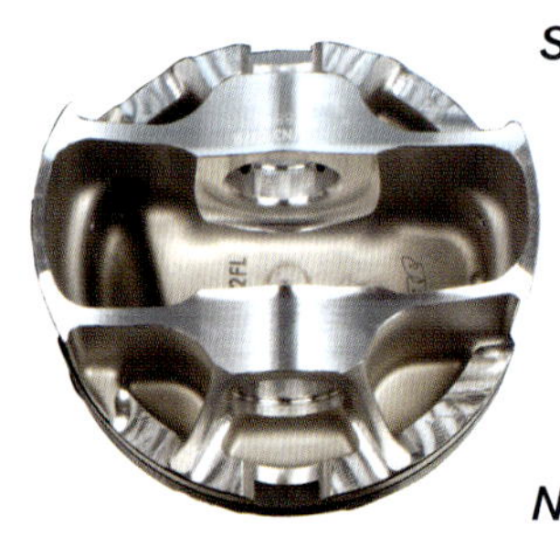

Some piston makers go to great lengths to reduce piston weight. Notice how this piston features a series of skeletonized machined reliefs, removing weight from areas where piston strength is not compromised. Reducing reciprocating weight frees up energy for quicker revs and lessens starting at connecting rods and rod bearings.

rial from the underside of the piston in areas where strength is not compromised.

Other milling operations employed on some pistons involve a series of narrow, closely spaced grooves around the circumference of the piston between the dome and the top ring groove. These are intended to reduce the amount of contact area against the cylinder wall when the piston rocks over during the transition from TDC. Reducing this contact area theoretically helps tame the flame travel to reduce the chance of detonation.

A feature found on many aftermarket pistons is a noticeable radius-milled groove that's machined into the piston land between the top and second ring grooves. This isn't done for the sake of appearance. This

Notice the series of small grooves between the dome and the top ring groove. This feature slightly reduces the contact area between the top of the piston and the cylinder wall during piston rock at/ from TDC.

Note the narrow radiused groove between the top and second ring grooves. Referred to as an accumulator groove, this captures blowby gasses that may pass the top ring, reducing the pressure applied to the second ring. This aids in reducing or eliminating second ring flutter.

Any machining performed on a piston has a purpose. Notice the series of small and tightly spaced horizontal grooves along the total area of the skirt. These tiny grooves aid in oil retention. Even if the skirts are coated with a dry film anti-friction treatment, these tiny grooves remain functional.

Oil holes drilled above the skirt areas are featured for oil drainback only.

groove, called an accumulator, provides added volume for residual combustion gas that blows past the top ring, reducing pressure between the top and second rings to aid in top-ring seating and reducing the potential for ring flutter.

To provide additional oil to the piston wrist pin, some pistons feature a series of small oil holes located on the floor of the oil ring groove. These are larger oil holes milled into the floor of the oil ring groove that deliver additional oil to the piston's wrist pin. To further enhance oil delivery to the pins, some pistons also feature a small passage drilled through the underside of each pin boss.

Full-Floating Pins

Rather than using a press-fit wrist pin to the small-end bore of the rod, a popular and common approach today involves the use of full-floating pins, where the pin is free to rotate in both the connecting rod's small end and the piston. This design also eases assembly and disassembly because no press or heat is required.

Since the pin is free to slide within the rod and piston bore, a method of retaining the pin in place is critical to prevent the pin from sliding out and hitting the cylinder wall. The outer ends of the piston's pin bores are machined with a small groove that is designed to accept a locking clip. Depending on the piston maker's design, this requires a single round-wire circlip at each end, a single flat-wound spiral lock at each end, or in some cases, two spiral locks at each end.

Split oil drain-back holes allow excess oil to bleed off of the oil rings. Notice the grooves at the floor of the oil ring groove.

Note the two orifices at the top of the pin bore. Oil is directly fed to the wrist pins via oil drain-back holes placed in the oil ring groove.

The use of full-floating wrist pins allows the rod to slide on the pin, allowing the piston to better retain its fore/aft position to the cylinder bore without forcing the piston forward or rearward, which reduces operating friction. Note the position of the oil ring support rail bump at the left.

The holes drilled into the rear wall of the oil ring groove, depending on the location, serve as oil drain-back holes or as passages that allow excess oil from the ring groove to force oil directly onto the wrist pins. Also notice the side relief machined across the pin bore area. This both reduces weight and provides a recessed location for the pins and pin locks, keeping them farther away from the cylinder walls.

Full-floating wrist pins require clips at each end to retain their position. Depending on the pistons at hand, this requires either flat-wound spiral clips or round-wire C-clips. Installing either style requires patience and the need to develop a knack for it. In skilled hands, the use of fingers and a small flathead screwdriver is all that's needed. First-time installers will likely experience frustration. The clips must fully engage into the pin bore groove.

Piston CD and the Oil Ring

Piston compression distance (CD) refers to the distance from the wrist pin centerline to the dome surface that is closest to the block deck at TDC. This distance will vary depending on piston design and the requirement to work in conjunction with the block deck height, crank stroke, and rod length. If the CD is short enough to result in the wrist pin bore being placed high enough to begin to intersect with the oil ring groove, a small void will exist at the bottom of the oil ring groove over each pin bore. To address this and to provide a completed footprint for the oil ring, the oil ring groove is milled taller to accept both the oil ring package and a support rail that is installed at the bottom of the ring groove. The support rail, to be installed before the ring package, features a small male dimple protrusion. The support rail must be installed with this tiny bump facing downward, directly over one side of the pin boss. This small bump serves as a stopper, preventing the support rail from rotating to prevent the rail's end gap from entering into the void at the top of the pin bore.

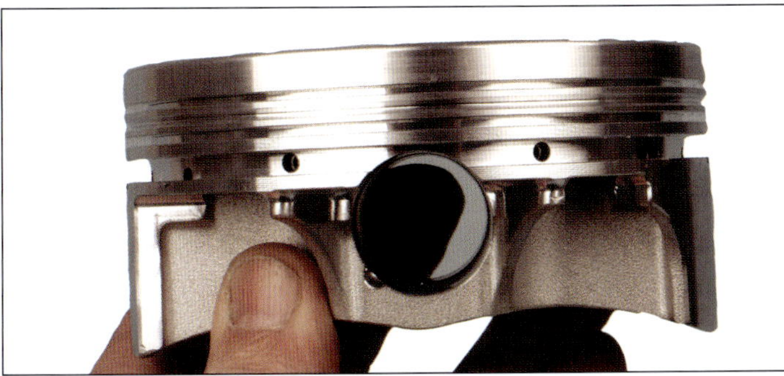

Flat-top domes are preferred, but inverted dish or high-dome designs may be required to achieve the desired compression ratio based on your cylinder head combustion chamber volume.

This view shows the support rail and oil ring package installed. If the pin bore intersects with the oil ring groove, the groove is machined wide enough to accept both the rail and oil ring package.

If a support rail is required, it must be installed with its small bump facing downward, directly above one of the pin bores. This prevents the rail from rotating, avoiding the end gap from entering this void area. If the rail begins to rotate, the small bump will serve as a stopper.

Determining Compression Ratio

This information is also included in CarTech's engine blueprinting book titled *Modern Engine Blueprinting Techniques: A Practical Guide to Precision Engine Building*. The compression ratio represents the volume of the cylinder when the piston is at BDC compared to the volume when the piston reaches TDC.

The factors involve cylinder displacement (bore diameter and crank stroke), the deck clearance, volume provided by the head gasket, and volume of the combustion chamber.

A simple formula is used to determine engine displacement:

Bore x Bore x Stroke x 0.7854 x Number of cylinders

Example: Let's say you're dealing with a 4.125-inch bore and a 4.000-inch total crank stroke in an 8-cylinder engine.

Determining Compression Ratio *(Continued)*

4.125 x 4.125 x 4.000 x 0.7854 x 8 = 427.65 ci

To consider the piston's dome and dish/valve reliefs, subtract piston high-dome volume or add dish or valve pocket volume.

Formula to Determine Compression Ratio

Cylinder volume + deck volume + gasket volume + net chamber volume = BDC factor

Deck volume + gasket volume + net chamber volume = TDC factor

BDC factor divided by the TDC factor = compression ratio

Formula to Obtain Cylinder Volume

Bore x Bore x Stroke x 0.7854 x 16.4 = cylinder volume

Example: Let's say that the bore is 4.000 inches in diameter and our stroke is 3.750 inches

4.000 x 4.000 x 3.750 x 0.7854 x 16.4 = 772.8336 cc ■

Piston Dome Volume

Quality piston makers provide dome volume figures for their pistons. You can rely on those figures or you can measure them for yourself.

Measure piston dome volume with the piston installed and with at least the top compression ring installed to seal the bore.

Rotate the crank to bring the piston down in the bore near BDC. Then coat the cylinder wall with a thick lithium grease to aid in sealing at a point of about 1.50 inches below the block deck.

Rotate the crank to raise the piston to a point exactly 1.00 inch below block deck; use a depth micrometer to measure this. Wipe off any excess grease that might be on the top of the piston.

Smear lithium grease onto the block deck around the bore. Place a piece of stout, flat, clear plexiglass or acrylic with a small chamfered hole drilled in the plate (about a 1/4 inch in diameter) onto the block. Press the plate gently to obtain a good grease seal.

With the block's deck level, use a use a burette to add fluid (blue windshield washer solvent works well) until the cavity is filled and no air bubbles are trapped under the clear plate. Fill the burette to its top index mark. As you release fluid, monitor how much fluid it takes to fill the cavity. The burette may need to be refilled several times.

Note: Before adding fluid, place a clean piece of paper under the bore and watch for leaks. If fluid passes through the bore past the top ring, a false reading will occur.

Combustion Chamber Volume

The burette is used here again. With valves installed, place the head upside down on a workbench. Install a spark plug. Apply white lithium grease around the chamber and position the clear plate. Using the burette, add fluid and record how many cubic centimeters it takes to fill the chamber. Make sure that no air bubbles are trapped.

Once you record your data (combustion chamber volume, piston dome volume, head gasket volume, deck height volume, and cylinder swept volume), you're ready to do a bit of math to determine compression ratio.

C = combustion chamber volume
P = piston dome volume
G = head gasket volume
D = deck height volume
V = cylinder swept volume

In this example, a 302 Chevy engine is used where C = 64 cc, P = 7.92 cc, G = 4.24 cc, D = 3.09 cc, and V = 621.88 cc.

The formula for compression ratio (CR) is as follows:

$$CR = (C - P + G + D + V) / (C - P + G + D)$$

Example:

$$(64 - 7.92 + 4.24 + 3.09 + 621.88) / (64 - 7.92 + 4.24 + 3.09)$$

$$685.29 / 63.41 = 10.8$$

(in this example, compression ratio is 10.8:1)

Due to aluminum's faster heat dissipation, you can get away with a higher compression ratio with aluminum cylinder heads than cast-iron heads. Considering today's fuels (gasoline), you should be able to get away with as much as an 11.4:1 or so compression ratio on high-test pump gas before pre-ignition/detonation problems occur. If the compression ratio is any higher, higher-octane race gas or alcohol is required.

SAMPLE ENGINE BUILD: 422 CI

To provide an example of a small-block Chevy performance build, this chapter outlines one specific build from start to finish. This 422.2-ci engine build features the following components: a Dart SHP Pro Iron block with cylinders sized to 4.1642 inches, Trick Flow 18-degree cylinder heads, Icon flat-top forged pistons, 6.000-inch Scat forged H-beam rods, a Scat forged crankshaft with a 3.875-inch stroke, Morel solid roller lifters, a Comp Cams billet solid roller camshaft, Jesel 1.6:1 offset roller rocker system, Fel-Pro gaskets, Mahle Clevite main and rod bearings, a Melling oil pump, Jesel camshaft belt drive, Trend Performance pushrods, a Dart single-plane intake manifold designed for 18-degree heads, Meziere Enterprises electric water pump, MSD Pro Billet distributor, MSD crank trigger, Holley 850-cfm carburetor, MSD 8-mm spark plug wires, a Moroso Performance oil pan, Moroso Performance valve covers, a Fluidampr 6.250-inch crankshaft balancer, and ARP fasteners throughout the entire build.

The compression ratio was finalized at 13.557:1. The engine produced 735 hp at 7,100 rpm and 575 ft-lbs of torque at 6,250 rpm.

The 422-ci engine boasts 13.5:1 compression.

Compression Ratio of Our 422-ci Small-Block Build	
Bore	4.1642
Stroke	3.875
Piston CD	1.062
Gasket Bore	4.200
Gasket Thickness	0.052
Rod Length	6.000
Chambers	56 cc
Static Compression Ratio	13.557:1

Block Prep and Modifications

The Dart iron block selected can be bored and honed to accept 4.125-inch bores but can safely be sized to 4.165 inches while maintaining sufficient cylinder wall thickness. In our case, since the 18-degree cylinder heads require a minimum bore size of 4.155 inches for adequate valve to block deck clearance, we opted for the larger 4.165-inch bore size. Before machining, the crankshaft was test fitted to check the counterweight clearance to the block's pan rails, and rods were test fitted to check for the rod's big end clearance.

The block of choice for the sample build is Dart's SHP Pro iron block (part number 31161212).

The Dart block features 350 main caps and is designed to use a two-piece rear main seal and a larger cam bore, requiring a camshaft that features big-block Chevy journals. The raw deck height is 0.9025 inch. The block is initially intended for 4.125-inch cylinder bores but may be overbored to a safe maximum of 4.165 inches.

Aftermarket blocks may be obtained that accept either a 350 or 400 main bore. We opted for the 350 mains to reduce rotating mass.

While a traditional factory block is specified for a 9.025-inch deck height, to arrive at a zero deck with our crank stroke, rod length, and piston height combo, we milled our decks to 9.001 inches.

The block features three oil gallery holes at front and rear, all of which must be plugged. Dart included all the freeze plugs, NPT plugs, and dowel pins that are required.

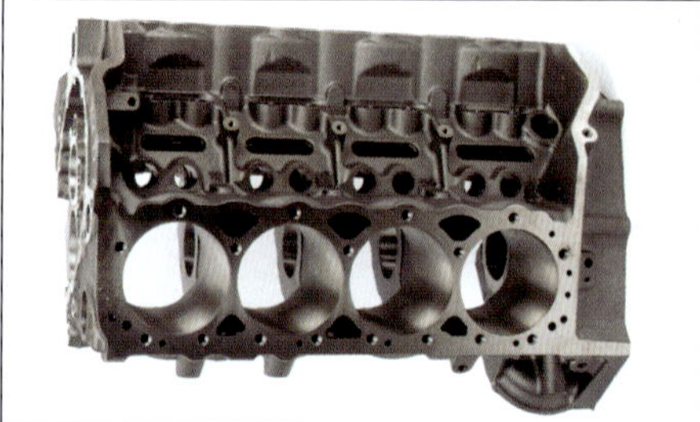

Taking advantage of today's high-quality aftermarket blocks simply makes sense. The material is of a higher quality, often with a high nickel content for strength, the machining is more accurate, and the blocks are designed from scratch for high-performance and racing applications with superior oiling systems, stronger main caps, and thicker decks with racing mods in mind. Options allow for a variety of larger-than-factory bore sizes, taller decks, raised cam bores, clearance notches for strokers, etc. Rather than trying to bring a factory block up to speed, starting with an aftermarket block that already features what is needed saves precious time and money.

Block machining was performed by Scott Gressman of Gressman Powersports in Fremont, Ohio, on the shop's dedicated engine block CNC machine. The block was delivered with a raw deck height of 9.027 inches. To achieve a zero deck with the pistons at TDC, the decks were milled to achieve a finished deck height of 8.9995 inches (stock deck height for a small-block Chevy is 9.025 inches). This was determined by factoring in the crankshaft stroke, connecting rod length and piston compression distance. Since the total crank stroke was 3.875 inches, half of the total stroke was considered, which in this case was 1.9375 inches. Added to this was the 6.000-inch rod length and the piston compression distance of 1.062 inches, which totaled to 8.9995 inches.

Before milling the decks, the CNC machine's digital probe first measured the existing decks, recording the height from the front to the rear and side to side, which was followed by probe measuring all cylinder bores for both the existing diameter as well as the bore centerline locations. Once all of the dimensions were recorded, the decks were milled to our desired height. Our example block was milled to achieve a finished deck height of 9.001 inches.

Scott Gressman, owner of Gressman Powersports in Fremont, Ohio, sets up our block on his CNC milling center.

During digital probing on CNC, block measurements are obtained and referenced to a program specific to our block. Once all of the data has been obtained, adjustments can be made with regard to the desired deck height and cylinder bore diameter.

During the initial inspection, the CNC digital probe first references the block's main bore centerline, establishing a precise reference.

The digital probe measures the raw cylinder bores, obtaining the true centerline and revealing any off-center tolerance. This aids the boring process to achieve a precise center during milling.

The CNC probe measures the deck height in preparation of milling to achieve the desired height and true squareness. Decks were cut to a height of 9.001 inches using a slower slow speed with a carbide cutter.

Once the decks were milled, the bores were initially cut to 4.150 inches, which was followed by a second phase at 4.1587 inches, leaving 0.0055 inch for honing.

CNC boring was performed precisely at the center relative to the main bore centerline.

Before cylinder boring, all pistons were measured for skirt diameter. Never assume that the desired bore size will be correct for the pistons at hand. Always measure the pistons to verify and to determine the required final cylinder bore size. Always measure the piston diameter at the precise location specified by the piston maker. Due to the slight barrel-shaped profile of the pistons, each piston maker specifies the point at which the piston must be measured.

In our case, the Icon pistons were measured at a skirt location that is in line with the bottom of the pin bore housing. This provides the target cylinder bore size after final honing to provide the piston-to-wall clearance specified by the piston maker.

Our piston skirt diameter, measured at the precise point specified by Icon, measured 4.1587 inches. With that in mind, the bores were CNC milled with a carbide cutter to an initial 4.160 inches, leaving 0.0042 inch for the final honing. Once all bores were milled, the tops of the bores were lightly chamfered on the CNC center. Providing a light chamfer of the top bore edges eases piston and ring installation by eliminating the sharp upper edges.

The advantage of CNC machining, which was not commonly available back in the day, involves both precision and repeatability. Before machining, the block is set up on the CNC machining center, which is followed by digital probing of existing deck height and squareness, cylinder bore centers, and lifter bore centers. If any deviations are present in terms of factory machining or casting shift, instead of assuming that bores are precisely centered, a computer program compares the readings to the block specifications.

In the process, for example, if cylinder bores were, say, 0.0005 inch off-center, the boring operation follows the intended bore centerlines, correcting any off-center issues if they existed. When the decks are milled, this not only achieves the desired deck height from the main bore centerline to the deck surfaces but also establishes a true parallelism of the decks with the main bore centerline, having equal dimensions on both right and left bank decks. It simply doesn't get any better than this.

With CNC machining now being much more widely available among upper-level machine shops, the entire process of machining and correcting for cylinder bore, lifter bore, and deck dimensions can be accomplished with a degree of precision and time savings without the need to move the block among different machining centers. Once decking

Our piston skirts measured 4.1587 inches. Our finished bores at 4.1642 inches obtained a wall clearance of 0.0055 inch.

After the decks have been cut and before installing the deck plates, all head bolt holes are lightly chamfered to eliminate the sharp edges created during deck milling.

Deck plates are torqued to 65 ft-lbs to stress the block, simulating installed heads. This allows for superior cylinder wall roundness during honing, compensating for cylinder wall distortion.

and boring operations are complete, the block simply moves to a honing station for surface completion of the cylinder walls.

Not all shops have these rather expensive CNC machining centers even though prices have come down over the past decade. Granted, a high degree of precision can be achieved using traditional equipment, including boring bars and surfacing machines, along with the use of specialty precision fixtures. But with a multi-axis CNC machining center, all operations can be accomplished in one setup. Considering the speed at which a CNC operator can machine a block, this is also a real time saver for a shop.

Once all CNC milling operations were complete, Scott moved the block to his Peterson honing station, where honing plates were secured to each deck. The use of honing plates, also called deck plates, simulate the distortional effect of installed cylinder heads. While it may seem that a block is rigid enough to prevent cylinder wall movement, in reality, even the strongest blocks can experience slight cylinder bore distortion when the cylinder heads are installed. The honing plates mimic the installed state, allowing honing to be more precise to provide a more uniform bore in a fully assembled condition.

The Icon piston skirts measured at a diameter of 4.1587 inches. To achieve a piston to wall clearance of 0.0055 inch, our cylinders were honed starting with 200-grit diamond stones to a final dimension of 4.1642 inches. This was followed by four light passes with 500 stones, finishing with one pass using plateau honing brushes to establish a more uniform surface finish, minimizing microscopic peaks and valleys for superior oil retention and to aid in faster piston ring seating. Each bore received a single pass with the

The cylinders are final-honed to size, followed by a single pass with plateau brushes to provide better ring seating.

plateau brushes. This essentially cleans the high points left by the honing while leaving enough of a surface profile to allow the piston rings to properly seat.

Aftermarket blocks tend to be produced with lifter bores a bit on the tight side to allow the machinist to obtain the ideal lifter-to-bore oil clearance. Our lifter bores initially measured 0.9040 inch. Our

Morel solid roller lifters measured 0.9038 inch. Morel specifies clearance at 0.0015 to 0.0018 inch, so Scott milled the bores by 0.0014 inch to size all of the lifter bores at a finished diameter of 0.9054 inch to achieve oil clearance of 0.0016 inch. Morel also calls for lifter bore taper at no more than 0.0002 inch. Our bores were finished with zero taper.

Once the block was back in my shop, all of the threaded holes were checked to verify they were thread tapped deep enough. No corrections to straight thread holes were required. We also checked the depth of all National Pipe Tapered thread (NPT) holes at the front and rear of the block as well as oil holes in the lifter valley. Only one hole at the front required to be slightly further tapped by a mere two threads to allow the threaded plug to seat deep enough to avoid contacting the timing cover.

Since the cylinders had been bored and honed, sharp edges were left at the bottom of the cylinder bores. The bottom edges were carefully deburred to eliminate any sharpness. This helps to avoid potential scratching of the piston skirts and eliminates potential stress riser areas.

Our attention then turned to checking the crankshaft and connecting rod clearance relative to the block. With the upper main bearings installed and lightly oiled, the crankshaft was installed and carefully rotated to verify that no counterweight-to-block clearance issues were present. Our tightest clearance was a healthy 0.100 inch. A minimum clearance between the counterweights and block pan rail area and cylinder bottom areas is approximately 0.060 inch.

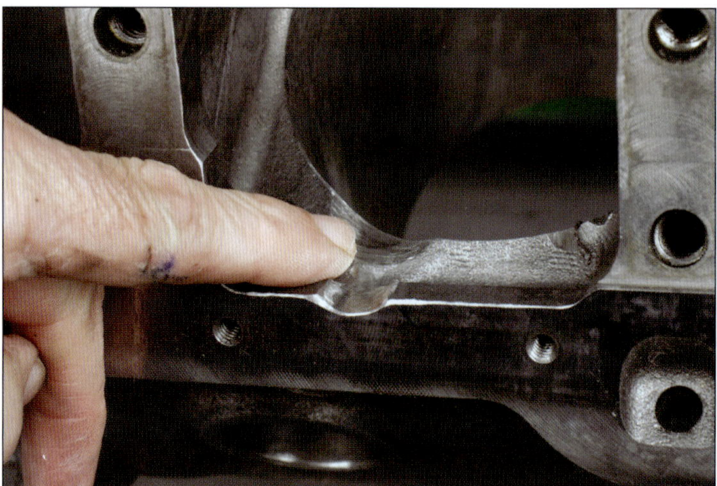

While the Dart block already featured starter reliefs for the rod's big end clearance, these required slight enlargement to gain sufficient clearance for our stroker crank and rod combo.

The crank is then checked for endplay. With all of the main caps loosened, the crank is knocked back and forth using a dead-blow hammer. This aids in squaring up the rear main cap where the thrust bearing is located. The caps are then fully torqued to 65 ft-lbs on all 7/16-inch nuts and 35 ft-lbs on the outer bolt location on the number 1 and 5 caps. A dial indicator with a magnetic base is attached to the block face. Using a flathead screwdriver, the crank is pushed forward to a gentle stop. The dial indicator gauge is then set at zero. The crank is then pushed rearward to a stop. This was repeated several times to verify the reading. In this case, our crank endplay was measured at 0.006 inch. Generally speaking, acceptable endplay should be in the range of 0.004 to 0.008 inch.

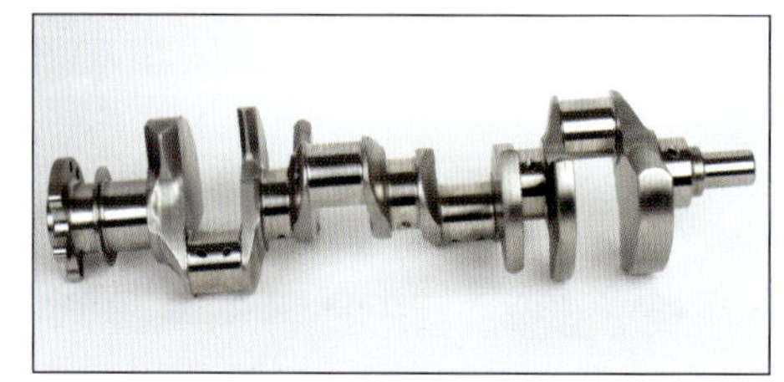

Our Scat forged lightweight crank features a 3.875-inch stroke and 2.100-inch rod journals.

The profiled Scat crank counterweights are radiused at the leading edges for more efficient dispersion of parasitic drag from oil cling.

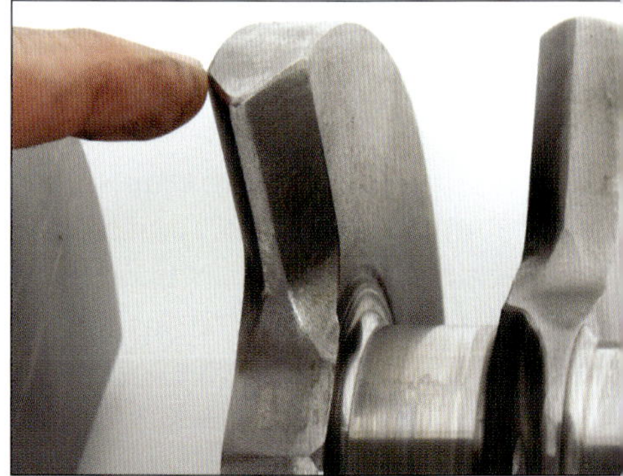

The trailing edge of each counterweight is knife edged to aid in slinging off parasitic oil. The bull-nosing of the leading edges and tapered knife edging of the trailing ends is similar to the profile of an airplane wing, creating a vortex at the trailing edge.

When it was installed with all bearings and main caps torqued, the crank end-play measured 0.006 inch.

After cleaning/wiping the cylinder bores, the pistons and rods were temporarily assembled along with a lightly oiled upper and lower rod bearing. The rods/pistons were then installed to each cylinder, and the rod caps were torqued lightly to about 20 ft-lbs. While slowly rotating the crank, we checked the rod's big end clearance at the pan rail and upper web areas. Not surprisingly, light contact at the outboard side of each cylinder location was found due to the increase in the crank stroke. This is nothing unusual. Clearancing is commonly required when a larger-than-stock stroke is used. All areas were marked. The rod and crank were removed, and the tight spots were easily relieved using a pneumatic die grinder and a milling bit. With the crank and checking rod reinstalled, clearance was again checked and verified at 0.080 to 0.100 inch.

At this point, the block was then initially cleaned in a jet wash, followed by a final and time-consuming cleaning using very hot water and Dawn dishwashing liquid. The block was scrubbed using a nylon bristle brush. All oil passages, lifter bores, and cylinder bores were washed using appropriately sized bristle rifle brushes from Goodson Tools & Supplies, which was followed by repeated rinsing and blowing with compressed air. Every oil passage was then carefully checked for flow at all main saddle to cam bore locations, all lifter oil passages, etc. Taking the time to thoroughly check eliminates any potential nasty surprises down the road. A cursory washing is simply not good enough. The only acceptable result is a block that is 100 percent clean and free of any and all foreign particles.

Once they had been cleaned, rinsed, and dry, exposed machine surfaces were lightly coated with WD-40 to prevent surface oxidation. The block's exterior surfaces were lightly coated with SEM self-etching primer to prevent unwanted surface rusting before painting.

Machined surfaces were then carefully masked, including the decks, pan rails, front timing cover, and water pump mounting surfaces, etc. Then, two coats of Seymour IMO industrial enamel paint in the IHC red color were applied. This paint is preferred as opposed to rattle-can engine paints, primarily because many of today's engine paints don't provide what we deem as acceptable coverage. While this industrial paint requires a longer drying period, the results are worth the extra time.

Crankshaft Balancing

Once block clearance was verified, we had the Scat crank balanced at Medina Mountain Motors in Creston, Ohio. Owner Jodi Holtrey first weighed all of the components to establish the correct bobweights. This included each rod's big end, small end, and total weight; one pair of rod bearings; a set of piston rings and the piston support rail; wrist pin and spiral pin locks; and each piston.

In the old days when OEM parts were used, it was commonly required to determine the lightest connecting rod to establish a baseline and then grind material from the remaining rods to obtain a set of equal weight. The same procedure was commonly required to match piston weights. Thankfully, today's high-quality aftermarket rods and pistons are so closely weight matched by the manufacturers that little or no corrections are necessary.

Our Scat H-beam rods weighed in with a tolerance range of a mere 0.7 grams, and our Icon pistons revealed a range of only 0.2 grams. While no machining corrections were needed, each rod and piston was matched and labeled to compensate for these small differences, mating lighter pistons to the heaver rods, resulting in a close-to-zero tolerance for these matched components. In this balance job, bobweights were set at 852.5 grams. Due to the light weight of our pistons and the weight-relieved Scat crank, Jodi was forced to add two small slugs of tungsten into the front and rear counterweights, with a 28-gram slug in the front counterweight and a 20-gram slug in the rear. Our final crank balance result was -0.9 gram in the front and -0.5 gram in the rear, which is within the ideal range.

While some may assume that it's necessary to obtain an absolute zero tolerance for the balance of the crankshaft, this simply is not necessary. This is because during engine operation oil will cling to and leave the crank and rods, fluctuating crank dynamic balance by a few grams, so obtaining crank balance to within 4 or 5 grams is more than adequate. Since our result was -0.9 and -0.5 gram, we were delighted. Bear in mind that a single US currency bill weighs 1 gram. With that in mind, it's easy to understand how only a few grams of out of balance is more than acceptable.

Our example balance job weights were recorded as follows (in grams):

Rod big end	429
Rod small end	186
Rod bearings (for one piston)	86
Piston	406
Piston pin	117
Piston pin locks (for one piston)	3
Rings and rail	41
Total	1,697
1/2 total	848.5
+ 4 g oil cling	852.5 grams

Once rods, pistons, pins, rings, rod bearings, and locks were weighed, bobweights were assembled and installed to the crank.

The crank spins on the balancer with bobweights installed. After correcting for the bobweights, the crank's static and dynamic balance was extremely close to zero thanks to the efforts of balancing whiz Jodi Holtrey of Medina Mountain Motors in Creston, Ohio.

Due to the lightweight pistons and the lightened crankshaft, a tungsten heavy metal slug was required in each of the end counterweights.

Our crank's final balance provided a -0.09 gram front and -0.05 gram rear weight differential, which is more than adequate.

Locating the heavy metal required cross drilling through the counterweights and reaming to size to provide an interference fit.

The Icon pistons weighed in at a mere 406 grams.

Block Plugs

Once all the machining of the Dart block was accomplished, the bare block was thoroughly washed. It was washed in a jet wash; handwashed using hot water, Dawn dishwashing liquid, and a series of bristle brushes from Goodson Tools & Supplies; rinsed thoroughly in hot water; and rinsed in cold water. An application of cold water helps to reduce surface rusting.

All surfaces, including all oil and cooling passages, were blown dry with clean compressed air. Cylinder walls, main saddles, decks, and lifter bores were lightly coated with WD-40 to prevent surface rust.

All block plugs were installed. Water jacket plugs involved ten $1^5/8$-inch brass expansion plugs, one 2.215-inch rear cam bore expansion plug, ten 1/4-inch NPT threaded plugs, and one 1/8-inch NPT plug. Expansion plugs were treated to a thin film of RTV on the outer contact surfaces before installation. All NPT plugs, were coated with Permatex Teflon pipe sealant. Before installing the freeze/expansion plugs, a thin film of RTV was applied to each plug hole. The RTV provides additional insurance against tiny leaks and provides a lubricant for easier plug installation.

Oil plugs include three 1/4-inch NPT at the block front, three 1/4-inch NPT at the block rear, one 1/4-inch NPT above the oil filter housing, one 1/4-inch NPT at each water jacket hole on the block sides, one 1/4-inch NPT, and one 1/8-inch NPT at the front of the lifter valley. The top rear oil sender hole just behind the block's rear intake rail is threaded for a 1/8-inch NPT oil pressure sender.

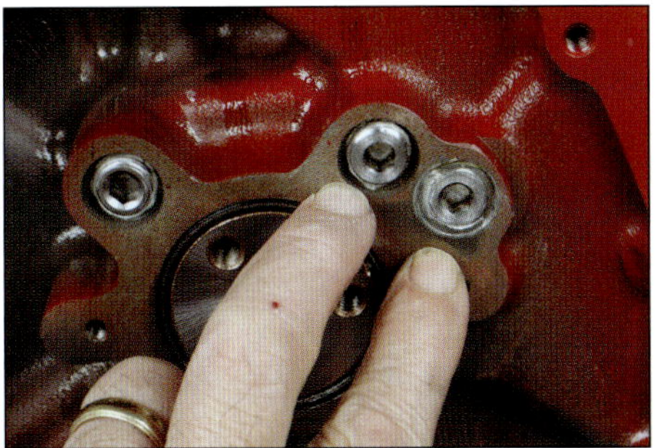

The front three oil gallery plugs must be installed flush or below flush to clear the Jesel belt drive cover plate. This needs to be verified before the block is final washed. Tapping the 1/4-inch NPT threads a bit deeper is usually all that's needed if they protrude. I also shaved two of the plugs on my lathe to obtain a flush fit.

Cam and Bearings

The Dart SHP Pro Iron block features a big-block Chevy cam bore. The correct cam bearings are provided with the block, Dart part number 32210010 (2.120 inches). All five cam bearings are the same size, so there is no specific bore location requirement because all of the cam journals are the same diameter. These bearings are anti-friction coated and feature three oil holes

At the front of the lifter valley are two NPT holes that must be plugged. The hole on the right side accepts a 1/4-inch NPT plug, while the hole on the left side requires a 1/8-inch NPT plug.

and a continuous oil groove on the outside diameter.

When installed, make sure that one of the bearing oil holes aligns with the oil feed holes at the upper main saddles. With the bearings installed, the cam was inserted to verify fitment with our cam rolling effortlessly like hot butter. After the cam was gently removed, all journals and lobes were liberally coated with Royal Purple Max-Tuff assembly lube and carefully reinserted.

The camshaft of choice for this build is Comp's billet roller (part number 12-000-11). Lobe lift is 0.432 inch for the intake and 0.430 inch for the exhaust. With our use of 1.6:1 Jesel roller rockers, our effective valve lift is a 0.648-inch intake and 0.645-inch exhaust. Duration at 0.50 inch of travel is 263 degrees intake and 272 degrees exhaust. While the intake centerline is 108 degrees at straight-up zero timing, we advanced the cam by 2 degrees to achieve an intake centerline of 104 degrees for a bit more low/mid-range torque.

Once the Dart moly-coated cam bearings were installed and checked for cam fitment, our Comp Cams billet roller cam was carefully inserted with its journals and lobes coated in Royal Purple max Tuff assembly lube.

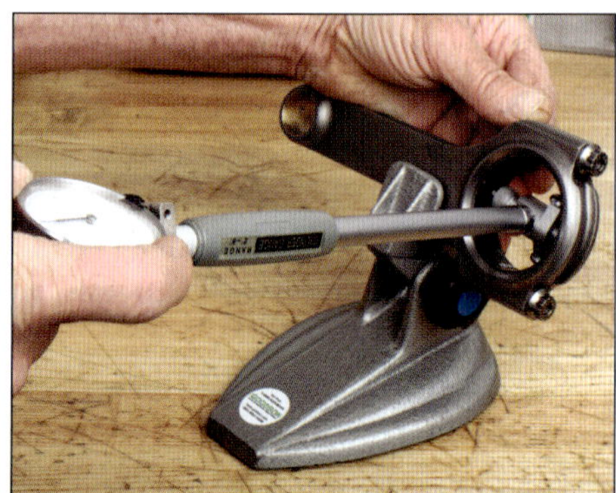

Never assume that crank journals are correctly sized. Our check of the finely finished Scat forged crank revealed an exact 2.450-inch diameter on all five main journals with no taper.

Bearing Clearance

It's critical to achieve proper main and rod bearing oil clearance. A general rule of thumb is 0.001-inch clearance for every inch of journal diameter.

In our application, our Scat crankshaft features main bearing journals with a 2.4500-inch diameter and rod journals with a 2.100-inch diameter. Plastigauge compressible plastic wire can provide a close approximation of clearance. For example, when checking main bearing clearance, lay a short piece of Plastigauge on the journal oriented front-to-rear. Apply oil to the bearing face and install the bearing-equipped cap to the block and torque it to specification. Remove the cap and check the crushed width of the Plastigauge using the index on the Plastigauge wrapper.

However, to obtain a much more accurate clearance measurement, measure the journal diameter with a calibrated micrometer and record that dimension. Install the upper main bearing to the block's saddle, install the lower bearing to the main cap, and install and fully torque the main cap. Adjust a bore gauge to match the journal's diameter. Insert the bore gauge onto the installed bearings and note the difference. In our case, the main journals measured

2.4500 inches. With our micrometer set at 2.4500 inches, a bore gauge was set up to that distance, zeroing the gauge to provide our reference of 2.4500 inches. Inserting the bore gauge to the installed main bearings showed a difference (from our gauge zero) of 0.0025 inch greater than zero, indicating that our oil clearance is 0.0025 inch.

Follow the same procedure for the rod bearings by installing the rod bearings to the rod and rod cap and fully torquing the rod bolts. In our case, our crankshaft's rod journals measured 2.100 inches. Initial checking with Mahle Clevite CB663HN standard upper and lower bearings revealed an oil clearance of 0.002 inch. I prefer to allow a slightly looser rod bearing clearance, so I ended up using a mix of a standard bearing shell in the upper location and an X bearing shell in the lower position, Mahle Clevite CB663HXN, which provided an oil clearance of 0.0025 inch.

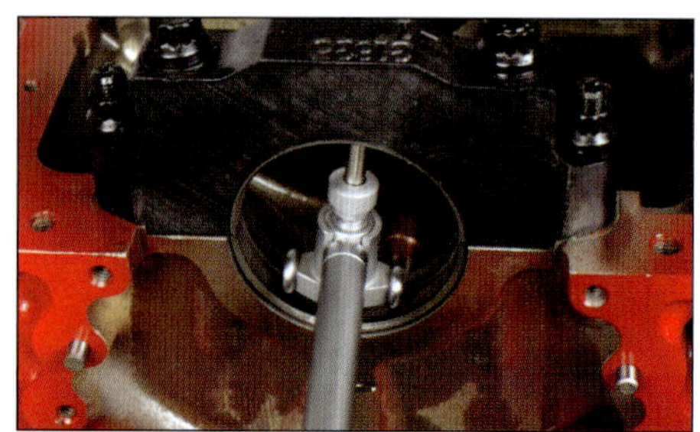

With standard upper and lower rod bearings installed to the rods and with the rod bolts fully torqued, the initial measured rod bearing oil clearance was 0.002 inch. With an engine intended to see high revs, we like our rod bearing clearance a touch on the loose side. To accomplish this, standard bearings were installed in the upper position with 1X bearings in the lower cap locations. Using a 1X bearing shell in combination provided an additional 0.0005 inch of rod bearing oil clearance for a final clearance of 0.0025 inch.

With a bore gauge indexed and zeroed to the micrometer that was used to measure the main journal diameter, our main bores, with bearings installed, revealed an acceptable 0.0025-inch oil clearance, which is exactly what we wanted.

The rod journals also measured exactly on spec at 2.100 inches.

Mixing rod bearing thicknesses to achieve the desired bearing clearance is an accepted practice. In this build, the standard thickness upper rod bearings were installed and mated with 0.001-inch undersize lower bearings. Shown here is a lower 1X bearing.

Shown here is a standard bearing installed to the upper position. The X designates the undersize. By using a standard bearing along with a 1X upper bearing, oil clearance is increased by 0.0005 inch.

By the way, there's nothing wrong with mixing standard thickness and X undersize bearings on the same rod. By using a standard bearing mated with an X bearing, you gain 0.0005-inch of additional oil clearance. With X bearings at both upper and lower locations, you'd gain an additional 0.001-inch clearance. When bearings are mixed on the same rod, some builders prefer to install the thicker standard bearing shell in the upper rod saddle and the X bearing shell in the lower cap location. It really doesn't matter as long as you are consistent on all of the rods. Mixing bearing thickness is a common practice among racing engine builders to fine-tune oil clearance. In this build, the standard bearings were placed in the lower locations and the X bearings were placed in the upper cap locations.

A dial indicator is then positioned at the front of the crank. Using a clean flathead screwdriver, the crank is pushed rearward. The dial indicator gauge is then set to zero. The crank was then pushed forward, noting crank thrust. This check was performed several times to verify thrust movement. Our recorded crank thrust was measured at 0.006 inch, which was within our desired range of 0.005 to 0.008 inch.

Once crank thrust was determined, the crankshaft was rotated to check for rolling resistance. We were able to easily rotate the crank with one hand. If the crank resists turning easily, carefully check to make sure that all main caps are in their correct positions and orientation.

The main caps and crankshaft were then removed. All main bearings were cleaned again, removing all of the oil film. Royal Purple Max-Tuff assembly lube was then applied to all main bearing exposed surfaces, including the thrust shoulders on the number five rear main bearing.

Our block and crank are designed to accept a two-piece rear main seal. The upper half of the rear seal was installed into the block's seal groove, making sure that the angled lip of the seal faced toward the front of the block. The upper seal was installed slightly cocked with one end protruding out about 1/8 inch. The lower seal was installed to the rear main cap with its opposing end protruding out of the cap by the same amount (about 1/8 inch). This allows a seal-to-seal mating above and below the main cap to block parting line, helping to protect against a potential oil leak.

The crankshaft was then carefully installed, followed by the main caps. Before installing the rear main cap, a small bead of RTV (about 1/8-inch wide) was applied to the block's inner corners where the main cap seats against the block. Main cap fasteners were again tightened in stages, knocking the crank fore and aft once the main caps were initially seated. The main caps were finalized at 65 ft-lb. The crank was again checked for freedom of rotation.

Crankshaft Installation

All main caps on the Dart SHP Pro Iron block feature 4-bolt clamping. All 7/16-inch fasteners are torqued to 65 ft-lbs, while the outboard 3/8-inch fasteners on cap numbers 1 and 5 are torqued to 35 ft-lbs. Our block features main cap studs. The studs are installed to the block finger tight. The washers, fine threads and nut undersides are lubed with CMD lube. Never torque the studs to the block. The clamping load is achieved as the nuts are tightened.

Make sure that all bearing saddles are dry. Install the upper main bearings, then apply assembly lubricant to the exposed bearing surfaces. Note: Apply lube to the thrust surfaces of the number 5 bearing before installing the thrust bearing because access to the rear thrust face is difficult after the bearing is installed.

Once all upper main bearings are in place, apply a coat of assembly lube. I prefer Royal Purple Max-Tuff synthetic assembly lube, but there are several excellent assembly lubricants available.

Install the lower main bearings to the main caps and lube the exposed bearing surfaces. Install the upper rear main seal to the block, making sure that the lip faces forward. Install the seal cocked in its groove with one side about 3/8-inch below flush and the opposite side the same distance above the cap mating surface. Install the lower seal into the number 5 cap in an opposite clock position. This allows the seal halves to meet above and below the mating surfaces, eliminating the chance of oil seeping between the seal haves and leaking out. Lightly oil the seal lips before installation. Note that this build features an external vacuum pump that pulls about 15 inches of vacuum in the crankcase. While a standard rear main seal should suffice, some recommend a seal that is specifically designed for high-vacuum applications. In this build, we used Fel-Pro 2912 rear seal.

Note: Before installing the crankshaft, make absolutely sure that the crank is clean. Run a fast-drying

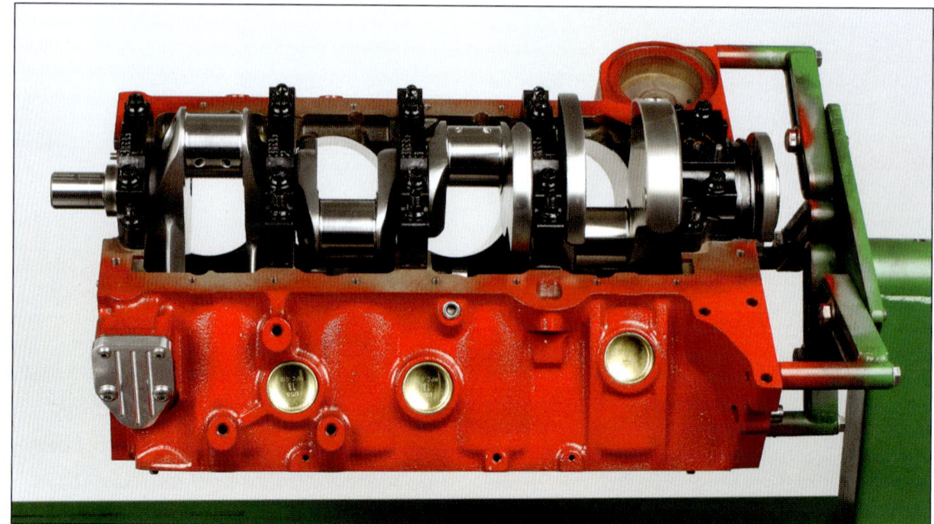

With the crank fully installed and main bearings lubed with Royal Purple Max-Tuff assembly lube, the main cap stud nuts were torqued in three progressive steps to 65 ft-lbs. Thanks to Dart's accurate align boring and Scat's precision machining of the crank, it rolled like butter and was easy to turn with two fingers on the snout.

solvent through all of the journal oil passages, run a clean, soft brush through all passages, and blow it with compressed air. While the shop that balanced the crank should have cleaned it, never assume. Make absolutely certain that there is no debris trapped in the oil passages. Wipe and inspect all journal surfaces.

Carefully lay the crank onto the upper main bearings. Avoid nicking the journals on the main saddle edges. Install the main caps and torque the main cap fasteners in stages: at the 7/16-inch fasteners, start at 20 ft-lbs, then 35 ft-lbs, then 45 ft-lbs, and finish at 65 ft-lbs. The 3/8-inch fasteners at the outboard locations on the number 1 and 5 caps are torqued to 35 ft-lbs. If using main cap bolts, apply a high-pressure assembly lube, such as CMD or ARP, on the bolt threads and to the underside of the bolt heads. If using main cap studs, apply lube to the exposed fine threads and to the underside of the nuts.

Although we checked crankshaft endplay previously during test fitting, once the main caps were fully torqued, we checked again to verify. Our endplay was confirmed at our previous measurement of 0.006 inch.

Once the cam and crank have been installed, the cam timing system was installed using a Jesel belt drive system.

Jesel Belt Drive

While the use of a timing chain set is certainly adequate, for this build we opted for a belt drive system from Jesel. A belt drive offers increased cam timing accuracy and minimizes the transference of crankshaft harmonics to the cam and valvetrain because the toothed belt absorbs vibrational frequencies, providing increased ignition timing stability. The belt drive system features a machined aluminum base cover that seals against the block, allowing the belt and sprockets to run exposed.

The belt drive mounting base attaches to the block with ten 1/4-20 fasteners. Instead of using the supplied socket head cap screws, a set of ARP studs (part number 334-1401) is available. These are specifically designed for use with a Jesel belt drive plate. The use of studs provides additional installation ease, providing 10 fixed mounting points to allow easier alignment of the base plate onto the block.

Depending on the race application and if driving will take place on paved surfaces where dirt is at a minimum, the belt and gears are exposed, making it easier to adjust cam timing. For abrasive operating environments, such as dirt/off-road, a dust cover is available to prevent debris from contaminating the system. Note that wet belt drives are also available, installed and sealed off with an outer cover similar to the installation of a chain drive. Specially formulated belts are used in a wet system. Dry belt systems are more commonly used in racing applications.

Belt drives are available for a wide variety of popular engine applications. Citing small- and big-block Chevy engines as examples, drive kits are offered for the standard cam height or raised-cam height, and crank gears are offered for either crankshafts that feature standard small-block snouts or small-block cranks that feature beefier big-block snouts. Note that belt drives are also available that incorporate a belt idler pulley for those who feel the need for this enhancement.

Before starting to install the system, the machined mounting plate should first be test fitted to the block to verify that it mates flush. Depending on the aftermarket block at hand, slight interference may be found in one or more spots that may require relieving of the block. Obviously, all

With the cam in place, a Fel-Pro gasket is installed to the block. I lightly coated each side of the gasket with Permatex Ultra Black RTV, locating the gasket to the block's two dowel pins.

The Jesel cover plate is then installed with the supplied socket-head cap screws. This seals off oil with the exposed belt running dry.

While there's nothing wrong with using a chain drive, we opted for a Jesel cam belt drive. This provides superior timing event accuracy. The kit includes everything required for installation, including the cover plate, which seals to the block, a cam nose adapter, an upper spider plate and cam pulley, a crank pulley, toothed belt, cam thrust shims, and cam endplay shims.

test fitting must be done before the block is final washed. Also, make sure that any NPT plugs that seal off oil passages on the front of the block are threaded deep enough to avoid contact with the mounting plate.

During our build, two of the 3/8-inch NPT plugs at the front of the block protruded a bit, so the plug faces were shaved down on a lathe, removing about 0.040 inch to properly clear the belt drive base plate. Once a flush mounting is verified, the mounting plate is secured to the block using an OEM-type gasket and a thin layer of RTV, securing the ten 1/4-20 socket head cap screws at a final 96 in-lbs.

An alternative is to install ARP studs (part number 334-1401), which provides additional ease of mounting because the studs offer guides for plate positioning. Note that some builders prefer to eliminate the cut gasket and use only RTV to seal the plate to the block, feeling that this provides better consistency in terms of plate-to-block angle, wherein a gasket might vary somewhat in terms of thickness when clamped, which can affect the angle of the plate relative to the belt pulleys.

Note: If the block has been line bored, a misalignment may be encountered between the crank seal and crank snout. If so, the dowel pin holes in the mounting cover may be enlarged. Loosely install the cover bolts before driving the crank pulley gear into place. During installation of the crank pulley, this will ensure that the crank seal is centered around the crank snout.

The kit includes two bronze thrust washers for the cam. Note that these are supplied in two different sizes. The rear bronze thrust washer is lightly lubricated on both sides and installed onto the step of the camshaft snout. This thrust washer measures 2.950 inches in outer diameter with a 1.880-inch inside diameter at a thickness of 0.031 inch. This is followed by installing the cam nose adapter.

For sealing purposes, a thin coat of RTV is applied to the rear recessed face of the adapter where it meets the cam nose face. The adapter secures to the camshaft nose with three Torx-drive 5/16–18 x 3/4-inch socket-head cap screws. Apply RTV to the screw threads; install and torque them to 26 ft-lbs. A Jesel spanner wrench (TOL-39260) is available to hold the cam while tightening these screws. Use a T-45 Torx bit to tighten the screws.

The Jesel kit includes two bronze thrust washers. The washer with the smaller ID installs to the step on the camshaft nose. The larger-ID washer will install to the front of the cam adapter.

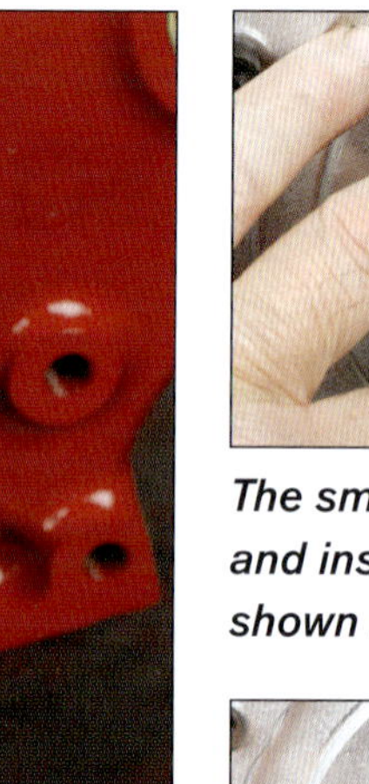

The smaller-ID thrust washer is lubed and installed to the cam nose as shown here.

The cam adapter secures to the cam with three Torx-drive screws. To hold the adapter and cam in place during tightening, Jesel offers a spanner tool. The two round heads of the tool engage into the recessed holes in the adapter. Note that the larger-ID bronze thrust washer is installed to the front perimeter of the adapter.

Before installing the cam adapter to the cam, apply a light coating of RTV to the rear recess area of the adapter. This provides additional insurance against potential oil leaks.

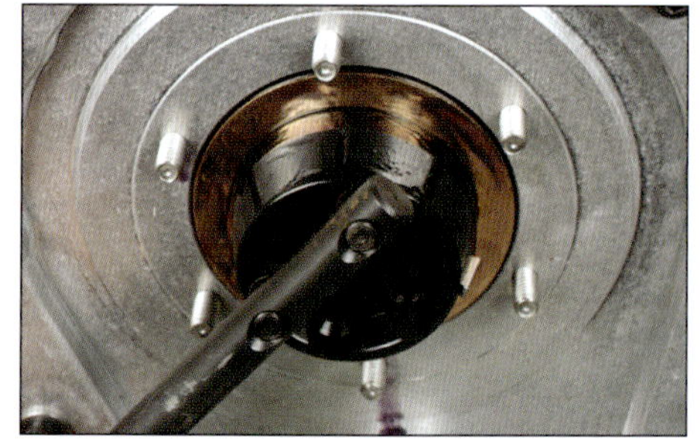

The 5/16-inch Torx-drive screws are tightened to 26 ft-lbs while using the tool to hold the cam from rotating.

Next, the outer bronze thrust washer is installed to the outside perimeter face of the adapter. This outer thrust washer has a 2.950-inch outer diameter x 2.260-inch inside diameter x 0.031-inch thickness. Oil both sides of the thrust washer before installing it.

Next, locate the three camshaft thrust shims. These feature a series of six holes that mount to the studs on the base cover. The three shims feature thicknesses of 0.010, 0.015, and 0.020 inch. Initially install all three shims dry with no oil or sealant. Then, install the cam thrust plate that features a built-in seal. The thrust plate features six holes that slip over the baseplate's studs. Be careful not to nick the seal when installing it to get it past the small key on the cam adapter. A safer method is to simply pop the key out of the cam adapter and reinstall it once the thrust plate has been installed for the final time. Secure it with six 14-20 nyloc jam nuts torqued to 96 in-lbs.

With all three shims in place, check camshaft endplay by installing a dial indicator that contacts the face of the camshaft adapter. When setting it up, preload the indicator by about 0.050 inch to ensure adequate movement range of the indicator probe. By carefully prying on the camshaft from the lifter valley drain hole access or through a lifter bore, carefully move the cam fully rearward. Next, zero the dial indicator gauge. Then, move the cam fully forward and note the distance on the indicator.

Adjust the endplay by removing select shim(s) until cam endplay is between 0.006 and 0.012 inch. When using a roller cam, adjust to the tighter side of the specification range. Minimizing camshaft endplay obviously has a positive effect with regard to roller lifter life. Preventing the camshaft from thrusting front-to-rear keeps the lifter rollers from side loading on the roller bearings. In this sample build, only the 0.015- and 0.020-inch-thick shims were used, eliminating the 0.010-inch shim, which resulted in cam endplay of 0.006 inch.

To adjust camshaft endplay, Jesel provides three shims at 0.010-, 0.015-, and 0.020-inch thickness.

Here all three shims are installed onto the six cover plate studs. Note the key on the adapter. This can interfere with the retaining plate's seal. It's best to remove this key until the shim package has been finalized.

The retaining plate slips onto the six studs and captures the shims. This retainer features a seal that must be kept dry during installation. Do not lubricate this seal.

During test fitting, install all three shims for the initial camshaft endplay measurement. After measuring each shim thickness, mark each for easy identification.

Once shims were finalized, the retainer plate nuts were torqued to 96 in-lbs and the key was reinstalled to the cam adapter.

Note that the key in the cam adapter has been removed. This avoids accidentally nicking the retainer plate seal. With all three shims installed, the retainer plate secured, and a dial indicator contacting the adapter, move the cam back and forth to determine existing cam endplay. We finalized ours at 0.006 inch by using only the 0.015- and 0.020-inch shims.

A retaining washer and bolt are then installed to the center of the cam adapter, securing the spider. Note that this 7/16-inch bolt features a left-hand thread. This bolt is tightened to 70 ft-lbs.

Once the cam endplay procedure is finished, the cam pulley is attached to the spider with the cam pulley's four studs protruding outward. Engage the spider to the cam adapter by aligning the adapter's key to the spider keyway and install the left-hand-thread center bolt and washer.

Once the shims required are established, remove the thrust plate and the shims. Lightly coat between the shims with RTV. Reassemble them using the supplied 1/4-inch x 20 nyloc jam nuts, tightening these to 96 in-lbs. Note: Do not oil the cam thrust plate's seal. This is a Teflon seal and must be installed dry.

Next, the crank gear drive pulley is installed, registering onto the crank snout's keys. Installing the crank pulley is an interference fit, requiring an aluminum driver, which is available from Jesel (part number TOL-39310), or you can make your own driver. Starting with solid bar stock of 2.400- to 2.500-inch OD and an overall length of 4.500 inches, turn the OD down to 2.372 inches and bore a hole in one end at an inside diameter of 1.872 inches at a depth of 2.500 inches. A slight step-down should be cut at the outside diameter of the hollow entrance end at an outside diameter of 2.310 inches. Make the length of this step cut 0.800 inch.

If you opt to fabricate your own aluminum driver, the dimensions are as follows. The example here applies to a standard-length Chevy crank snout:

Outside diameter	2.372 inches
Overall length	4.500 inches
Inside diameter	1.872 inches
Depth of inside	2.500 inches
Step-down OD at hollow end	2.310 inches
Step-down length from end	0.800 inch

The crank pulley features an interference fit. Align the pulley keyway to the snout key, and using an aluminum driver, such as the Jesel tool shown here, and a dead-blow hammer, tap the pulley onto the crank snout until it bottoms out against the crank snout fillet.

Do not lubricate the cover housing's crank snout seal. This is also a Teflon seal that must be installed dry. Coat the crank snout with anti-seize paste. Apply a thin layer of RTV to the inner chamfer of the crank pulley to prevent potential oil seepage. Align the crank pulley's keyway with the crank snout keys. The aluminum driver tool mates flush with the crank gear and allows tapping the gear into place with a dead-blow hammer. Drive the crank pulley fully onto the crank snout until it dead-stops.

The Jesel aluminum driver aids in installing the press-fit crank pulley. This is readily available, but if you opt to make your own, all that is needed is a chunk of bar stock and a lathe.

The belt drive has been installed. In this photo, the cam is positioned in the straight-up zero location. Note the timing mark at the top of the spider is at zero.

The bottom of the cam pulley features a dot that aligns with the small dot on the top of the crank pulley.

This closeup shows the timing mark on the cam pulley that is aligned with the zero mark on the spider. Each mark on the spider represents 2 degrees, allowing advance or retard as needed. To adjust cam timing, loosen the four nuts that secure the cam pulley to the spider, rotate the cam pulley, and retighten the nuts to 22 ft-lbs.

Rotate the crankshaft to position the number-1 cylinder at top dead center (TDC). Rotate the camshaft to position the key on the cam adapter at the 12 o'clock position.

Install the camshaft's aluminum pulley spider into the camshaft pulley. Align the timing marks on the spider with the timing line on the cam pulley. Loosely install the 7/16-inch left-hand-thread cam bolt and retaining washer. Install and hand-tighten the four 5/16–20 12-point flanged nuts. Carefully tilt the top of the camshaft pulley down and slide the toothed drive belt onto the two pulleys. Make sure the spider keyway is engaged onto the cam adapter's key.

Installing the belt is a tight fit, so exercise patience. Note that you need to align the spider with the cam pulley by aligning the thin white line, located on the underside of the cam pulley edge, with the zero mark on the spider. Remember that the cam bolt features a left-hand thread, so turn counterclockwise to tighten.

Once the timing belt is in place with both dots aligned with the cam gear dot at 6 o'clock, the crank gear dot at 12 o'clock, and the cam adjuster marks set at zero, tighten the cam gear's center left-hand-thread bolt to 70 ft-lbs. Note that the timing dot on the crank pulley is a very small black dot and is not highlighted in white. The white dot on the cam pulley is very visible. A 12-point 5/8-inch socket is needed for the cam center bolt, and the crankshaft needs to be held in place during bolt tightening. Now, you're ready to degree the cam.

Once the cam timing is adjusted, using a 3/8-inch 12-point wrench, tighten the four cam pulley nuts to 26 ft-lbs. Rotate the crankshaft two full turns, verifying that the timing marks are repeated.

Cam timing adjustments are performed by loosening the four nuts on the spider. Turn the crankshaft clockwise to retard the camshaft or counterclockwise to advance. Each mark on the spider gear equal two degrees at the crankshaft.

If the belt needs to be cleaned, do not use solvents. Wash it with soap and water only.

Dry Belt Care

Replace the belt if it ever gets contaminated with engine oil or harsh chemicals, such as gasoline, brake cleaner, etc. Belt replacement is recommended every other year for street/strip use, every 200 passes on the dragstrip, or annually if the vehicle is used in circle track applications.

Notice that the Jesel belt drive is exposed. With the water pump removed, adjustment for cam timing is readily accessible. If the vehicle is planned to run in a dirty environment, a dust cover, which is available from Jesel, is highly recommended.

Belt Drive Fastener Torque

Using a small-block Chevy as an example:

Upper (cam) pulley nuts	22 ft-lbs	Cam seal thrust plate nut	96 in-lbs
1/4–20 front cover bolts	96 in-lbs	7/16–20 left-hand cam bolt	70 ft-lbs
		5/16–18 cam adapter bolts	26 ft-lbs

Crank Balancer Installation

OEM crankshaft balancers feature a two-piece construction with an elastomeric (rubber) cushion ring to help absorb vibration harmonics. The OEM units are not well balanced, and the rubber tends to dry out and crack over time. For any performance build, don't even consider it. Spend the extra dough and buy an aftermarket balancer that features a viscous material inside that serves to balance dynamically and absorbs harmonics, such as Fluidampr or ATI Performance Products, to mention two examples.

Installing a balancer requires drawing it onto the crank snout slowly and evenly. Under no circumstances should you strike the balancer. Leave the hammer in the drawer. The fit will involve a slight interference of 0.001 to 0.003 inch, depending on the manufacturer and application.

Our example build uses a Fluidampr 6.25-inch balancer that features timing marks. Our Scat crank snout OD measured 1.2465 inches, and our Fluidampr bore measured 1.2445 inches, providing us with a very nice 0.002-inch press fit. Always measure, as it's possible that a manufacture's crank snout and/or balancer bore may provide a variable that will result in an excessive interference fit. If the fit is too tight, although balancer makers advise not to modify, many builders tend to gently hone the balancer bore to achieve the specified fit. Also make sure to

The balancer chosen for this build is a 6.25-inch unit from Fluidampr, featuring a special internal fluid that self-balances the unit during rotation.

Apply anti-seize paste to the crank snout OD and to the ID of the balancer and start the balancer to the crank by aligning the keyway to the crank key. With the mandrel tip threaded into the crank snout, the plate is set flush to the face of the balancer. While holding the rear end of the mandrel steady with a wrench, the mandrel nut is turned clockwise to smoothly draw the balancer fully onto the crank. Our interference fit was just under 0.003 inch, which provided a secure fit and relatively easy installation. Never attempt to install a balancer by striking it with a hammer.

measure the installed height and width of the crank snout keys as well as the keyway in the balancer bore to verify clearance.

To draw the crank balancer onto the crank snout, a Moroso balancer installer tool is used. A 7/16–20 adapter from the kit is installed to the tool mandrel. This will engage into the crank snout threads.

The Fluidampr balancer is shown fully installed, bottoming out against the Jesel crank pulley.

Once clearances have been determined, coat the crank snout and the balancer bore with a high-quality anti-seize compound. Align the balancer to the crank snout, initially engaging the key. Use a balancer installation tool, such as the Moroso 61743 puller/installer kit shown.

Install the appropriate-size threaded adapter to the tool's threaded mandrel.

In the case of a small-block Chevy, this is the adapter that features a 7/16–20 thread. Apply oil or assembly lube to the adapter threads before assembly to prevent galling. Also lube the mandrel's threads and install the pusher nut onto the threaded mandrel. Insert the mandrel into the pusher plate with the flat side of the plate facing you. Screw the mandrel into the crank snout with the 7/16-inch adapter engaging the crank snout threads. The plate features a built-in bearing that the driver nut seats against.

While holding the hex at the exposed end of the mandrel steady using a 5/8-inch wrench, use a $1^{1}/_{16}$ open-end wrench to turn the driver nut clockwise. This pushes the balancer onto the crank snout. Make sure that the balancer is square to the snout. Avoid any angles that would result in galling the crank snout. Draw the balancer fully into place until it dead-stops against the crank gear, or in this case, the Jesel belt drive crank pulley. Remove the tool. If the 7/16-inch adapter happens to remain in the crank snout, this is easily removed using a flathead screwdriver because the adapter features a slot at each end.

Piston and Rod Installation

Always check the piston ring end gap. In this build, our rings provided with the Icon pistons require a file fit. Their specification calls for a gap of bore diameter x 0.0045 inch. In our case, this calls for a gap of 0.0187 inch. Using a Summit Racing ring filer equipped with a diamond wheel, all top and second rings were carefully filed to achieve a snug end gap of 0.019 inch.

Once rings were file fit, the filed edges were carefully deburred using a small fine flat file and thoroughly cleaned. When checking ring end gap, insert the ring into a clean bore and square the ring at a depth of about 3/4 to 1 inch, using a ring squaring tool that pushes the ring down evenly. The entire ring circumference must be set at an equal depth in the cylinder to obtain an accurate gap measurement.

When filing, don't get carried away by removing too much material. It's better to creep up on the desired gap. Repeating the filing and checking process may take some time, but it beats ruining the rings and buying another set.

The cylinder walls must be meticulously cleaned with a fast-drying solvent and a lint-free towel and then lubricated before piston installation. When I say clean, I mean *clean*. Keep wiping with fresh lint-free towels until absolutely no residue if found on the towel, regardless of how long it takes.

Avoid using a synthetic lube because this can prove to be too slippery and can prevent the piston rings from properly breaking in and seating when the engine is running. Instead of coating the cylinder walls and drowning the ring package in 30W oil, we lightly coated the cylinder walls with Akerly & Childs Xtreme engine assembly lubricant. While there are a number of lubricants that are acceptable, we've favored this lube in recent years. Using the same lube, we applied this to the ring grooves and rings before

Pistons are secured to the rods with full-floating pins. A single spiral lock is installed at each end of the pins.

The pistons and rods are ready for rings and bearings. Each rod and piston assembly was fitted to a specific cylinder with the bearing clearance and ring gap fitted per cylinder.

Piston rings are organized here on a per-cylinder basis. The top rings and second rings were file fit to a gap of 0.019 inch.

installing the rings. This provides enough lubrication for the rings without the need to make an oily mess during piston installation.

Since our pistons feature a fairly short CD, the oil ring groove intersects the piston wrist pin bore. To provide a stable floor for the oil ring package, a support ring is installed first at the base of the oil ring groove. Support rings feature a small male dot that must be oriented facing down and positioned directly above one of the pin bores. This dot prevents the support ring from rotating out of position, preventing its end gap from moving into the pin bore area. This is followed by the installation of the oil ring package, the second ring and the top compression ring. All ring end gaps must be clocked well away from each other to prevent end gap alignment.

Install the rod bearings. Examine each rod bearing carefully because these will be marked for position (upper and lower). The upper bearing shell installs to the rod saddle, while the lower bearing shell installs to the rod cap. The rod saddle and cap must be clean and dry. Do not apply lube between the bearings and their saddles.

Align the assembly tang of each bearing shell to the assembly notch on the rod and cap. Push the bearing shells into place fully with each end flush with the cap parting line. Apply a coat of assembly lube to the exposed bearing surfaces. A variety of lubes are acceptable, but my favorite is Royal Purple's Max-Tuff assembly lube. This is a synthetic lube that is thick, coats well, and has great cling, so it won't dry or drain off if the assembled engine isn't started for an extended period. It's also extremely slippery, making it great for bearing use. While it's great for bearings, do not use this on the cylinder walls because it's too slippery to achieve piston ring seating.

To install the pistons, the rings must be compressed to a point just slightly smaller in diameter than the bores. While several types of ring compressors are available, by

Our valve reliefs and dome flat surfaces were finely finished by Icon, requiring no additional deburring of relief pocket edges.

Our Icon forged pistons feature a relatively short skirt and lightweight construction while maintaining strength. The skirts are moly coated to provide both oil retention and reduced friction. Note the dot on the skirt. This dot on each skirt provides the skirt diameter measuring points. Due to diameter and barrel shape of a given piston, the manufacturer will indicate where skirt diameter must be measured.

Due to the short compression height of the pistons at 1.062 inches, the wrist pin bore intersects with the oil ring groove. A support rail is installed at the base of the oil ring land to complete the floor for the oil ring at each end of the pin bore. A male dimple on the support rail is positioned in one of the openings. This prevents the support rail from rotating too far, ensuring that the rail gap does not reach the open area.

far the best approach is to use a dedicated-size billet ring compressor that features a tapered inner wall. Insert the rod and piston through the compressor until it captures the ring packages. Align the rod's big end so that the chamfered side of the big end faces the appropriate fillet on the crankshaft's rod journal.

With the piston ring compressor held flush against the block deck, push the piston into its bore. When used correctly, you should be able to push the piston in with thumb pressure only and without the need to tap the piston with a hammer. If you must assist entry, use only very light tapping with a clean plastic piston hammer. If you feel the need to apply hard hits, stop and recheck.

Once the ring package has fully entered the bore, remove the compressor. Push the piston down while guiding the rod's big end carefully onto the rod journal to avoid nicking the journal. Once the upper bearing of the rod's big end makes contact with the journal, install the rod cap with the lower bearing and install the rod bolts.

Rod Bolts

For performance applications, always use high-quality aftermarket rod bolts, such as those made by ARP. When installing rod bolts, carefully follow the rod bolt or connecting rod maker's instructions. You have two choices when tightening rod bolts: by following the recommended torque value or by monitoring rod bolt stretch. It's important to understand that any high-tensile bolt stretches when a proper clamping load is achieved. The elastomeric stretch range is critical.

If there isn't enough stretch, a proper clamping load won't be achieved. If the bolt is stretched beyond its safe elastic range, the bolt will be overstretched and will weaken, unable to hold the clamping load. In simple terms, view the rod bolt as a rubber band. It needs to stretch to a specific range but not beyond. Monitoring rod bolt stretch offers a more precise method of determining clamping load as opposed to only monitoring torque. When you rely only on a torque application, you're trying to overcome frictional factors, such as thread friction and the bolt's underhead to the rod cap friction. By monitoring bolt stretch, the potential variables of friction are eliminated.

When a set of aftermarket performance rods is purchased, they will be equipped with high tensile strength rod bolts. The rod maker will provide a specification sheet with a recommended torque value and the maximum allowable bolt stretch based on bolt diameter and shank length. If you opt to tighten using a torque value, there will usually be two different recommended torque values based on the type of bolt lubricant used (oil or a specific high-pressure assembly lubricant, such as ARP bolt lube, CMD, etc.).

A torque value for oil differs from a torque value if a high-pressure lube is used. If a specific high-pressure lube is used, the torque value recommendation will be slightly lower than with oil because the special lube will reduce friction. Pay attention to this because the choice of lubricant wlll affect the torque value. It's best to use the lube that the rod and/or rod bolt maker specifies.

Regardless of the tightening method (torque or stretch), a quality lube must be applied to bolt threads and to the underside of the bolt head to reduce friction and prevent galling.

Tightening rod bolts with the stretch method is very simple, although admittedly more time consuming compared to tightening to the torque value alone. To tighten rod bolts by monitoring stretch, at least one (preferably two) dedicated rod bolt stretch gauges are needed. The process is very simple and involves one bolt at a time. The rod bolt features a centered dimple at each end

With the rod and piston passed through the ring compressor until the bottom of the piston skirts are exposed, insert the assembly into the bore, allowing the skirts to enter. Keep the ring compressor flush with the deck.

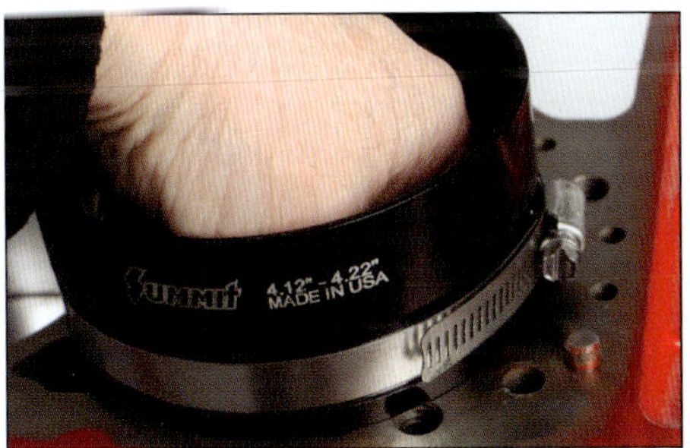

While holding the compressor against the deck, a firm push with the fist allows the piston to fully enter the bore. It's important to have the compressor adjusted to allow a smooth insertion. Ideally, a ring compressor made to the specific bore size should be used, but an adjustable compressor works fine as long as you pay attention to adjustment.

(at the head and at the shank tip). The rod bolt stretch gauge features a stationary pointed anvil and a spring-loaded pointer that face each other. Place the rod bolt onto the gauge, allowing the pointers to engage each end of the bolt. Rotate the gauge dial to set it at zero.

Without disturbing the dial indicator, remove the bolt and install it into the rod. Tighten the bolt to a base torque value. Let's say that the bolts in question call for a torque value of 70 ft-lbs. Tighten the bolt to a value of, say, 60 ft-lbs. Carefully install the stretch gauge onto the rod bolt. Any movement from the pre-set zero will indicate how far the bolt has

stretched. Let's say that the maker calls for a safe maximum stretch of 0.005 inch.

If the gauge shows that the bolt has not stretched beyond the pre-set zero mark, or maybe only about 0.0005 inch beyond zero, remove the gauge and tighten the bolt further. Reinstall the gauge to verify the stretch. Continue until the bolt has stretched (in this example) by no more than 0.005 inch. If the safe maximum stretch is listed at 0.005 inch, a final stretch at, say, 0.004 to 0.0045 inch would be okay.

Repeat the process with each rod bolt. Just remember to zero the bolt in its relaxed state on the gauge. Don't

assume that your zero mark obtained with the first bolt will repeat with all remaining bolts. Always establish a base by setting the gauge to zero with each bolt.

During the process, record each bolt's stretch for future reference. It's a bit easier with a pair of rod bolt stretch gauges, which will save time when installing each rod's pair of bolts. Use one gauge to zero one of the rod's bolts in its relaxed state and to monitor that bolt as it is tightened. Use the other gauge to address the rod's other bolt. Just be careful not to mix up the gauges. It's critical to keep each gauge dedicated to a specific bolt.

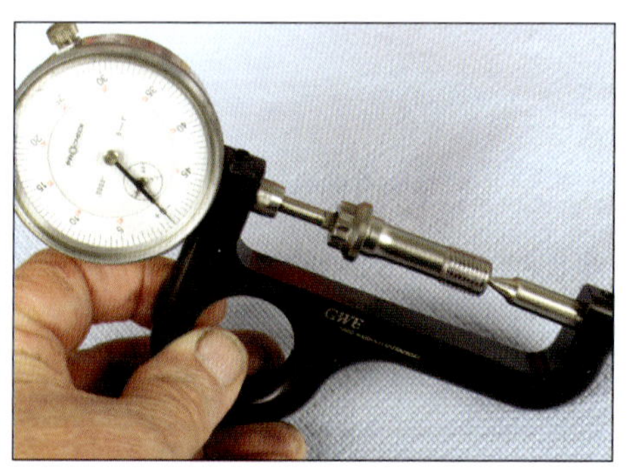

Each rod bolt was first indexed at zero on the stretch gauge before installation. This provides a reference during torqueing to observe the bolt stretch.

Before installation, the rod bolt threads and underhead areas were coated with ARP assembly lube. This reduces friction and provides a more accurate applied torque.

The rod is carefully pulled onto the journal, keeping the rod saddle aligned until the bearing surface makes contact. Avoid pounding the piston downward to avoid an abrupt impact.

The rod bolts were tightened to 70 ft-lbs, which revealed average bolt stretch of 0.0045 inch.

With both rods installed to a common journal, rod side play measured 0.016 inch.

A first-time user of a stretch gauge may complain that he or she set the indicator to zero on one bolt, and after fully installing that bolt, when they set the next bolt onto the gauge, it doesn't read zero. That user may assume that the bolts are faulty by not being of equal length. The purpose of the stretch gauge is not to measure the relaxed length of all bolts. Even the best rod bolts will not be exactly the same length and may vary by a thousandth or so because of tolerances during manufacturing. This minute variance in relaxed length is not important. The bolt length needs to be established by zeroing the gauge to establish a baseline to see how far each individual bolt stretches. The gauge must be reset for each individual bolt.

In theory, the maker's specifications for torque value should result in obtaining the recommended amount of bolt stretch. For instance, if the rod bolt is specified for 70 ft-lbs of torque and a maximum stretch of 0.005 inch, by torquing to 70 ft-lbs, the bolt will likely stretch to its recommended range. However, by monitoring stretch, we can accurately verify the clamping load. Down the road, during a rebuild, the initial records can be used as a reference to show how much torque achieved a specific amount of stretch.

For instance, during initial assembly, we may have stretched the bolt by 0.005 inch by applying, say, 70 ft-lbs of torque. During the rebuild, we may find that the bolt now stretches by, say, 0.007 inch. In this case, the bolt should be replaced, since it has stretched beyond the specified maximum.

In this sample build, the rod bolts supplied with the Scat rods were ARP 2000 with a 7/16-inch thread size and a shank length of 1.450 inch. Scat recommends a torque of 70 ft-lbs. Stretch is not to exceed 0.005 inch.

Engine builders may establish a routine of cycling the rod bolts, bringing the bolts to less-than-max stretch several times to condition the bolt before final installation. Keeping accurate records of each and every rod bolt's amount of stretch will help to determine when it's time to replace the bolts.

Once each pair of rods is installed to a common journal, use a feeler gauge to check the rod side play. In this build, side play measured 0.016 inch. A range of 0.014 to 0.019 inch is generally acceptable.

Oil Filter Adapter

The oil filter requires a mounting adapter that is bolted to the block's filter base. Install a pair of 5/16 inch x 18 bolts at a length of 7/8 inch. Apply a dot of medium-strength thread locker to the bolt threads and torque the bolts to 18 ft-lbs. Note that to obtain enough clearance for a socket wrench, the bolt heads must be smaller than 1/2 inch. Use bolts that feature a flanged 3/8-inch hex head. Using standard 5/16-inch bolts that feature 1/2-inch hex heads will not allow the use of a 1/2-inch socket wrench.

Wet Sump Oil Pumps

Many (if not all) aftermarket performance engine blocks feature priority main oiling, which means that oil is first delivered to the mains, followed by oil being delivered to the cam and valvetrain. Some of these blocks are so efficient in terms of oil delivery that they do not require high-pressure or high-volume oil pumps and may actually specify the use of a standard pressure/standard volume oil pump. Do not take this recommendation lightly.

If the pump produces too much volume, excess oil can be delivered very quickly to the upper end of the engine and can momentarily starve the main bearings. This is because the volume of oil is pushed up quickly and does not drain back to the sump fast enough, potentially lowering the oil level in the sump to the point where the oil pickup begins to suck air. If the block maker specifies the use of a standard pressure/standard volume pump, believe it. Don't select a high-pressure or high-volume pump just because the word *high* sounds like a good idea.

For this build, I chose a Melling pump (part number 10553ST). Its new high-pressure/standard volume shark-tooth design offers more consistent pressure and smoother operation. This pump is equipped with a purple high-pressure spring and includes an optional lower-pressure yellow spring. Since Dart recommends avoiding high-pressure and high-volume pumps for their block's ultra-efficient oiling system, the yellow spring was swapped out, which will drop pressure (compared to the high-pressure spring) by about 10 psi, essentially converting the pump to a standard-pressure pump.

The pump cover plate is secured with four screws requiring a T-30 torx bit. The cover is removed for access to the small press-fit pin that secures the spring. Once the cover was reinstalled, the screws were torqued to 103 in-lbs with a drop of medium thread locker on the threads.

The oil pump pickup, which must be compatible with the depth of the oil pan, is Moroso part number 24350 and is recommended for their pan (part number 20200). This pickup features a feed tube that press fits into the pump and a bracket that shares two of the oil pump cover screws. Granted, since the bracket prevents the pickup from working loose, the tube was tack welded to the pump body anyway for added insurance.

Before mounting the oil pump, an ARP oil pump driveshaft was lubed and installed. Note that many performance aftermarket oil pump driveshafts do not click onto the pump's driven shaft. Once the engine is upright and before installing the distributor, verify that the driveshaft is engaged with the pump by turning the driveshaft with a long screwdriver.

While General Motors used a bolt to secure the oil pump to the number-5 main cap, we opted for an ARP stud. Install the stud finger tight to the main cap. With the pump in place, apply ARP assembly lube to the exposed threads and to the underside of the nut. A 1/2-inch 12-point socket wrench is required to torque the nut. Since the pickup prevents a straight access to the nut, use a 2-inch extension that features a 1/2-inch 12-point box wrench.

Since leverage is now added to the torque wrench, the additional leverage needs to be compensated for by reducing the torque value setting on the torque wrench. The OEM spec for the oil pump fastener is 60 ft-lbs. Since we're using ARP assembly lube, that value drops to about 56 ft-lbs. To obtain an applied 56 ft-lbs of torque, the torque wrench was adjusted to 49 ft-lbs. The wrench's setting depends on the length of the torque wrench from the center of the head to the center of the grip. Following is an easy formula:

TW = L / (L+E x desired setting T)

TW The value set on your torque wrench

L Length of the torque wrench

E Length of the wrench extension

T The desired torque value

If the torque wrench length from center of the drive head to the center of the grip is 14 inches and the wrench extension is 2 inches long, L is 14 and E is 2. In this case, we wanted to achieve 56 ft-lbs, which is TW.

In our example, 14 / (14 + 2 x 56) = 49, so the torque wrench was adjusted to 49 ft-lbs. The setting on the torque wrench is simply lowered to compensate for making the wrench longer when the extension is added.

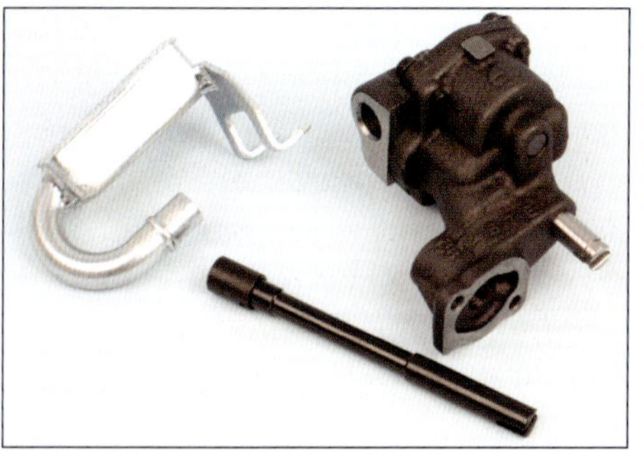

The Melling shark-tooth oil pump was fitted with a Moroso pickup designed for use with a specific Moroso oil pan. Due to the efficient oil delivery system in the Dart block, the high-pressure spring was removed from the pump and the supplied standard-pressure spring was installed.

Rather than using an OEM-type bolt, the oil pump is secured to the number-5 main cap with an ARP stud, a washer, and a 12-point nut.

The oil pump pickup was sourced from Moroso to be compatible with the Moroso oil pan. The pickup tube is an interference fit into the pump and brazed in place, and the pickup bracket shares two of the pump cover screws.

Cam Timing

Our camshaft used in this sample build is a solid steel roller from Comp Cams (part number 12-000-11). The specs are as follows:

Valve adjustment	0.016 intake; 0.020 exhaust
Gross valve lift with 1.5:1 rockers	0.648 intake; 0.645 exhaust
Gross valve lift with 1.6:1 rockers	0.691 intake; 0.688 exhaust
Valve timing at 0.050	Intake open 24 deg BTDC; close 60 degrees ABDC
	Exhaust open 64 degrees BBDC; close 28 degrees ATDC
Intake center line	108 degrees
Duration at 0.050	Intake 263 degrees; exhaust 272 degrees
Lobe lift	0.432 intake; 0.430 exhaust
Love separation	108 degrees

When checking cam degree, it's critical to first establish accurate top dead center (TDC). Using a piston stop that mounts to the deck, drop the piston down in the cylinder by about 0.200 inch or so. Adjust the threaded piston stop screw so that it protrudes below deck by about 0.100 inch or so. Slowly rotate the crank clockwise until the number-1 piston stops against the piston stopper and note the pointer location at the degree wheel.

Rotate the crank counterclockwise until it stops against the piston and note the mark on the degree wheel.

Count the number of total degrees between the two stops and divide that in half. Turn the crank to align that midpoint degree to the pointer. Then, adjust the wheel without turning the crank so that the zero mark on the wheel aligns with the pointer. Remove the piston stop and rotate the crank again in both directions to verify TDC.

Continue to check the cam timing to determine if it can be left at straight up or if advance or retard is needed to compensate. There isn't room here to provide a step by step, but the procedure is easy to look up in a number of CarTech books or online. In our case, the cam intake lobe lift was checked using a lift plunger that features a dial indictor in conjunction with our Goodson Tools & Supplies DW-11 degree wheel.

The plunger, which contacts the lobe, was allowed to drop 0.050 inch on either side of max lift. By counting the number of degrees between these two points, the halfway mark was noted, which showed the centerline at 108 degrees, exactly matching the cam card. The max lobe lift measured 0.432 inch, which also exactly matches the cam card. At max lobe lift, the exhaust lift was noted at 0.430 inch, which was on spec with the card. At 0.050 inch of lobe lift, the degree wheel noted 24 degrees before top dead center (BTDC) and 60 degrees closing after bottom dead center (ABDC). All of the checks matched the Comp Cams spec card.

During piston-to-valve clearance checking, there was 0.210-inch intake clearance (excessive) and 0.080-inch exhaust clearance (too tight). The cam was advanced 2 degrees to move the intake centerline to 104 degrees, which would gain low/mid-range torque and allows us to obtain 0.146-inch intake valve-to-piston clearance and 0.124-inch exhaust valve-to-piston clearance.

Advancing decreases the intake valve-to-piston clearance and increases the exhaust valve clearance, while retarding increases intake and decreases exhaust clearance.

True TDC is found by installing a piston stopper on the deck. With the stopper's adjustable stop protruding out by about 0.100 inch or so, turn the crank clockwise until the piston stops and note the index pointer location on the degree wheel. Rotate the crank counterclockwise until it stops again and note the reading. The total degrees divided in half is true TDC. The wheel is then adjusted to the TDC mark. The cam was advanced by 2 degrees to tighten the intake centerline to 104 degrees.

After degreeing the cam and verifying the specs on the cam card, we advanced the cam 2 degrees to move the torque band slightly towards the low- and mid-range.

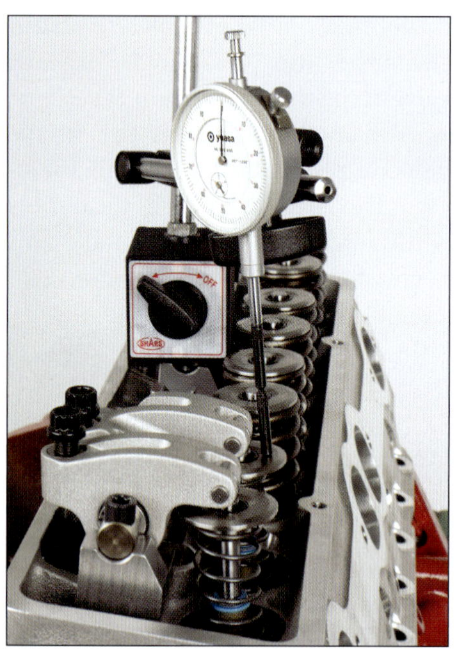

Intake valve-to-piston clearance is checked with the crank at 10 degrees ATDC. A dial indicator contacts the valve retainer and is set at zero. With a light checking spring in place, the valve is pushed down until it stops. Note the distance traveled on the gauge. Exhaust valve-to-piston clearance is checked at 10 degrees BTDC.

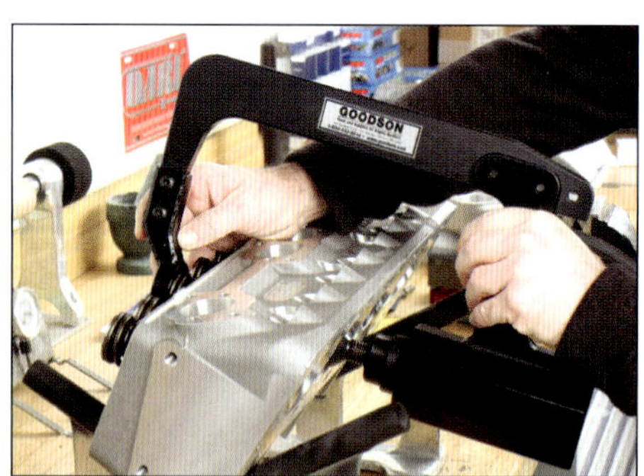

Goodson Tools & Supplies's MTI high-performance pneumatic valve spring compressor CF-3000B was used to compress and remove and install the valve springs when changing over to light checking springs during pushrod-length checking. The billet construction handles the high-pressure springs that are common with racing applications. The tool makes spring service easy and controllable.

Roller Lifters

Roller lifters feature a roller bearing that contacts the cam lobes. It is absolutely critical that the roller remains in plane with the lobe so that the roller bearing glides over the lobe. If the lifter is allowed to rotate within its bore, the roller bearing will contact the lobe at an angle that will quickly result in damage to the lifter and cam. There are several ways to maintain proper lifter orientation within the lifter bore, including the use of dog bones and a spider plate, the use of roller lifters that are paired together with a link bar, or roller lifters that are keyed to the lifter bore.

Dog bones are separate metal guides that feature two female U-pockets that have opposing flats. The flats mate to and guide the lifters that feature opposing flat surfaces on the lifter bodies. These flats keep the lifters in the proper plane with the cam lobes. To keep these flat guides in place, a sheet metal spider plate is installed that has tensioned fingers that push down onto the center of the dog bones. The plate secures to the lifter valley with a series of screws.

Keyed lifters require no additional guide plates. They feature a male key on the lifter body that engages to a female key slot machined into the lifter bore or lifter bushing. This obviously requires custom machining to create the key slot in the lifter bores.

If the plan is to run roller lifters, the easiest and most direct method is to use lifter pairs that are bridged together with a pivoting link bar. The lifter pair (each pair features an intake and exhaust lifter) simply drops into the lifter bores with no custom machining or use of separate guide plates required.

If the lifter pairs feature a link bar, pay attention to the position and orientation of the link bar. The link bar must face the center of the lifter valley. Also, if the link bar features a stamped or laser-etched arrow, the lifter pair must be installed so that the arrow points upward. This allows proper pivoting of the link bar.

Lifter bore clearance is critical to maintain proper operating clearance and lubrication. The lifter manufacturer will specify the correct oil clearance because this can vary depending on the maker and the design of the lifters. However, a general rule of thumb is to obtain about a 0.0015-inch oil clearance.

Another factor to keep in mind is the design of the block being used because some aftermarket performance blocks feature taller lifter bore bosses that require 0.300-inch taller-than-stock lifters. Pay attention to the block maker's specification and assembly instructions before purchasing lifters.

For example, in the case of the Dart SHP Pro iron block used in this sample build, the block is intended for 0.904-inch diameter lifters, which also must be 0.300-inch taller than stock GM roller lifters. Aftermarket blocks for Chevy small-block applications may be intended for either 0.842- or 0.904-inch diameter lifters. Aftermarket blocks are typically machined at the factory to leave excess material in the cylinder bores, lifter bores and deck height, allowing the machinist to tailor these areas to accommodate the builder's plans.

In the Dart block, the lifter bores initially measured 0.9025 inch. The lifters of choice are the highly regarded Morel solid-roller lifters that measure 0.903 inch in diameter. The lifter bores were machined at 0.9045 inch to provide a 0.0015-inch oil clearance. This was accomplished on a CNC machining center, verifying that all lifter bores were not only sized to the desired diameter but also that all bores are accurately centered.

Lifters traditionally feature a pushrod cup that is centered within the lifter. In the case of the small-block Chevy, centered lifter cups are intended to accommodate the traditional 23-degree valve angle common in Chevy heads. However, if using a different valve angle, the intake lifter, or both intake and exhaust lifters, may require the use of offset lifter cups. An example is our build, which features 18-degree valves. This requires the use of a centered-cup exhaust lifter but an offset intake lifter to maintain a proper operating pushrod angle.

While the standard small-block Chevy lifter diameter is 0.842 inch, durability gains can be had by moving up to a 0.903-inch-diameter lifter because the larger diameter provides increased stability. One thing to consider is the lifter's roller wheel diameter. Moving from a standard 0.750-inch-diameter wheel to a 0.810-inch wheel, for example, has the effect of increasing duration and provides a faster rate of lift acceleration. This allows the use of more radical lift cams.

The example build features recently developed Black Mamba 0.903-inch Morel solid roller lifters equipped with 0.810-inch wheels. The lifter pairs are joined by pivoting link bars. Due to the requirements of our 18-degree cylinder heads, the intake lifters feature a 180-degree pushrod cup offset to maintain the pushrod angle and clearance. Exhaust lifter cups remain centered.

According to Morel, these lifters require a 25- to 30-minute break-in under no-load conditions, varying engine RPM from 1,800 to 2,200 rpm, after which time valve lash should be readjusted. In a cast-iron block, lifter bore clearance should be 0.0015 to 0.0017 inch, and lifter bore taper should not exceed 0.0002 inch. Morel recommends that no oil restrictors are used with these lifters.

Care must be taken when installing lifters that feature offset cups. As mentioned earlier, the 18-degree cylinder heads require offset intake

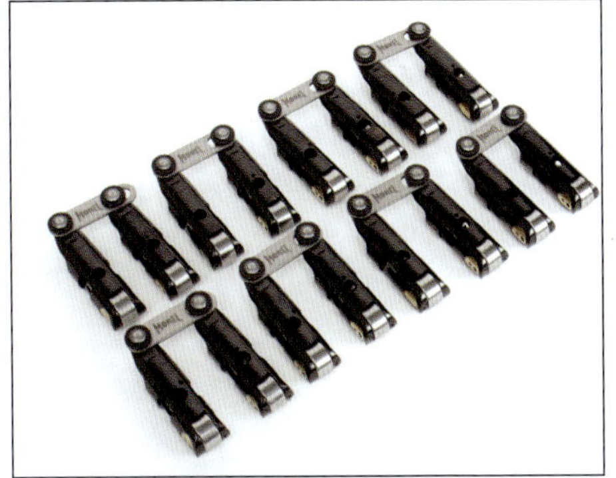

Our solid roller lifters are Morel's new Black Mambas. The diameter is 0.903 inch. The roller wheels are 0.810 inch in diameter. The increased body diameter provides additional stability, and the larger wheel size provides a faster rate of lift compared to OEM sizes. The bodies are skeletonized to reduce weight.

The rollers feature solid bronze axles, eliminating potentially fragile needle bearings.

and exhaust rocker arms. The Jesel intake rockers feature a 0.550-inch offset, requiring offset intake lifter cups. The exhaust rockers feature an offset of 0.220 inch; however, we're able to use non-offset, center-cup exhaust lifters.

When installing the lifters, it's critical to locate the paired link-bar lifters to place the intake offset cups in the proper locations. Starting from the front of the left bank (cylinder-1, driver's side), the order is as follows: the exhaust lifter with the centered cup is paired with the intake lifter with the offset cup biased toward the front of the engine.

Due to the 0.550-inch intake rocker offset, the intake lifters feature a 180-degree offset cup for proper pushrod alignment. Although the exhaust rockers are offset by 0.220 inch, we could get away with a centered cup on the exhaust lifters.

Lifter bodies are relatively short to reduce mass with vertical legs for link bar pivot attachment. Oil orifices align with the lifter gallery oil passages.

For cylinder-3, the intake lifter with offset biased to the rear is paired with the exhaust lifter. For cylinder-5, the exhaust lifter is paired with the intake lifter with the offset biased toward the front. For cylinder-7, the intake lifter with offset biased toward the rear is paired with the exhaust lifter. The passenger side order is the same, starting with the number-8 (rear) cylinder.

The Morel lifters are solid rollers, so no oil pre-soak is needed. Just make sure that the lifter bores are clean, apply oil to the lifter bodies and rollers and install them.

The lifter bores were finished to provide a 0.00155-inch oil clearance. Lifter bore taper was zero. The lifters drop in like warm butter.

Due to the 0.550-inch offset in the intake rockers, intake lifters feature a 180-degree cup offset as is seen on the lifter at the right in this photo.

Timing Pointer

An adjustable timing pointer allows for superior accuracy in terms of setting the timing reference at the crank balancer. Any timing pointer intended for use on a small-block Chevy application will suffice, providing a pointer designed to match the diameter of the crank balancer is obtained.

In the case of our Fluidampr 6.25-inch balancer, we chose a TCI adjustable pointer (part number 871001). This bolts directly to two of the Jesel belt-drive cover-plate bolt locations. Before installation of the cylinder heads, we used a TDC finder affixed to the left block deck and determined the exact top dead center of the number-1 piston. The timing pointer was then adjusted so that the pointer's needle aligned with the zero mark on the Fluidampr balancer.

Crank Trigger

Using a flying magnet crank trigger kit provides increased timing accuracy, since timing is controlled directly from the crankshaft. An aluminum trigger wheel, featuring four imbedded rare earth magnets, mounts to the face of the crank balancer. A pickup sensor mounts to the block with the pickup receiving crank position signals as the crank rotates.

Picking up the timing signal directly from the crankshaft eliminates potential variables, such as distributor gear backlash, wiggle, camshaft endplay, etc., for a much more accurate timing signal. The distributor advance must be locked out, since the distributor will not be used for timing adjustment. In this build, an MSD Pro Billet distributor (part number 85551) was chosen that already features a lock-out, designed for use with a crank trigger.

Rather than relying on adjusting and maintaining ignition timing via the distributor, this build features an MSD flying magnet crank trigger assembly. The kit includes everything needed for installation, including the magnet wheel, pickup sensor, and the required brackets and fasteners. By obtaining timing directly at the crank, ignition timing and control is much more accurate and more stable.

Installing the crank trigger is relatively simple, but precautions must be followed. Mount the pickup's bracket to the engine block, using the two 3/8–16 threaded holes on the block's front right side (passenger's side). The pickup bracket mounts to the main bracket and the pickup mounts to the adjustable bracket. Before mounting the trigger wheel, bring the number-1 piston to TDC, then rotate it to the initial firing position (about 12 degrees). Mount the wheel to the damper so that one of the rare earth magnets in the wheel somewhat aligns to the pickup.

The pickup adjustable bracket offers about 20 degrees of timing adjustment, but one of the wheel magnets needs to be placed as close to the pickup as possible to take advantage of the pickup's adjustment range. The wheel features multiple mounting holes to position it in the most favorable location. Place the pickup in about the center of its adjustment range and mount the wheel so that a magnet aligns as close as possible to the pickup. Then adjust the pickup exactly aligning to that magnet. Also, the center of the pickup should be at the center of the wheel's thickness. Shimming the bracket may be required to accomplish this. Make sure that the arrow engraved on the face of the wheel faces outboard.

Installing the wheel backward will let the engine fire but will result in false triggering at high RPM. Before mounting the wheel, note that the kit includes an aluminum centering adapter. This features a step register that locates the wheel centered to the crank balancer. This is critical to avoid wheel runout. Secure the wheel to the damper with the three 3/8–24 screws provided, torqued at 40 ft-lbs. Apply a dot of medium thread-locker compound to the bolt threads before installation. Once everything is installed properly, ignition timing is easily adjusted by moving the pickup in its slot to fine tune the ignition advance.

Adjust the air gap between the tip of the pickup and the edge of the trigger wheel to 0.050 to 0.080 inch. Setting the gap at 0.065 inch is a good rule to follow. Hold the pickup's hex using a 3/4-inch wrench steady while tightening the jam nut with a 1-inch wrench to secure the gap setting.

Cylinder Heads

For this build, 18-degree heads were chosen instead of the traditional Chevy 23-degree heads. The use of popular 18-degree heads offers several advantages. The angle number refers to the angle of the valves in relation to the head deck surface. The shallower valve angle in 18-degree heads allows the use of a smaller combustion chamber for increased compression without the need to use high-dome pistons.

Another advantage of 18-degree heads involves the valve location.

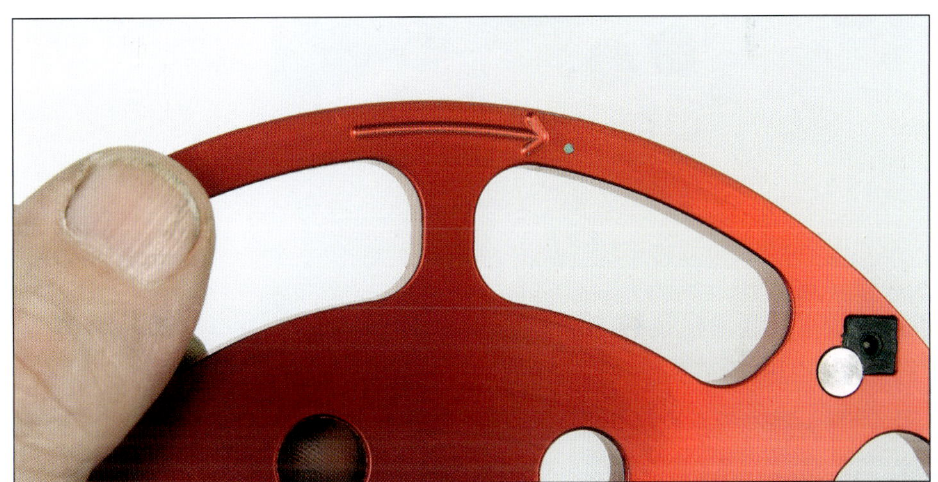

The magnet wheel features an engraved arrow. The wheel must be installed with this arrow visible. Mounting the wheel backward will result in false triggering at high RPM.

The trigger wheel must be mounted hub-centrically. The kit includes a centering adapter that step-registers the wheel to the damper. This ensures that the wheel will run with no runout relative to the crank balancer.

The pickup is adjusted to obtain an air gap of 0.065 inch between the pickup and the wheel. Note that the wheel was mounted properly so that the arrow is visible.

In a 23-degree head, the valves are located 0.275 inch from the cylinder bore centerline. When the valves are close to maximum lift, they are slightly shrouded by the combustion chamber and cylinder wall, which is detrimental to flow. Intake valves on 18-degree heads are located directly on the bore centerline, and exhaust valves are slightly closer to the cylinder wall. This eliminates the shrouding effect and allows the use of larger intake valves. In a nutshell, 18-degree heads flow better than traditional 23-degree heads. More information regarding cylinder heads is found in the cylinder head chapter.

Using 18-degree heads requires an intake manifold specifically designed for 18-degree heads, an offset shaft-mounted rocker-arm system, a solid-roller cam and lifters, and head-specific exhaust headers.

The heads used in this sample build involve Trick Flow Ultra 18 250 heads, which are 100-percent CNC machined and feature 250-cc intake ports runners. For information and a comparison, data on the Dart Pro 1 18-degree heads with 252-cc intake runner volume is also included. During test fitting, both heads were installed and checked for fit.

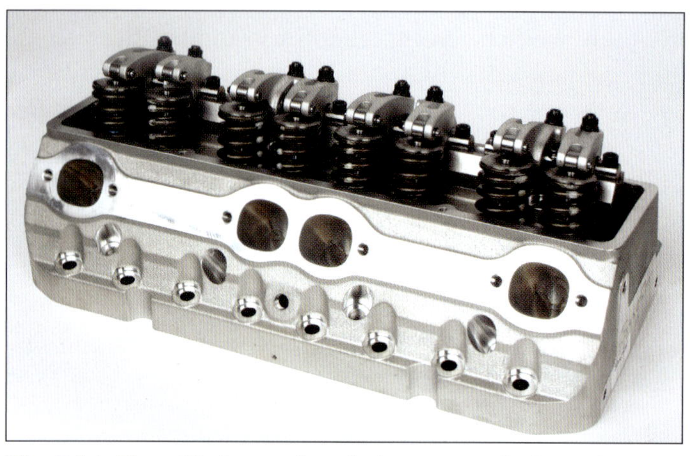

The Trick Flow 18-degree heads feature angled spark plugs and require gasketed plugs. Special exhaust headers are required for 18-degree heads due to exhaust port locations.

The Trick Flow heads, as well as Dart 18-degree heads, require offset shaft-mounted rockers with exhaust rockers featuring a 0.220-inch offset and intake rockers at 0.550-inch offset.

Installing the washer to the center 3/8-inch stud cannot be done with the stud in the way due to the limited space between springs. The washer must be installed before the head is installed; then, lower the head over the stud. Be aware of this to avoid wasting time installing the head only to discover that you have to remove it again. If the head is installed with the stud in place, the washer will not be able to be installed afterward.

On the exhaust side of the Trick Flow heads, coolant is open to center-located 1/4-inch NPT holes and a 10–24 hole just above the deck. The 1/4-inch NPT port can be plumbed to the water pump is desired, or simply plug the hole if the engine won't be used in long endurance racing. The small 10–24 hole must be plugged. This feature replicates the Chevy Motorsports 18-degree heads. The Dart heads do not include these ports, so no plugging is needed.

Instead of using the supplied 10-24 set screws provided with the heads, we installed 10–24 socket head cap screws with applied thread sealant.

The Trick Flow heads are 100 percent CNC machined. Intake runner volume is 250 cc and exhaust port volume is 100 cc. Valve springs are rated at 700 pounds max. Open pressure is 600 pounds.

Dart Pro 1 18-Degree Heads

An alternative head choice is Dart's Pro 18-degree head. This head also requires a minimum cylinder bore size of 4.155 inches, due to the larger intake valve and valve layout. A specific Jesel or T&D shaft-mount rocker system is required as well as a specific ARP head stud kit.

Trick Flow 3181T001-C01	
Ultra 18 250 18-degree valves have the following specs:	
Material	A356-T6 aluminum alloy
Intake port volume	250-cc competition ported
Intake port dimensions	1.350 x 2.200 inches
Intake seat material	Ductile iron
Intake valve	2.150-inch, 11/32-inch stem, 5.560-inch overall length
Combustion chamber volume	56-cc CNC profiled
Exhaust port volume	100-cc CNC ported
Exhaust port dimensions	1.760 x 1.460 inches oval
Exhaust seat material	Copper bronze alloy
Exhaust valve	1.600-inch, 11/32-inch stem, 5.570-inch overall length
Exhaust flange pattern	Standard GM 18 degree
Plug location	Standard GM 18 degree
Spring pocket diameter	1.660 inches
Valve guide material	Manganese bronze
Seals	Viton fluoroelastomer
Locks	10-degree with recess for lash caps
Retainers	10-degree titanium 1.550 inches
Valve spring ID locators	1.550-inch x 0.060-inch thick
Springs	1.560-inch OD double spring with dampers 240 pounds at 2.000-inch installed height 500 lbs/inch rate 0.700-inch max lift 600 pounds open pressure
Minimum bore diameter	4.155 inches
Requires shaft-style rockers with 0.550-inch intake offset and 0.220-inch exhaust offset. Also requires intake manifold designed for 18-degree heads.	

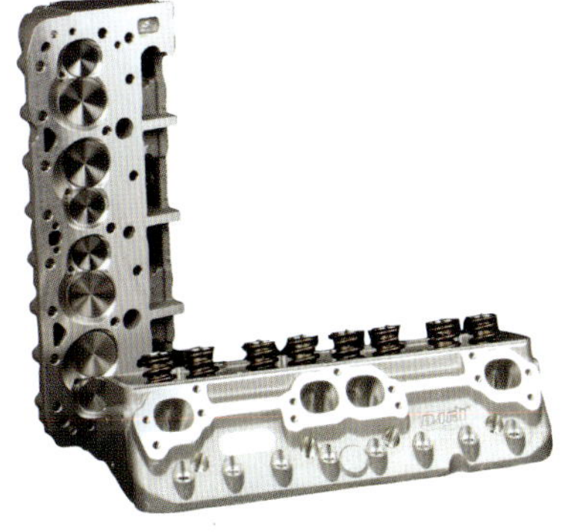

Dart's 18-degree heads feature intake port volume at 252 cc with exhaust port volume at 108 cc.

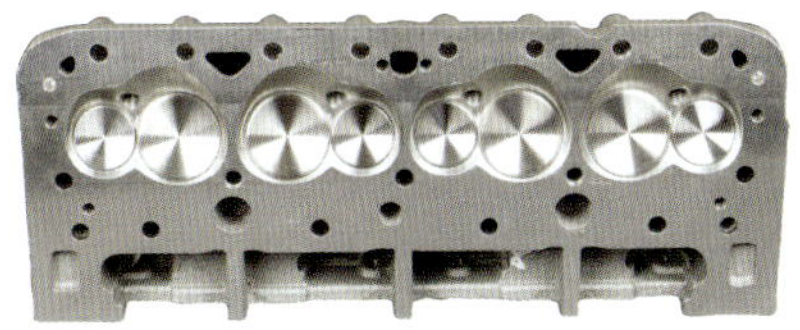

Dart's 18-degree heads feature 65-cc combustion chambers, 2.150-inch intake valves, and 1.600-inch exhaust valves.

Dart Pro 1 18-Degree	
Part Number 11992133	
Material	RMR cast aluminum
Combustion chamber	65 cc
Intake valve diameter	2.150 or 2.180 inches
Intake port volume	252 cc
Intake port dimensions	2.150 x 1.290 inches
Intake port location	raised, 5-degree intake face (stock is 10 degrees)
Intake gasket	Mr. Gasket 143
Exhaust valve diameter	1.600 or 1.625 inches
Exhaust port volume	108 cc
Exhaust port dimensions	1.740 W x 1.500-inch H
Exhaust port location	Raised and spread, GM & Stahl pattern
Exhaust gasket	Dart 65222000
Flow, intake	371 cfm at 0.750-inch lift, 28 inches
Flow, exhaust	261 cfm at 0.750-inch lift, 28 inches
Lifter	180-degree offset required
Manifold	Dart 42711000
Pistons	Most aftermarket 18 degrees
Retainers	Titanium, 10-degree lock
Spark plugs	Angled, 0.750-inch reach, gasket type
Spring cups	1.550-inch ID locator
Spring pockets	1.550-inch OD (0.030-inch deeper max)
Springs	1.550D = 215 pounds at 1.950 inches, 0.680-inch lift max; or 235 pounds at 1.950 inches, 0.750-inch lift max
Head studs	Dart 66110012
Valve angles	18 degrees
Valve length	5.550 inches, 0.250-inch tip
Valve stem diameter	0.3415 (11/32 or 5/16 inch)
Valve guides	1/2-inch OD manganese bronze, cut for 0.530-inch PC seals
Valve guide length	2.250 inches
Valve guide clearance	0.0014 to 0.0020 inch (with 0.3415-inch valve stem)
Valve guide spacing	1.935 inches
Valve seats	Ductile iron or copper infiltrated
Valve seat dimensions	Intake 2.250 x 1.850 x 0.375 inch; exhaust 1.680 x 1.350 x 0.375 inch
Valve seat angles	Intake 38–45–60–70–80 degrees; exhaust 38–45 degree radius
Torque	7/16-inch head stud nuts 70 ft-lbs, 3/8-inch 50 ft-lbs; manifold 35 ft-lbs
Fuel injection down nozzle bosses provided	

Note: The Dart 18-degree heads require Jesel shaft-mount rockers featuring a 1.6:1 intake arm ratio, 1.55:1 exhaust arm ratio, 0.550-inch intake arm offset, 0.220-inch exhaust arm offset; or T&D rockers with 0.550-inch intake offset and 0.170-inch exhaust arm offset.

Installing the Cylinder Heads

Note that 18-degree heads often require a set of head bolts or studs that are designed for use with a specific manufacturer's heads. In this sample build, our Trick Flow and Dart 18-degree heads required a set of ARP studs (part number 234-4721). The set included four different lengths of studs (5, 4³/₄, 4, and 2¹/₂ inch). All studs feature 7/16–14 threads that engage the block. All but three studs feature 7/16–20 fine threads at the top for nut engagement. Three studs feature a neck-down to 3/8–24 thread at the top.

This smaller-diameter shank and upper thread size is due to tight nut access at the middle-row center three hole locations. A row of eight studs are installed at the exhaust side. All studs are installed to the block finger tight. Never torque the studs to the block.

With ARP Ultra-Torque Fastener Assembly Lubricant applied to the upper fine threads and underside of the nuts, the 7/16-inch nuts are torqued to 80 ft-lbs, and the three 3/8-inch nuts are torqued to 60 ft-lbs. Tightening is done is three equal steps, following the torque sequence specified by ARP. The 7/16-inch nuts were tightened at 25, then 50, then 80 ft-lbs. The 3/8-inch nuts were tightened to 25, 40, and 60 ft-lbs.

The use of 18-degree heads takes advantage of smaller combustion chambers and oversized valves. The 2.150-inch intake valves necessitate a minimum 4.155-inch cylinder bore diameter to allow intake valve clearance.

Note: The three $4^3/_4$-inch studs that neck down from 7/16-inch

Our Fel-Pro MLS head gaskets feature 4.200-inch bores for adequate valve clearance and provide a 0.053-inch thickness. The special coating reduces friction during operation, allowing the aluminum heads to expand and contract while also providing additional sealing performance. The use of ARP head studs provides superior clamping force. Studs are installed finger tight to the block. Stud nuts are torqued to 80 ft-lbs on all 7/16-inch nuts, and 60 ft-lbs on the three necked-down 3/8-inch stud nuts.

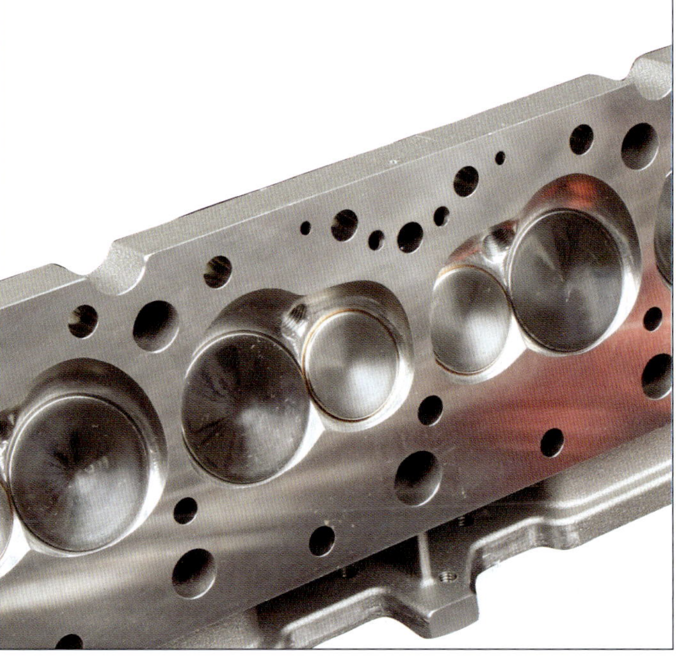

The Trick Flow 18-degree heads feature 56-cc combustion chambers and stainless steel 2.150-inch intake and 1.600-inch exhaust valves.

The ARP head stud kit for the Trick Flow 18-degree cylinder heads involves four different lengths. From left to right in this photo, each head requires four 5-inch, three $4^3/_4$-inch, two 2-inch, and eight $2^1/_2$-inch studs. All lower threads are 7/16–14. All studs except the three $4^3/_4$-inch long studs feature 7/16–20 upper threads. The three $4^3/_4$-inch studs neck down to 3/8-inch, featuring 3/8–24 upper threads. The smaller diameter and smaller nut size accommodates the tight access at three locations.

Bolt Torque Sequence

This is the head fastener tightening sequence. Tighten the bolts in three equal steps to a final 80 ft-lbs for the 7/16-inch nuts and 60 ft-lbs for the three 3/8-inch nuts using ARP Ultra-Torque lube.

thread to 3/8-inch thread must be installed to the block before installing the head. Refer to the sequence drawing for locations 9, 1, and 6. Also, the center neck-down stud's washer must be placed in its pocket on the head before placing the head onto the block.

Due to the tight space between the two adjacent valve springs, you will not be able to install this washer with the stud passing through the head. The option is to grind a flat on opposing sides of this washer to clear the springs.

Also be aware that it will be difficult to install the 7/16-inch nuts onto the two 4-inch-long studs at the front and rear of the head because of the close proximity of the valve springs. Refer to the stud sequence image for stud locations 17 and 14. Once the washer is dropped over each stud, I used a hemostat to start the nuts onto the studs. A thin-wall, 12-point, 1/2-inch socket is then required to tighten the nuts.

Caution: Due to the water crossover design between the two center exhaust ports that is common on GM 18-degree NASCAR heads as well as the Trick Flow heads, there is a small water crossover loop that allows plumbing water from between the two center cylinders back to the water pump. This can be handled by installing a 1/4 male to -4 or -6 hose end and hose. The heads feature a 1/4-inch NPT threaded hole between the two center exhaust ports. If the engine is not going to be run in long endurance applications, this plumbing is not needed. Simply plug the hole with a 1/4-inch NPT plug.

Also, a small 10–24 threaded hole exists on the exhaust side of the head just above the deck, below the 1/4-inch NPT hole. This small 10–24 hole must be plugged. The Trick Flow heads include a 10–24 set screw that is to be installed, with sealant, flush to the outer surface. If it is screwed in too far, it can fall into the block's water cavity. Install 10–24 socket head cap screws with sealant. This allows for a fully tightened installation without the worry of dropping the screw inside the water jacket.

The Dart 18-degree heads do not have this feature, so no mods are needed.

Rockers

In this build, the cylinder heads feature 18-degree valves, requiring offset intake and exhaust rocker arms. The application calls for an intake rocker offset of 0.550 inch and an exhaust rocker offset of 0.220 inch. The rockers of choice are pro-level aluminum full-roller rockers from Jesel that are fitted with heavy-duty roller bearings and precision hardened pushrod cup adjusters.

The standard Chevy rocker arm ratio is 1.5:1. Since the camshaft lobe lifts measured 0.432-inch intake and 0.430-inch exhaust with a 1.5:1 ratio, the effective valve lift would be 0.648 intake and 0.645 exhaust. We opted to increase lift by going to a 1.6:1 rocker arm ratio, which provides a 0.691-inch intake and 0.688-inch exhaust lift. This is still within the max range of the Trick Flow valve springs, which are rated at 0.700-inch or greater max lift.

The Jesel rocker system features a full-length steel rocker stand that bolts to the head, featuring precisely located positions for each pair of shaft-mount rockers. The stands are secured with eight 7/16-inch screws that feature female Torx drives. Be aware that the bolt holes in the heads on each intake side are open to the lifter valley, requiring the use of thread sealer on these intake locations. The recommended torque value for all 7/16-inch stand mount screws when using ARP lube is 52 ft-lbs if the head has thread inserts, or 48 ft-lbs with tapped threads, using a T-50 Torx bit.

To establish correct arm geometry, four 0.025-inch thick shims were installed under the rocker stands. Shims of three different thicknesses are provided with the rocker set. The offset configuration of the rockers is specifically designed for the Trick Flow heads. Each rocker shaft is secured to the stand with three Torx-drive screws. The stand provides an absolute ideal fit to our heads and maintains all rocker shafts in perfect alignment.

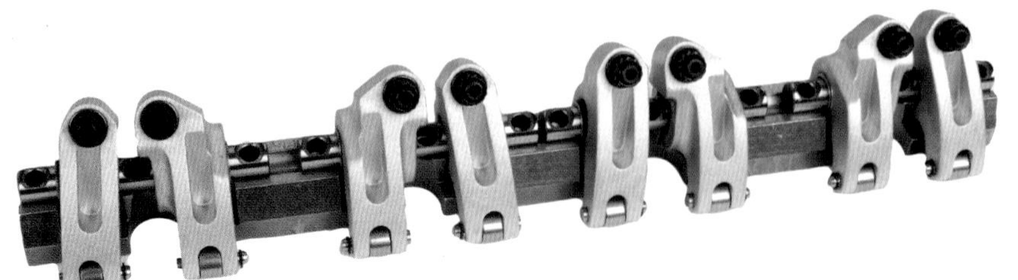

The Jesel shaft-mount roller-rocker system features high-strength rockers with each pair mounted to a common shaft. The shafts are secured to a steel stand that bolts to the heads.

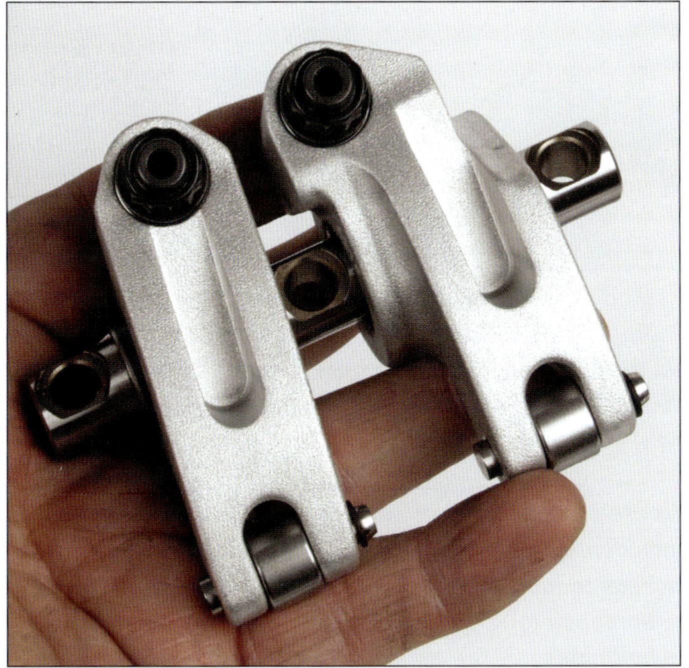

The Jesel roller rockers feature intake and exhaust rockers that share a shaft mount. Heavy-duty precision bearings at the trunnions and tips are designed to withstand high spring pressures and high engine speeds. The CNC machined and shot-peened bodies provide high strength to avoid bending/flexing. These are pro-level rocker assemblies, far surpassing any OEM setup in terms of performance, durability, and operating precision.

Note the visible offset at the intake rocker by comparing the roller tip to the adjuster nut. Both rockers feature an offset with the exhaust at 0.220 inch and intake at 0.550 inch.

The Jesel roller rockers are shaft mounted and secured to a rocker stand that bolts to the head. The stand is precision machined to exactly locate the rockers. Note the visible offsets of the exhaust and intake rockers.

Before rocker arm installation, be sure to apply Jesel's high-pressure lube to the adjuster cups.

Rocker shafts are secured to the stand with Torx screws that require a T45 bit. The stand screws are torqued at 60 ft-lbs, while the rocker shaft bolts are torqued to 26–28 ft-lbs. Exhaust rockers (seen here at left) feature a 0.220-inch offset and intake rockers feature a 0.550-inch offset. This is to accommodate the valve sizes and spring diameters.

Apply lubricant to the rocker arm shaft bolt threads and under-head. If using ARP lube, torque the bolts to 21 ft-lbs; if using oil, torque them to 30 ft-lbs.

Jesel provides rocker stand shims in three thicknesses, including 0.025, 0.050, and 0.100 inch. Depending on the specific application, shims may be needed to establish the correct rocker-arm geometry to gain a center sweep of the rocker-arm roller to the valve tip. In our build, the 0.025-inch-thick shims provided the necessary fit.

The rocker stand shims are placed on the head followed by positioning the stand. The 7/16-inch screws require a T-50 Torx bit and are tightened to 60 ft-lbs. Note that the bolt holes on each intake position are open to the lifter valley. Apply thread sealer to the intake-location screws.

Each pair of rockers is shaft mounted. Each shaft is secured to the rocker stand with three 5/16–18 Torx-drive screws, requiring a T45 Torx bit. These screws are torqued to 21 ft-lbs when lubed with ARP assembly lube or 26 ft-lbs if lubed with 30W oil. For the initial break-in, Jesel supplies a special high-pressure lube to be applied at the pushrod to cup adjuster surfaces. Once valve lash is set, Jesel recommends that the adjuster nuts be torqued at 25 ft-lbs with oil or 20 ft-lbs with ARP lube.

To torque the adjuster nuts, a 7/16-inch 12-point wrench is needed with a center opening to hold the adjuster in place. In our build, Comp Cams suggests exhaust lash at 0.020 inch and intake lash at 0.016 inch. Make sure that both lifters are on the cam base circles and that the rocker lash adjusters are backed fully off before torquing the rocker shaft bolts. Do not torque the bolts if there is any preload on the springs. Then, proceed with lash adjustment.

Lash was adjusted as follows on cylinder-1:
- Rotate crank until exhaust valve just starts to open
- Adjust intake lash at 0.016
- Rotate crank until intake just starts to come off of full lift
- Adjust exhaust lash at 0.020
- Repeat for remaining cylinders

Pushrods

Determining pushrod length is a simple but critical task. The intake valve tips were painted with a black marker to provide a witness mark during rocker travel. With light checking springs installed, an adjustable pushrod checker was installed between the intake lifter and rocker. With the lifter contacting the intake lobe at its base circle, the checking pushrod was adjusted to achieve zero lash at the rocker. Initially our checking pushrod measured at 8.707 inches, but the mark on the intake valve tip was slightly inboard toward the center of the engine. This indicates that the pushrod is too short.

Cold valve lash is set at 0.016 inch for the intake valves and 0.020 inch for the exhaust valves. Do not overtighten the adjuster nuts, using a maximum of 24 ft-lbs.

Using the shim kit provided by Jesel, we installed 0.025-inch-thick shims under the rocker stand and checked again, still using the 8.707-inch pushrod length. The crank was again rotated two full turns, and the rockers were removed, revealing an on-center witness mark on the valve tip. To allow adequate lash adjustment travel, final pushrod length was determined at 8.650 inches with 0.025-inch shims under the rocker stands. This provided one full turn of travel on the rocker adjusters with plenty of room to establish valve lash. One full turn of the adjusters equals 0.042 inch of depth movement for the adjuster cup. Our Comp Cams card calls for valve lash of 0.016 inch for the intake and 0.020 inch for the exhaust.

Total rocker sweep to the valve tip should reveal center contact as seen on this witness mark.

Our Trend pushrods feature a length of 8.650-inch, a 3/8-inch diameter, and a 0.135-inch wall thickness. The 270-degree ball ends provide additional pivoting for better clearance.

Each pushrod is clearly laser marked for dimensions.

When installing the lifters, keep in mind that the intake lifters are offset. The lift cup must be biased toward the offset intake rocker. In some locations, the Morel logo on the link bar will be upside down.

To gain a more stout pushrod to reduce deflection under stress, we opted to step up from 5/16-inch diameter to 3/8-inch pushrods. Especially due to the offset lifter and rocker setup, it's important to check the pushrod clearance where it passes through the cylinder head. The Trick Flow heads already featured a large enough passage, so no removal of head material was needed. However, due to the 0.550-inch offset of the intake lifter cups, 3/8-inch pushrods do get a bit close to the upper vertical section of the lifter bodies where they join the link bar, but they do clear to the tune of about 0.008 inch. Pushrods were ordered from Trend with a 3/8-inch diameter, length of 8.650 inches, and wall thickness at 0.135 inch. The ends feature a slight taper with 210-degree ball ends.

Intake Manifold

While a wide selection of intake manifolds is readily available for small-block Chevy applications, including those for carburetion and fuel injection, for this sample build, Dart's single-plane manifold specifically designed for use with 18-degree heads was chosen. The intake manifold height is 6.400 inches and the plenum accepts 4150-style carbs. Using airflow technology developed on NASCAR and NHRA engines, this manifold flows up to 10 percent more air than many comparable manifolds. The air-gap style has a raised water crossover to insulate incoming air, an optimized intake runner cross-section to maximize high mixture velocity and extended runner dividers to equalize port lengths.

Intake ports measure 1.186 inches wide and 2.250 inches high. The manifold was installed with Fel-Pro (part number 1282) intake gaskets and ARP 12-point stainless steel bolts; all 3/8–16

x 1-inch bolts were tightened to 25 ft-lbs per Dart specs. Do not use bolts longer than 1 inch because longer bolts protrude into the pushrod passages, potentially contacting the pushrods. Note that all intake threaded holes in the heads are open to the lifter valley, except for the far front and rear holes, which are blind.

All bolts were coated with thread sealant to equalize friction during tightening. Note that the four center manifold bolts must be torqued using a torque wrench extension, due to limited vertical access. Using a torque wrench that features a 14-inch length (measured from the center of head to the center of the grip) and a 2-inch-long wrench extension, the four center bolts were torqued with the torque wrench adjusted to 21.8 ft-lbs, which achieved an effective 25 ft-lbs. The formula for using a torque wrench extension is as follows:

Divide the length of torque wrench by the length of torque wrench plus length of the extension, and multiply that number by the desired torque value. In this case:

$$14 / (14 + 2) \times 25 = 21.8$$

Once the intake manifold was installed, the manifold was plumbed with Earl's Performance Plumbing -8 AN plumbing to move hot coolant from the rear of the heads to the water neck and return to the radiator. The manifold features four 1/2-inch NPT threaded holes: two at the front and two at the rear. The front holes were plugged with 1/2-inch NPT plugs, applying thread sealant. At the rear holes, 1/2-inch NPT male to -8 male straight fittings were installed. A pair of 90-degree -8 hose ends attached to these rear fittings.

The -8 Earl's Performance Plumbing black braid hose was routed forward along the outside of the manifold. At the Meziere water neck spacer, which features a pair of 3/8-inch NPT threaded holes, a pair of 3/8-inch NPT to -8 90-degree fittings was installed connecting the hose to the fittings with -8 120-degree hose ends. The water neck spacer was positioned with the 3/8-inch NPT holes facing rearward. Hoses were connected to the hose end barrels via a Koul Tools fixture, which makes hose to hose end installation a breeze, allowing you to simply push the hose into the hose end just short of the female threads. Place the hose end barrel into the two-piece clamshell tool and affix the tool in a bench vise. The tool's funnel tapered opening guides the hose right in with no hassle.

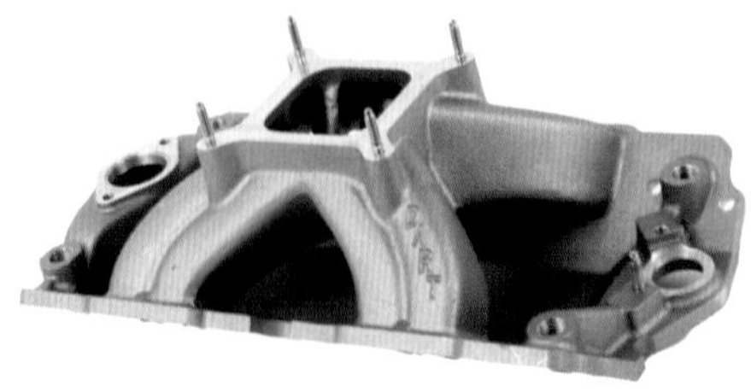

The Dart single-plane intake manifold is designed for use with 18-degree heads. The height is 6.400 inches. Installation requires 3/8–16 x 1-inch bolts. Do not use longer bolts because they will enter the pushrod passages, potentially rubbing against the pushrods. Bolt torque is 35 ft-lbs.

The Dart intake manifold features high-flowing runners. Intake ports measure 1.186 inches wide and 2.250 inches high.

The Moroso valve covers were sealed with Fel-Pro (part number 1628) metal-core formed gaskets. These are marked for "pushrod side," because one side features inboard cutouts for pushrod clearance.

Earl's Performance Plumbing -8 AN plumbing was used to transfer coolant from the rear to the water neck. The 90-degree hose ends are installed at the rear corners. At the water neck, a pair of 90-degree 3/8-inch NPT to -8 fittings are installed connected to 120-degree hose ends. The front corner water holes in the manifold are plugged with 1/2-inch NPT plugs.

Coolant is routed from the rear corners of the intake manifold to the thermostat housing base with -8 AN Earl's Performance Plumbing hose assemblies.

Carburetor

A Holley 4150 double pumper race-bred Ultra XP 850-cfm carb was mounted using a set of ARP stainless steel carb studs and torqued to 60 in-lbs. This carb features an aluminum construction that weighs over 4 pounds less than traditional Holley carbs and has mechanical secondaries, no choke, four-corner idle adjustment, fuel bowl sight glasses, an integrated idle bypass for compatibility with radical camshaft profiles, a billet aluminum baseplate, and 20-percent increased-capacity fuel bowls to avoid starvation issues.

The use of 18-degree heads requires a special intake manifold that is designed to accommodate the 18-degree heads. The standard 23-degree heads feature an intake manifold mounting flange angle of 10 degrees, while an 18-degree head features a 5-degree mounting flange. In this photo, the engine is test fitted with Dart 18-degree heads and a Dart single-plane intake manifold. Bolt hole alignment was perfect. The intake ports on this manifold measure 1.130 inches wide and 1.960 inches high. Depending on the heads being used, some port matching may be desired. Using the Dart 18-degree heads require no extensive port matching, although some material from the entrance of the cylinder head ports may be desired to maximize flow. With this manifold installed to the Trick Flow heads, the ports on the heads are slightly larger. If port matching is desired, the intake manifold's ports can be slightly enlarged.

For this build, we chose a Holley Ultra XP 4150 carbure-tor (part number 80804RDX), which features 850 cfm, mechanical secondaries, a billet baseplate, and no choke. The Ultra XP aluminum construction is about 38 percent lighter than comparable models, saving about 4 pounds.

This Holley carb features 1.750-inch throttle bores and 1.567-inch venturis and high-capacity fuel bowls to eliminate starvation.

This racing carburetor features a down-leg booster, an integrated idle bypass for a good idle even with radical camshafts, and four-corner idle adjustment.

The Holley 850 racing carb is secured with radius-nosed ARP studs. Adding a 1-inch-thick spacer will likely gain an additional 5 to 8 hp at high engine speeds.

Distributor

Since we're running an MSD crank trigger ignition, the advance mechanism in the distributor needs to be locked out. The MSD Pro Billet distributor (part number 85551) was chosen, which already is locked out and is specifically designed for use with a crank trigger. To ensure cam gear compatibility, an MSD bronze gear to the distributor was installed. MSD 8.5-mm plug wires were custom cut to length.

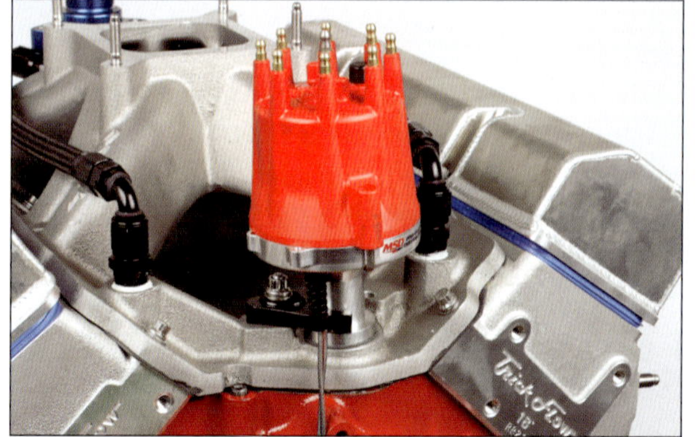

The MSD Pro Billet distributor is secured using a billet aluminum hold-down clamp secured to an ARP distributor stud and nut. The distributor was outfitted with an MSD bronze gear for cam gear compatibility. Distributor depth was carefully checked to insure proper gear mesh. Since we're running an MSD flying magnet crank trigger, this distributor features no advance/retard adjustment. Timing is done by adjusting the front-mounted crank trigger pickup.

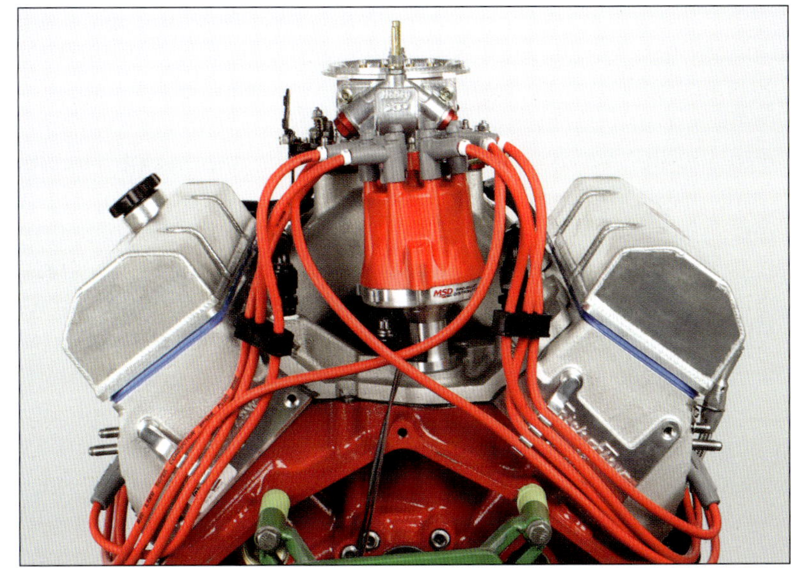

The MSD Pro Billet distributor features an advance lock-out, since timing is adjusted by moving the MSD flying magnet crank trigger system's pickup in relation to the trigger wheel. 8.5-mm MSD plug wires were custom-trimmed to length.

The fill cap threads into the welded-in bung. An O-ring provides sealing. This provides a fill location for adding oil.

Valve Covers

Note: Be aware that special valve covers are needed to clear the rockers on 18-degree heads. Standard small-block Chevy valve covers will not fit, since the inboard intake-side walls will contact the rockers and not allow the covers to mount. Billet rail fabricated covers are required that feature a wider inboard-to-outboard wall dimension. This places the bolt holes on the covers passing through the valve cover roof instead of on an outer flange. These covers are available from sources such as Dart, Brodix, Moroso, Hamburger's Performance Products, Canton, Trick Flow, and CTS.

For this sample build, Moroso fabricated aluminum valve covers (part number 68328) were chosen. They were sealed with Fel-Pro 1628 reinforced silicone gaskets and 1/4-inch studs with nuts torqued to 80 in-lbs. These covers feature no breather holes, allowing the builder to modify as needed.

Since we're running a Jones Racing Products vacuum pump and sealing the crankcase, the valve covers have been outfitted accordingly. On the left bank cover, a 1.800-inch hole was drilled and a female-threaded bung was TIG-welded that seals with an Earl's Performance Plumbing threaded fill cap, which provides an oil fill port. The front wall of each valve cover was drilled with a 3/4-inch hole and fitted with Earl's Performance Plumbing -12 weld-in fittings that allows plumbing the valve covers to the Jones Racing Products vacuum pump.

Since we're running a Jones Racing Products vacuum pump, the crankcase is sealed, using no passive breathers. The -12 AN male fittings are TIG welded to the front of each valve cover. This allows plumbing from each cover to the vacuum pump.

Due to the increased inboard/outboard width, the perimeter fastener locations are recessed to align with the cylinder head's threaded holes.

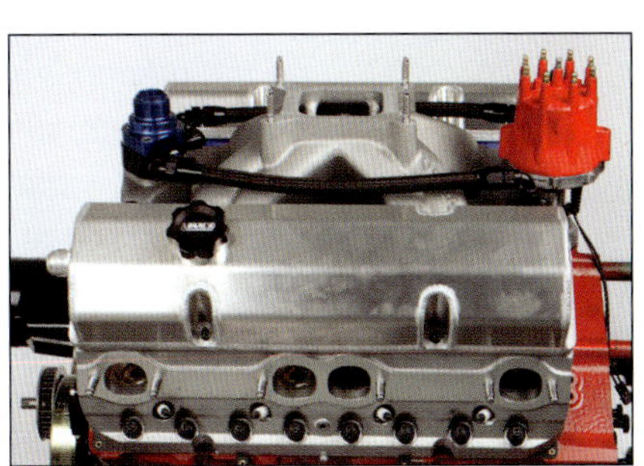

Due to the 18-degree heads and offset rockers, valve covers that are wider inboard-to-outboard are needed for clearance. We chose a pair of Moroso fabricated aluminum covers that feature inboard billet lips. A fill cap was added to the left cover using an Earl's Performance Plumbing weld-in bung.

Oil Pan

The oil pan of choice for this build is Moroso's 20200 road-racing pan. This 7-quart pan is designed for racing applications where hard cornering and braking are anticipated. The sump is extended, or "kicked out" at the sides for additional capacity with a lightly spring-loaded trap door at the front of the sump. This allows easy drainback of oil from the front of the pan back to the sump, while the one-way trap door eliminates oil from being thrown to the front, out of the sump, during hard braking.

The side kick-out design features angled walls that reduce the potential for oil to rise up out of the sump during hard turns. The sump depth is 8.250 inches. A perforated windage screen is mounted above the sump. Note: If you use a Lokar dipstick that features a flexible shaft and a swedged tip, the tip will hang up and get caught on the inside lip that's located just above the screen. Before mounting the pan, you'll need to remove material from this lip to prevent this problem. Cut a slot about 1/2-inch wide in the lip, deburr the cut, and carefully wash the pan to eliminate all metal particles.

If the plan is to use a traditional flat-blade dipstick, this is not necessary. Note: While I've experienced poor bolt-hole alignment on some oil pans, the Moroso pan dropped onto the Dart block perfectly with no time-wasting mods for fit. A Fel-Pro one-piece silicone formed gasket seals the pan to the block. ARP stainless steel 12-point bolts secure the pan.

Vacuum Pump

Rather than installing crankcase breathers and relying on passive evacuation of crankcase pressure, a vacuum pump was installed. This allows the engine to be sealed, using the pump to create negative crankcase pressure, allowing the crankcase to breathe and reducing parasitic oil windage concerns, minimizing crankcase pressure caused by blowby past the rings. An external vacuum pump provides a number of benefits including reduced friction, improved piston ring sealing by relieving crankcase pressure under the rings, reduced windage around the rotating assembly, improved oil scavenging and reduced oil contamination. An external vacuum pump typically results in horsepower gains of 10-35 hp.

Our pump selected for this build is a 2-stage vacuum pump from Jones Racing Products (part number VP-9100-C). This is a gear-style pump with built-in heat sinks that allows the passage of oil, fuel, or moisture without pump damage. Mounting involves a bracket (VP-9100-L-BM), a 38-tooth radius tooth pulley (FP-6106-38-5/8), a 38-tooth radius tooth pulley (BG-6108-38S), a radius tooth belt (760-10 HD), and a multi-part drive hub assembly that

The Moroso oil pan 20200 features a 7-quart capacity, kick-out extensions at the sump for increased oil retention in the sump during hard cornering and acceleration, and a spring-loaded door to prevent oil from leaving the sump during hard braking.

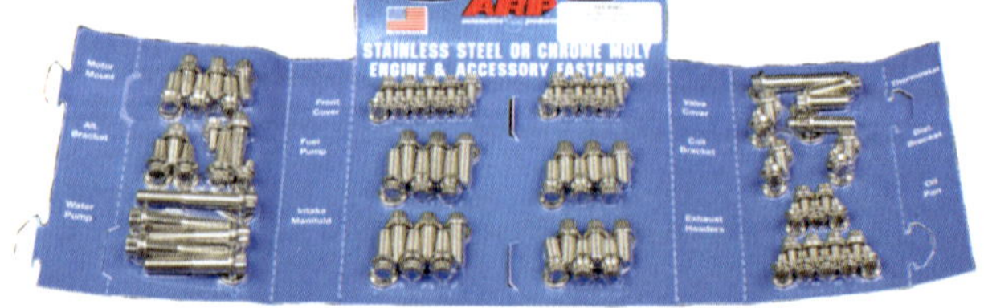

ARP offers an engine assembly kit that features stainless steel 12-point fasteners for a variety of locations, including the oil pan, valve covers, intake manifold, water pump, motor mounts, alternator bracket, front cover, fuel pump, coil bracket, exhaust headers, thermostat, and distributor hold-down. Since the kit is designed for use with a stock OEM engine assembly, some bolts may be too short or too long, depending on the use of OEM-type valve covers or cast/billet valve covers, aftermarket water pump, etc. However, even with aftermarket components, this provides a great start, especially if you want the function and appearance of these high-quality fasteners. The intake manifold bolts in this kit feature the correct length for the Dart 18-degree intake manifold.

attaches to the crank balancer. An adapter secures to the crank snout, which registers the MSD trigger wheel on center and provides a center register for the drive hub. The drive hub then secures to the Fluidampr via three 3/8–24 bolts that also pass through the MSD trigger wheel.

Because the pump's 0.500-inch-thick bracket sandwiches between the block and the MSD 8600 trigger pickup bracket, it was necessary to mill 0.500 inch of material from the rear of the MSD bracket to maintain the pickup sensor alignment with the trigger wheel, since the pump bracket caused the pickup to move 0.500 inch forward of the trigger wheel.

The pump features two -12 AN inlet ports and one -12 exhaust port. The inlets connect to the front of each valve cover via -12 AN Earl's Performance Plumbing 90-degree hose ends and black braided hose.

The Jones Racing Products drive hub features radius tooth pulleys for the vacuum pump and alternator. The fore/aft adjustment of pulley locations are enabled with the use of supplied spacers to align with the pump and alternator pulleys. During final installation, the small drive pulley was placed behind the larger pulley. The small drive pulley is aligned to the vacuum pump pulley; the larger drive pulley is aligned to the alternator pulley.

The exhaust is easily routed to a remote vacuum pump breather tank.

When test fitting the vacuum pump, check for possible interference between the pump's bracket and the block's fuel pump cover. If using an aluminum fuel pump cover, the bracket may interfere if the cover sticks out from the block surface, preventing the pump bracket from seating flush with the block. Mark the fuel pump cover and remove and grind clearance as needed.

The Jones Racing Products hub drive system features a vacuum pump and racing alternator, each of which is driven via radius-tooth belts and pulleys by the crank-mounted drive hub.

Racing Alternator

A Jones Racing Products 1-wire alternator is installed to the engine's left side with the bracket secured to the block's existing 3/8-inch holes in the lower left face of the block. Belt adjustment is provided with the lower slotted bracket. The Jones Racing Products alternator is rated at 80/140 or more max amps and is driven with a 24-tooth radius tooth belt and pulley.

The vacuum pump is mounted to the right front of the block with its bracket sandwiched between the block and the MSD crank trigger pickup mount. A pair of -12 AN hoses connect the pump to the front of each valve cover.

The belt-drive vacuum pump and alternator system is solid, durable and easy to access. The low mounting locations frees up space in the upper engine compartment.

The unit mounts to the block with a two-piece bracket assembly (part number AL-9101-BB-LM) and rear support (part number AL-9100-CL-HM-F). A heavy-duty switch (SW-9100-HD) protects the alternator charging system. This alternator is driven by the radius tooth belt–equipped crank hub that also drives the vacuum pump.

The Jones Racing Products alternator's small-block Chevy mounting bracket makes installation a breeze. The bracket secures to the block with two 3/8-inch bolts, using existing threaded holes at the block's lower left face.

The Jones Racing alternator mounts to the left front of the block. The alternator pulley is driven by the larger-diameter drive pulley on the drive hub.

Water Pump

I always favor using an aluminum electric water pump. This eliminates the need for a pump belt and the resulting parasitic drag on the crank. In this build, Meziere's part number WP301 was chosen, which produced a flow of 55 gallons per minute. It is fitted with a stainless steel shaft and ceramic seal and weighs in at a mere 7 pounds. The pump directly mounts to the block using a pair of Fel-Pro gaskets and

four 3/8–16 x 1$\frac{1}{2}$-inch bolts torqued to 25 ft-lbs.

Dyno Run

Only one session was available for the dyno. The best results in this single session produced 735 hp at 7,100 rpm and 575 ft-lbs of torque at 6,250 rpm. We're confident that further tweaking would likely gain another 10 to 15 hp. The #88 jets were installed in both primary and secondary carburetor circuits.

The alternator belt adjustment range from the center of the drive hub to the center of the alternator pulley is 8 to 8$\frac{1}{2}$ inches, allowing a 1/2-inch adjustment range. The adjustment range for the vacuum pump belt is 8$\frac{3}{4}$ to 9$\frac{3}{4}$-inches, providing a 1-inch range of adjustment. When adjusting belt tension, avoid extreme tightness. The belts are driven by radius teeth as opposed to surface tension.

The Meziere electric water pump weighs only 7 pounds and offers a high flow rate of 55 gallons per minute, eliminating the need for a belt.

Dyno Results			
RPM	**Corrected Torque**	**Corrected HP**	**Oil Pressure**
4024	499	511.7	70.3
4193	526	524	70.4
4661	537.5	534.2	72.2
4706	542	542.8	70.4
4900	544.6	598.8	70.1
5300	546.3	615.2	70.3
5700	552.8	643.5	70.1
6100	572.1	660.9	70.1
6250	**575**	676.3	70.2
6340	574.5	698.2	70.2
6500	566.8	703.8	70.1
6832	549.4	717.1	70.0
6993	518.3	729.4	70.1
7100	512.1	**735**	70.2

Parts Used in This Build

Parts Used in This Build	
Block	Dart SHP Pro Iron (P/N 31161212)
Cylinder Heads	Trick Flow 18-degree (P/N 3181T001-C01)
	Dart 18-degree (P/N 11992113)
Crankshaft	Scat 4-350-3875-6000-2
Connecting Rods	Scat 2-350-6000-2100-SA
Pistons	Icon (forged, 4.165 bore) (P/N IC966.040)
Camshaft	Comp Cams solid roller (P/N 12-000-11)
Lifters	Morel solid roller Black Mamba (P/N MP6654/S0-43019)
Rockers	Jesel shaft-mount offset (P/N KPS-10509)
Cam Belt Drive	Jesel (P/N KBD-31000)
Pushrods	Trend 8.650 X 3/8, wall 0.135, tapered
Oil Pump	Melling (P/N 10553ST)
Oil Pump Dowel	Dart 0.250-inch diameter
Water Pump	Meziere (P/N WP301)
Intake Manifold	Dart 18-degree single plane (P/N 42711000)
Distributor	MSD Pro Billet (P/N 85551)
Distributor Hold-Down	BSP-BLK65920
Bronze Distributor Gear	MSD (P/N 8471)
Crank Trigger	MSD (P/N 8600)
Ignition Control	MSD (P/N 6201)
Spark Plug Wires	MSD (P/N 31239)
Spark Plugs	Autolite 3932 or Autolite AR3933X
Carburetor	Holley 0-80804RDX
Vacuum Pump, Two-Stage	Jones Racing Products (P/N VP-9100C)

Parts Used in This Build *(Continued)*	
Vacuum Pump Plumbing	Earl's Performance Plumbing -12
	Hose 350612ERL
	90-degree hose ends AT809112ERL (4)
	Weld-in fittings 997112ERL (2)
	Weld-in fill bung with cap 166018ERL
Racing Alternator	Jones Racing Products (P/N AL-9101-E-NS)
Oil Pan	Moroso (P/N 20200)
Oil Pickup	Moroso (P/N 24350)
Oil Filter Adapter	Melling (P/N MFA-350)
Bolts for Filter Adapter	5/16-18 x 1.125 (2)
Oil Filter	Moroso 22460
Valve Covers	Moroso (P/N 68328)
Main Bearings	Mahle (P/N MS909H)
Rod Bearings	Mahle CB663HN & CB663HXN
Cam Bearings	Dart (P/N 32210010) (coated 2.120 inches)
Crank Balancer	Fluidampr (P/N 62260D) (6.250 inches)
Head Gaskets	Fel-Pro MLS (P/N 1144-053)
Intake Gaskets	Fel-Pro (P/N 1282)
Oil Pan Gasket	Fel-Pro (P/N 1881)
Valve Cover Gaskets	Fel-Pro (P/N 1628)
Hi-Vacuum Rear Seal	Fel-Pro 2912
Cylinder Head Studs	ARP (P/N 234-4721)
Crank Bolt	ARP (P/N 134-2501)
Accessory Fastener Kit	ARP (P/N 534-9501)
Carb Studs	ARP (P/N 400-2401)
Distributor Stud	ARP (P/N 430-1701)
Oil Pump Stud	ARP (P/N 230-700)
Exhaust Header Studs	ARP (P/N 400-1402)
Oil Pump Shaft	ARP (P/N 134-7901)
Timing Pointer	TCI 871001
Water Neck	Meziere WN0028S
Dipstick	Lokar ED-5018 (for Dart SHP block)

Water Plumbing for Dart Manifold:	
-8 Hose, Black, 6 Foot	Earl's Performance Plumbing 390608ERL
90-Degree -8 Hose End, Black	Earl's Performance Plumbing AT809108ERL (2)
-8 120-Degree Hose End, Black	Earl's Performance Plumbing AT812008ERL (2)
1/2 NPT Plug, Black	Earl's Performance Plumbing AT993205ERL (2)
1/2 NPT To -8 Fitting, Black	Earl's Performance Plumbing AT981688ERL (2)
3/8 Npt To -8 90-Degree Fitting	Earl's Performance Plumbing AT982208ERL (2)

Aftermarket Block Sources

Brodix
479-394-1075
brodix.com

Dart Machinery
248-362-1188
dartheads.com

Donovan
310-320-3772
donovanengines.com

World Products
877-630-6651
pbm-erson.com

Performance Crankshaft Manufacturers

Bryant Racing
714-535-2695
bryantracing.com

Callies Performance
Products
419-435-2711
callies.com

Crower Cams and
Equipment
619-661-6477
crower.com

Eagle Specialty Products
662-796-7373
eaglerod.com

Lunati
662-892-1500
lunatipower.com

Scat Crankshafts
310-370-5501
scatenterprises.com

Winberg Crankshafts
303-783-2234
winbergcrankshafts.com

Aftermarket Connecting Rod Manufacturers

Argo
02-4934-7099
Argorace.com.au

Arrow Precision
+44(0)1455 234200
arrowprecision.com

Bill Miller
775-887-1299
bmeltd.com

Brian Crower
619-749-9018
briancrower.com

Callies Performance
Products
419-435-2711
callies.com

Crower Cams and
Equipment
619-661-6477
crower.com

Dyers
800-867-7637
dyersrods.com

Eagle Specialty Products
662-796-7373
eaglerod.com

GRP
303-935-7565
grpconrods.com

Howards Cams
920-233-5228
howardscams.com

K1 Technologies
440-497-3100
k1technologies.com

Lunati
662-892-1500
lunatipower.com

Manley
732-905-3366
manleyperformance.com

Oliver
231-237-4515
oliverracingparts.com

RPM Machinery
317-856-3000
rpmmachinery.com

Scat Crankshafts
310-370-5501
scatenterprises.com

Wagler Competition
812-636-0391
waglercompetition.com

Superchargers

Accelerated Tooling
616-885-3626
acceltool.com

Alan Johnson Performance
Engineering
805-922-1202
alanjohnsonperformance
.com

Bill Miller
775-887-1299
bmeltd.com

Blower Drive Service
562-693-4302
blowerdriveservice.com

Dyers Superchargers
708-496-8100
dyersblowers.com

Eaton
877-386-2273
eaton.com

Edelbrock
888-799-1135
edelbrock.com

Kenne Bell
Sales: 909-941-6646
Tech: 909-941-0985
kennebell.net

Littlefield Blowers
714-992-9292
littlefieldblowers.com

Magnuson Products
805-642-8833
magnacharger.com

Paxton Superchargers
805-247-0226
paxtonauto.com

Procharger
913-338-2886
procharger.com

The Blower Shop
208-985-7650
theblowershop.com

Vortech
805-247-0226
vortechsuperchargers.com

Weiand Automotive
Industries
866-464-6553
weiand.com

Whipple Superchargers
559-442-1261
whipplesuperchargers.com

Turbochargers

AFI Turbo
480-231-3324

Banks Power
800-601-8072
bankspower.com

BorgWarner Turbo Systems
+49 (0) 6352/403 5800
turbo.borgwarner.com

Forced Performance
972-984-1800
forcedperformance.net

Garrett
turbobygarrett.com

Innovative Turbo Systems
805-526-5400
innovativeturbo.com

Precision Turbo
855-996-7832
precisionturbo.net

ProCharger/ATI
913-338-2886
procharger.com

Turbo Engineering
860-726-1962
turboengineeringintl.com

Turbonetics
805-581-0333
turboneticsinc.com

Fuel Injection Component And System Sources

Accel/Mr. Gasket/Prestolite
    Performance
216-688-8300
mrgasket.com

AEM
310-484-2322
aempower.com

Bosch
708-865-5200
boschusa.com

DSR Fuel Systems
317-490-3410

Edelbrock Corp.
310-781-2222
edelbrock.com

EFI Technology
310-793-2505
efitechnology.com

Electromotive
800-843-3889
electromotive-inc.com

EPI (Engine Performance
    Injectors)
800-893-2260
fuelinjectors.com

Fast
877-334-8355
fuelairspark.com

GoTech EFI
561-271-1770
gotechefi.com

Holley Performance
    Products
270-781-9741
holley.com

HP Tuners
661-644-4624
hptuners.com

Injen Technology
866-946-5264
injen.com

Katech
586-791-4120
katechengines.com

Magnafuel Products, Inc.
800-321-7761
magnafuel.com

Motec Systems USA
714-897-6804
motec.com

Painless Performance
    Products
800-423-9696
painlessperformance.com

Professional Products
323-779-2020
professional-products.com

SCT
sctflash.com

Snow Performance, Inc.
866-365-2762
snowperformance.net

Wilson Manifolds
954-771-6216
wilsonmanifolds.com

Coating Sources

Anatech
704-489-1488
anatechltd.com

Calico
704-483-2202
calicocoatings.com

Cerakote
866-774-7628
cerakotehightemp.com

Diamond Pistons
877-552-2112
diamondracing.net

JE Pistons
714-898-5114
jepistons.com

Mahle Motorsports
888-255-1942
us.mahle.com

Polydyn
888-765-9396
polydyn.com

Swain Tech Coatings
585-889-2786
swaintech.com

Wiseco
800-321-1364
wiseco.com

Piston Sources

CP–Carrillo
949-567-9000
cp-carrillo.com

Diamond Pistons
877-552-2112
diamondracing.net

ICON
800-648-7970
uempistons.com

JE PISTONS
714-898-5114
jepistons.com

Mahle Motorsports
888-255-1942
us.mahle.com

ROSS PISTONS
310-536-0100
rosspistons.com

Wiseco
800-321-1364
wiseco.com